HOW TO COMPENSATE EXECUTIVES

How to compensate executives

Revised Edition

JAMES E. CHEEKS
GORDON D. WOLF

DOW JONES-IRWIN
Homewood, Illinois   60430

ISBN 0-87094-172-0
Library of Congress Catalog Card No. 78-74885

Printed in the United States of America

1 2 3 4 5 6 7 8 9 0 K 6 5 4 3 2 1 0 9

Preface

Every enterprise has a number of jobs that involve making critical decisions. These jobs must be filled with qualified, effective executives if the firm is to survive and grow.

This book presents a guide to planning a compensation program that will insure the continuity of qualified leaders and decision makers necessary for profitable growth. It focuses throughout on the true cost to the company of an executive compensation program and the program's aftertax benefit (or true value) to the executive.

We have written this Revised Edition of *How to Compensate Executives* as an aid to planning for anyone associated with executive compensation, but it is the chief executive officer who should be most mindful of its contents—not for his own aggrandizement, but because executive retention and continuity is the one responsibility he cannot delegate.

May 1979   **James E. Cheeks**
                              Gordon D. Wolf

Contents

keep the option qualified. Accounting for stock options: *Options with a value at grant. Options for restricted stock. Discounted stock options.* In summary: *Stock appreciation rights. Accounting considerations.*

tions by employees. The deduction rules. Distribution of pension plan benefits. Plans integrated with Social Security. Insurance benefits. Choosing a profit-sharing plan: *Profit-sharing contributions for employees. Vesting and forfeiture. Distributions or withdrawals from profit-sharing plans.* Thrift, savings, and other contributory plans. Other pension and profit-sharing considerations: *IRS approval of the plan. Subchapter S corporations. Partnerships, proprietorships, and the self-employed retirement plan. Master or prototype plans.*

Objectives of
compensation policy

Compensation planning has three basic goals: to retain, to stimulate, and to attract. First, it must *retain* present company personnel. This is essential. Second, it should *stimulate* useful or profitable effort for the current and future benefit of the business. Third, it should be able to *attract* necessary additions to the staff.

This book will analyze and demonstrate how to achieve each of these objectives when planning the compensation of executive employees. It should be understood at the outset that planning an executive's pay package moves well beyond the considerations of broad-based salary administration and the design of benefits for the company rank and file. To be sure, these are very important elements of any organization's human resources and they establish a general foundation upon which the executive compensation program is built. But executive compensation planning in practice proves to be a highly complex and challenging area, requiring special knowledge and special skills.

What makes executive compensation planning so delicate a task is the nature of the executive as an individual—his or her knowledge, wants, and temperament—and the nature of the executive's relationship with the company. At this point, it seems wise to define the concept of executive, for purposes of compensation planning. In this book, an executive is a particular person whom the company considers important to retain or acquire as an employee, who occupies a position which can affect the success of the business and influence its future, and who can be stimulated to further valuable effort for the company.

In some companies this definition will include individuals who are not usually thought of as executives. In the field of executive compensation planning, whether a person is an executive will not depend on the person's title, but on the way the company thinks about the individual and on the fact that it thinks about him or her as a unique individual.

Some companies may have dozens of such executives; the very smallest may have only one or two. The number involved does not affect the need for compensation planning. Obviously, the fewer the executives, the more important they are, and the more important compensation planning for them becomes. Of course, the number of executives will affect what is planned for them—the diversity of the alternatives, and the degree of personalization that can be accommodated. It will also affect who does the planning. In larger companies, planning is done by personnel officers, an individual executive (such as a vice president of personnel or finance), a team of executives, or a management consulting firm. In small firms, it may be done by the owner of the business, an attorney, an accountant, or other outside counselor. Whoever does the initial planning, it is essential that the plan be thoroughly reviewed and fully understood by the company's chief officers.

NONCASH REWARDS IN COMPENSATION PLANNING

All executives expect to be paid in cash, and preferably lots of cash. But some are willing to forego a certain amount of cash in favor of certain other benefits, now or in the future.

For one prominent executive, a noncash reward of major importance was the opportunity to buy company stock at bargain rates, coupled with a low-interest company loan toward the purchase price. For another, it was the postponement of receipt of a certain amount of salary until a later year, with the postponed amount treated as if invested for his benefit in securites he designated. For still another executive, it was company-paid counseling services, which gave him tax planning advice resulting in a tax saving of over $60,000.

For many thousands of executives, important elements of their compensation package, though not paid to them in immediate cash, would include:

1. Coverage under a pension, profit-sharing, stock bonus, or savings or thrift plan.
2. Coverage of their medical bills, and those of their families.
3. Life insurance coverage.
4. Stock options or alternative forms of equity participation.
5. Company cars and other perquisites.

There are noncash rewards to fit every need of compensation planning. Most of them will help retain the executive in the company; some will stimulate the attainment of the company's financial goals; and most can be useful in attracting valuable executive recruits.

Executives are shrewd, knowledgeable people, and they will know what rewards your company's competitors are offering. Of course, your company will not be able to match each and every benefit that might be offered by each and every competitor. Your executives realize this, but still expect you to be fair in meeting their needs with a package that is at least competitive with those of other similar organizations. In fact, liberal noncash rewards can be granted to executives in most cases without undue strain on company finances. This book will examine all important noncash benefits, stressing those which can add significantly to the executive's estate, comfort and job satisfaction at low cost to the company.

THE TRUE COST OF EXECUTIVE COMPENSATION

There may be nonmonetary considerations in an individual's compensation package—considerations of prestige, glamour, or image—which have little, if any, cost to the company. But by *true cost,* something more practical is meant. As used here, the true cost to a company of compensation it pays its executive is the net *dollar amount* it must give up to obtain the executive's services. To the individual executive, the true value of compensation is the net amount received, which is not necessarily what the company parts with. Federal income taxes often play the decisive role in determining true dollar costs.

For instance, suppose a corporation pays an executive a straight cash salary of $50,000 and nothing more. The true cost is not the $50,000 the company pays, but much less. The typical corporation in the United States pays a federal income tax on profits at a rate of about 46 percent. Thus, with some qualifications, every dollar of cost reduces tax by 46 cents *if* that cost item is deductible for tax purposes. If the company pays $50,000 in compensation, the true cost is only $27,000, since $23,000 (46 percent of $50,000) is absorbed by the federal government where the $50,000 is deductible compensation. To the executive, the true value of the $50,000 is what is left after federal taxes are paid. A typical $50,000-a-year executive with average personal deductions and exemptions would expect to keep about $38,000 after federal taxes.

Within limits, the compensation planner could design an all-cash compensation plan. The true dollar cost to the company is only about half (54 percent) of what it pays the executive, assuming the payment qualifies as a tax deduction. The true dollar value to the executive is the dollars received less the tax he or she must pay on those dollars.

Compensation planning takes on greater importance when the company decides to provide the executive with something more than cash, as most companies do. For example, it typically provides group life insurance. The company can obtain such insurance coverage at a cost lower than the executive could arrange personally. This is a net dollar saving even apart from any tax advantage. But just as with cash compensation, the tax deduction makes the true cost to the company only 54 percent of what it pays for the insurance, while the executive has no cost of any kind. The same principle would apply to medical and hospitalization coverage paid for by the company.

With other forms of noncash compensation, the planning considerations become complex. Suppose the company decides to reward the executive with a bonus of ten shares of company stock. Here the company may believe it has no dollar cost at all. It is paying its executive something which it may have created without any expenditure. Yet there may be a substantial, even prohibitive, true cost in such payment. The company could sell that stock in the marketplace, now or in the future. By giving the executive the stock, it is surrendering a valuable profit opportunity of its own, and one which is doubly valuable because there is no federal tax on the proceeds a company receives when it sells its own stock.

These brief examples indicate the challenge facing the compensation planner. The true cost to the company of any given compensation plan must be weighed against its true value to the executive, balancing the company's need for economy and financial responsibility against the ambitions and economic desires of valuable executive personnel.

Whatever the compensation package decided on, the executives should be told, periodically and in full detail, what the company is providing or paying out in benefits. This is sometimes necessary for legal or tax reasons, as will be seen in later chapters; but the authors recommend full and direct communication, whether necessary or not. Each executive should receive a statement detailing the dollar amount expended on his or her personal behalf for cash compensation, group insurance, medical plans, company contributions to pension plans and profit-sharing plans, and the cash value of stock, services or other benefits the company provides.

RETHINKING THE COMPANY'S
COMPENSATION PACKAGE

Many major new rules have come into effect in recent years. Policies and programs from the past may now be dangerously outmoded. Among the new rules affecting the compensation picture are:

Reduced capital gains taxes. These can enhance compensation plans involving direct payments in stock, stock options, and stock purchase plans. They also affect lump-sum withdrawal from pension, profit-sharing, and similar plans.

Reduced tax on current compensation. This encourages increased cash compensation and tends to discourage certain forms of compensation involving a postponement of benefit.

Tax on "tax preferences." This has an adverse impact on certain stock options. An alternative minimum tax on the capital gains tax preference (and excess itemized deductions) adversely affects programs leading to capital gains tax treatment.

Phasing out of qualified stock options. This has caused an increase in the use of nonqualified options and a rethinking of the purpose and design of these programs.

These and other new and changing tax, legal, and accounting rules are considered in depth in the following chapters, and their full impact on compensation planning is reflected. Also considered are the new and developing compensation devices (such as financial counseling and performance shares and units), and not-so-new devices (such as phantom stock) now taking on added interest.

PLANNING FOR THE OWNER

All too often in smaller companies the business owner overlooks self in the compensation planning operation. Yet if the owner holds down a job in the corporation, as chief executive or otherwise, personal compensation planning is at least as important as for any other present or prospective employee. Compensation planning factors in this book apply to the owner-executives as well as other executives. Any problems or special considerations arising because the executive is a controlling stockholder are pinpointed, with suggestions for surmounting these difficulties.

2

The tax context: Basic tax rules of executive compensation

The approach taken in this book is to consider all important laws and rules—business management, state corporate law, federal securities law, and federal tax law—that bear on compensation planning. Each relevant rule or principle is considered in place, as particular compensation devices or plans are developed or analyzed.

But some readers may welcome the following material devoted exclusively to the most complex aspect of compensation planning: federal income taxation. This is an orientation chapter, setting forth the rules compensation planners and executive advisers should be aware of before compensation planning begins. Applications of these rules can be seen throughout the balance of the book.

THE EXECUTIVE'S TAX PICTURE

Amounts executives receive from their employers for services are compensation income. This income is subject to full, regular income tax rates, without relief or reduction except that under the personal service income (maximum tax) rules discussed below, it generally cannot be taxed at more than 50 percent.

An executive, or for that matter any other employee, reports compensation in the year it is received or is made available so that it can be withdrawn at will. If payment is made by check the amount must be reported in the year the check is received, even though the executive may not cash it until the next year.

Around year's end, executives may be advised by unsophisticates to have their salaries for the last few weeks of the year postponed to the following year. This would be done to postpone for a year the need to pay tax on the salary (apart from withholding tax). For example, suppose an executive draws $6,000 a month. Instead of taking the December 1979 salary in 1979, the executive postpones receipt of that salary until January 1980, when both the December and January salaries are paid. Since the check for the December 1979 salary is not made out until 1980, it is claimed that the tax on the amount collected in 1980 is not due until the 1980 return is filed in 1981. Legally, this advice is unsound. If the company is solvent and the executive is entitled to the money, the Internal Revenue Service will require the taxes to be paid as if the money had been received when it was due — the executive is deemed to be in "constructive receipt" of the 1979 salary.

Executives are sometimes given advances or drawing accounts. For executives, the term *drawing account* is usually just a synonym for regular salary, implying that other payments may be made later as a bonus or a division of profits. If so, the drawing account is taxable when received, as regular salary. If the executive is not absolutely entitled to the advance or "draw," but must repay all or part of it if it is not earned through performance of services (for example, if the executive is a sales manager and must repay any advance in excess of sales commissions earned), it is taxable only when it is earned.

A bonus, like regular salary, is taxable to the executive when it is received or made available. If a bonus based on this year's performance is not legally payable under the terms of the bonus arrangement until the next year, it is not taxable until next year. As long as such an early withdrawal would violate the terms of the arrangement and is not actually made, this would hold true even though the executive might be in a position to withdraw the funds during the current year because of his or her management position and a controlling interest in the stock of the company.

The executive's compensation includes amounts the company pays to someone other than the executive, which are paid for the executive's benefit, unless those amounts are expressly tax exempt or tax deferred (such as pension or hospitalization contributions). Thus, the executive must report and pay tax on company payment of taxes, living expenses (e.g., reimbursing commuting expenses), or other similar benefits. Amounts withheld from the executive's salary and set aside for future benefit—such as voluntary pension or savings plan contributions—are also included as income.

PERSONAL SERVICE INCOME (MAXIMUM TAX RELIEF)

Personal service income is income qualifying for tax relief for persons in relatively high brackets. It is income or compensation received for services performed personally by the recipient, as contrasted with income derived primarily from the employment of *capital* or from putting one's money to work. Thus, salaries, bonuses, and other forms of executive compensation are personal service income, while interest, dividends, and other income received from investments or business interests are not.

A 50-percent maximum tax rate applies to personal service income; the 70-percent ceiling rate continues for ordinary income derived from investments and the deployment of capital. In practical terms the personal service income benefit only applies to those taxpayers—primarily executives—above the 50-percent bracket; that is, taxpayers whose taxable income exceeds:

$60,000—in the case of a married person filing a joint return.

$41,500—in the case of a single person.

$30,000—in the case of a married person filing a separate return.

Because of various computation factors the personal service income relief does not in practice produce benefits unless such income is somewhat above these figures.

For executives, personal service income is the sum of the taxable amounts paid them or for their benefit: salary, bonus, payments in company stock or other property or bargain purchases of such items, taxable insurance premiums, and so forth.

If the Revenue Service decides that what a company calls compensation to an executive is in fact a nondeductible dividend, it can be expected to deny the executive maximum tax relief for the dividend portion. Presumably, if some compromise figure is worked out during the audit of the company's return, the executive could also compromise at that amount. But if it comes to litigation, the figure treated as compensation for the company may differ from that for the executive, who is a different taxpayer.

TAX PREFERENCE ITEMS

Tax preferences are normally tax-favored income or special deductions.[1] But one's tax preferences can subject one to special tax burdens as well as benefits.

There are two items of tax preference in the typical executive compensation package: (1) Long-term capital gains, which arise most often in stock option, stock purchase, or stock bonus plans, or other arrangements involving compensation paid in property, and in pension or profit-sharing plans (though executives normally elect out of long-term capital gain treatment here). Sixty percent of the long-term capital gain (over short-term capital loss) is a tax preference. (2) The bargain element—that is, the stock's value less the option price—in a qualified stock option (note this is not an item of income or deduction). Every dollar of the bargain is a tax preference.

These tax preferences are taxed in different ways. The qualified stock option tax preference is added to a number of other preferences which seldom arise for executives (e.g., excess depreciation deductions and intangible oil drilling costs). This group of tax preferences is subjected to a minimum tax ("add-on" minimum tax) which is added on to the regular income tax. This tax is 15 percent of total tax preferences reduced by half the taxpayer's income tax (or $10,000, if this is greater).

Example: Powell has taxable income of $60,000 and $25,000 of tax preferences. His income tax is $19,678. His minimum tax is $2,250 (that is, 15 percent of $25,000 less $10,000). Total tax liability: $21,928.

Tax preferences other than capital gains offset dollar for

---

[1] Tax preferences items are occasionally referred to as tax preference *income*, though almost all tax preferences are deductions rather than income.

dollar the personal service income qualifying for the protection of the maximum tax, thereby exposing that amount to tax at normal rates (up to 70 percent). This happens whether or not the minimum tax applies.

The use of tax preference items to reduce the income qualifying for maximum tax relief should influence executives' attitudes towards tax shelters and other tax-favored investments. Except for investments producing capital gain, such investments have a lower aftertax yield to the executive than they have to other persons in the same tax bracket whose income comes from investments or business operations but not personal services.

Example: Sheehan has taxable income of $215,400, of which $162,400 qualifies for maximum tax relief. Potter has $215,400 of taxable income all of which is from investments and business operations other than personal services. Assume Sheehan and Potter both invest in real estate which produces a net tax loss of $53,000 entirely attributable to depreciation in excess of straight line (a tax preference). Assume further that each is married and neither has any other tax preferences. For Potter, the $53,000 depreciation deduction yields a tax saving of $36,040. For Sheehan, the same deduction produces a tax saving of only $26,500, because of her loss of the maximum tax benefit for that $53,000.

Arrangements and investments generating tax preferences can still be desirable despite the minimum tax. This is because the regular income tax saved by the preference exceeds the tax cost of the minimum tax.

The capital gains preference is added to an adjusted (excess) itemized deduction tax preference (roughly, certain itemized deductions in excess of 60 percent of adjusted gross income less certain other itemized deductions) and subjected to an "alternative minimum tax." This alternative minimum tax is payable only if it exceeds the sum of the regular income tax and any regular (add-on) minimum tax. In situations involving highly compensated executives, the alternative minimum tax will seldom be imposed.

Broadly, the amount subject to alternative minimum tax (called alternative minimum taxable income) is taxable income plus the capital gains and itemized deduction tax preferences.

Tax is:

10 percent of alternative minimum taxable income over $20,000 but not over $60,000.

20 percent of alternative minimum taxable income over $60,000 but not over $100,000.

25 percent of alternative minimum taxable income over $100,000.

Example: Hunt has $85,600 of taxable income before capital gain. Capital gain is $100,000 of which $40,000 is added to taxable income, for a total taxable income of $125,600. Tax on this (assuming no add-on minimum tax and no benefit from maximum tax) is $57,912.

Alternative minimum tax (assuming no itemized deduction preferences) is $33,400 ($4,000 plus $8,000 plus $21,400). Since this is less than the regular tax, the alternative minimum tax does not apply.

This chapter is meant merely to describe the tax rules for executives and their employers, as a key part of the context in which compensation planning is done. Later chapters will detail how tax (and other rules) determine the planning of particular compensatory devices.

WHAT THE EXECUTIVE MAY NET AFTER TAXES

In determining what to pay or offer an executive, compensation planners should be able to compute, at least roughly, what tax the executive is likely to have to pay, so they can project what the executive will have left in spendable funds *after* taxes.

Tax and aftertax income can be approximated as follows:

Total compensation income	$_____
Add 10 percent of compensation income for outside income (dividends, interest, etc.)	$_____
Deduct 15 percent of compensation income for itemized deductions (state taxes, interest expense, etc.) reduced by the zero bracket amount ($3,400)	$_____
Deduct $4,000 for personal exemptions	$_____
Balance: Taxable income (approximate)	$_____

If taxable income is less than the amount qualifying for maximum tax relief ($60,000 for most married persons), the tax can be obtained from the tax table. (The table is reproduced at the end of this chapter.)

If compensation will qualify, or might qualify, for maximum tax relief, the computation becomes more complicated, and cannot easily be summarized.

The figures below show what the tax and aftertax amount on various salaries would be using the above assumptions about outside income and itemized deductions and assuming no tax preferences.

Salary	Tax
$ 40,000	$ 8,850
50,000	12,892
60,000	17,473
80,000	27,048
100,000	36,884

THE EMPLOYER'S TAX PICTURE

Corporations and other employers can take full tax deductions for amounts they pay as compensation to their employees, subject to requirements covered below. This includes compensation paid as salaries or bonuses and, sometimes within special restrictions, such staples of the executive compensation menu as pension contributions, stock option and stock purchase benefits and bargains, deferred compensation, medical and life insurance benefits, and so forth.

Deduction requirements are:

1. The compensation must be business-connected (no problem in practice here).

2. It must be for personal services. Normally no problem, though occasionally there is a question of whether a payment labeled as compensation is in fact partly to buy or rent some asset owned by an executive. For example, a corporation may acquire an executive by acquiring the executive's business. Though there will of course be a purchase contract assigning a purchase price to the business assets, the Revenue Service may claim that part of the amount paid the acquired executive as salary (and deductible) is in fact for the assets of his business (and not deductible).

3. It must be a reasonable amount. To the extent compensation is unreasonable or excessive, it is not deductible. The result is that the employer is taxable on this excessive amount, which it does not have because it has paid that amount out as salary.

Example: Apex Corporation pays its president $150,000, of which $70,000 is found unreasonable. Instead of a $150,000 deduction, Apex deducts $80,000 and is taxable on the $70,000 balance, which it does not have.

Apex must use other income or capital to pay the tax on the nondeductible $70,000.

Compensation planning aspects of the reasonableness requirement are explored in Chapter 3.

4. It must be for services actually rendered—which means rendered at or before the time deduction is being claimed. More on this also in Chapter 3.

1979 Tax Rate Schedules

SCHEDULE X—Single Taxpayers

If the amount on line 12, is:

Not over $2,300.......... The tax is: 0

Over—	But not over—		of the amount over—
$2,300	$3,400	14%	$2,300
$3,400	$4,400	$154+16%	$3,400
$4,400	$6,500	$314+18%	$4,400
$6,500	$8,500	$692+19%	$6,500
$8,500	$10,800	$1,072+21%	$8,500
$10,800	$12,900	$1,555+24%	$10,800
$12,900	$15,000	$2,059+26%	$12,900
$15,000	$18,200	$2,605+30%	$15,000
$18,200	$23,500	$3,565+34%	$18,200
$23,500	$28,800	$5,367+39%	$23,500
$28,800	$34,100	$7,434+44%	$28,800
$34,100	$41,500	$9,766+49%	$34,100
$41,500	$55,300	$13,392+55%	$41,500
$55,300	$81,800	$20,982+63%	$55,300
$81,800	$108,300	$37,677+68%	$81,800
$108,300	....	$55,697+70%	$108,300

SCHEDULE Y—Married Taxpayers and Qualifying Widows and Widowers

Married Filing Joint Returns and Qualifying Widows and Widowers

If the amount on line 12, is:

Not over $3,400.......... The tax is: 0

Over—	But not over—		of the amount over—
$3,400	$5,500	14%	$3,400
$5,500	$7,600	$294+16%	$5,500
$7,600	$11,900	$630+18%	$7,600
$11,900	$16,000	$1,404+21%	$11,900
$16,000	$20,200	$2,265+24%	$16,000
$20,200	$24,600	$3,273+28%	$20,200
$24,600	$29,900	$4,505+32%	$24,600
$29,900	$35,200	$6,201+37%	$29,900
$35,200	$45,800	$8,162+43%	$35,200
$45,800	$60,000	$12,720+49%	$45,800
$60,000	$85,600	$19,678+54%	$60,000
$85,600	$109,400	$33,502+59%	$85,600
$109,400	$162,400	$47,544+64%	$109,400
$162,400	$215,400	$81,464+68%	$162,400
$215,400	....	$117,504+70%	$215,400

Married Filing Separate Returns

If the amount on line 12, is:

Not over $1,700.......... The tax is: 0

Over—	But not over—		of the amount over—
$1,700	$2,750	14%	$1,700
$2,750	$3,800	$147.00+16%	$2,750
$3,800	$5,950	$315.00+18%	$3,800
$5,950	$8,000	$702.00+21%	$5,950
$8,000	$10,100	$1,132.50+24%	$8,000
$10,100	$12,300	$1,636.50+28%	$10,100
$12,300	$14,950	$2,252.50+32%	$12,300
$14,950	$17,600	$3,100.50+37%	$14,950
$17,600	$22,900	$4,081.00+43%	$17,600
$22,900	$30,000	$6,360.00+49%	$22,900
$30,000	$42,800	$9,839.00+54%	$30,000
$42,800	$54,700	$16,751.00+59%	$42,800
$54,700	$81,200	$23,772.00+64%	$54,700
$81,200	$107,700	$40,732.00+68%	$81,200
$107,700	....	$58,752.00+70%	$107,700

SCHEDULE Z—Heads of Household

If the amount on line 12, is:

Not over $2,300.......... The tax is: 0

Over—	But not over—		of the amount over—
$2,300	$4,400	14%	$2,300
$4,400	$6,500	$294+16%	$4,400
$6,500	$8,700	$630+18%	$6,500
$8,700	$11,800	$1,026+22%	$8,700
$11,800	$15,000	$1,708+24%	$11,800
$15,000	$18,200	$2,476+26%	$15,000
$18,200	$23,500	$3,308+31%	$18,200
$23,500	$28,800	$4,951+36%	$23,500
$28,800	$34,100	$6,859+42%	$28,800
$34,100	$44,700	$9,085+46%	$34,100
$44,700	$60,600	$13,961+54%	$44,700
$60,600	$81,800	$22,547+59%	$60,600
$81,800	$108,300	$35,055+63%	$81,800
$108,300	$161,300	$51,750+68%	$108,300
$161,300	....	$87,790+70%	$161,300

3

Determining a reasonable compensation level

One of the foremost problems currently facing top business management is the need to determine the proper or correct amount to pay key personnel, and to justify that amount to government authorities and stockholders. In practice, this means the ability to select and justify an amount which is not too much pay for the services rendered. True, executives can be paid too little as well as too much. An underpaid executive may hurt the employer by underperformance. Nonetheless, it is allegations of *over-payment* that invite adverse publicity and the danger of legal action. Avoidance of overpayment and the appearance of overpayment is therefore a primary concern.

If the company can take a tax deduction for the compensation it pays its executives and employees, its true cost of what it pays is, in most cases, only 54 percent of the actual payment. But the company can deduct only a reasonable amount as compensation. Anything in excess of that amount is nondeductible and therefore sharply increases the company's true cost of executive salary. Reasonableness is also the standard to be employed if a stockholder or group of stockholders questions a salary as being excessive. Thus, if a reasonable salary for a particular executive would be about $80,000, and she were paid $200,000, the company could tax-deduct only $80,000. Therefore, the true cost of this compensation to the company would be $163,200. Furthermore, stockholders might be able to recover the excess $120,000 for the company from the officers involved. Directors or officers authorizing executive salary should therefore be prepared to prove that the amount involved is reasonable.

From a business standpoint, the ideal cash compensation is the one that, at lowest cost to the company, leaves the executive in a kind of aggressive contentment. The exact amount depends on the particular individual and company involved and cannot be found by formula. But granting that this amount must vary from case to case, a constant feature of all compensation planning should be the aim to keep the federal tax collected on a compensation arrangement at not more, or not much more, than 50 percent. Putting the same goal another way, the amount that the executive nets after taxes should not be less than the company's aftertax cost. Assuming sizable amounts are involved, this goal is achieved only if compensation is found to be reasonable. This is true from the executive's standpoint as well as from the company's. If the company's payment is reasonable, 46 percent of that amount is, in effect, recovered by the company as a reduction in its income tax. And if it is reasonable, the executive cannot be taxed on any of it at more than 50 percent (with the qualifications discussed in Chapter 2).

Example: If a $100,000 salary is "reasonable," the $100,000 deduction saves the company $46,000 in taxes and its true cost is $54,000. To the executive who receives it, the tax on reasonable salary of $100,000 (disregarding other income and deductions and assuming a joint return) is $39,678. Thus, the executive gets $60,322 at a cost to the company of $54,000.

But if only $50,000 of the $100,000 salary is reasonable, the company's cost is $77,000—a bad bargain, which underscores the need for careful advance planning to establish that amounts paid are reasonable compensation.

In large publicly-held companies, reasonableness is almost never a problem. Salaries in the hundreds of thousands of dollars are passed without question by the Revenue Service. And, apart from the occasional outspoken stockholder at the annual meeting, reasonableness is not often an issue for the public company under corporate law.

It is in the closely held company that the reasonableness of compensation becomes most important to the compensation planner, principally for tax reasons. The explanation for this lies in what is often called the corporate double tax. An owner (stockholder) of a corporation sees a twofold federal tax on the profits of the enterprise: (1) the tax paid by the corporation on its profits, and (2) the tax the stockholder pays on corporate aftertax profits distributed as dividends. A stockholder who is also an executive employee of the business can see a way to minimize or eliminate twofold taxation in favor of a single tax, this way: Unlike dividends, compensation paid the stockholder-executive is deductible by the corporation, and hence not taxable to the corporation (thereby to that extent eliminating the corporate segment of the double tax). This provides the motive to maximize compensation to the stockholder-executive (and correspondingly minimize dividends).

But compensation is deductible for tax purposes only to the extent it is reasonable. The unreasonable or excessive part is nondeductible by the corporation and therefore subjected to double tax. Hence the motivation on the part of compensation planners serving closely held businesses to establish that the compensation paid is reasonable. This is generally done for executives only, since in practice reasonableness is a tax problem only for compensation paid a person with a significant equity interest in the business, or to someone related to such a person.[1]

Understandably, reasonableness depends on the circumstances of the particular case. But the key factors to be considered are:

1. Compensation being paid to executives in comparable positions by comparable companies. This is probably the most important factor, and one which seems easiest to establish. If the company pays what its competitors are paying, this is a very strong indication that its compensation is reasonable.

2. The executive's qualifications for the job. The amount and type of previous experience in this particular job is probably the most important qualification. Other qualifications would include experience in other jobs with the company, and in similar or different jobs in other companies. Education, degrees, professional licenses and other credentials would also be relevant.

3. The nature and scope of the work performed. The more responsible and demanding the job, the more the compensation that is deserved.

4. The size and complexities of the business. Running a large firm, or a large part of a large firm, tends to justify a sizable salary.

5. A comparison of salaries paid with the gross income

---

[1] Reasonableness can also be a problem in an unincorporated enterprise. Here the owner may seek to shift taxable income from the enterprise to a relative in a lower tax bracket who works for the enterprise, through payment of compensation. Standards of reasonableness are the same here as for corporate employers and the compensation planning principles spelled out in this chapter should be applied.

and the net income. If gross income is substantial but salaries to executives essentially eliminate or greatly reduce net income, this may indicate that salaries are unreasonable.

6. General economic conditions. Good times tend to support liberal compensation.

7. Comparison of salaries with distributions to stockholders. Large salaries as against small dividends tend to indicate that salaries are excessive. This is particularly true if the executive is also a stockholder, which may tend to suggest that amounts designated as salaries are in fact something else (e.g., dividends).

8. The company's salary policy as to all employees. There is something of a tendency to find that executives' salaries are not excessive if other employees are liberally paid. It is a sign that compensation is excessive if stockholders or the owners' families get more than other employees for the same work.

9. In the case of a small corporation with only a few officers, the amount of compensation paid to the particular executive in the previous year. A substantial increase over last year's compensation tends to show that this year's compensation may be excessive.

Compensation planning professionals and legal authorities agree that no single factor is decisive. Compensation may be justified though only a few of these conditions are met. But management and other company decision makers should be aware that their salary judgments will be subject to review by stockholders or the Revenue Service, or both, and possibly by courts as well. These second-guessers may well apply all nine standards listed above. Therefore, the directors or officers should be prepared to show which conditions indicating reasonableness of salary were satisfied, and which need not be satisfied, and why. It is wise to make and preserve a written record of this decision (say, as part of the minutes of a directors' meeting), which will be available to answer possible future challenges by the Revenue Service or by stockholders.

For the company whose directors or officers are seeking to set and justify a particular level of compensation for a particular executive, the authors recommend the following approach:

First, find out what other firms in the same line of business are paying comparable executives (test 1, above). While this will already be known in a general way, dig deeper. Compensation ranges and norms can be obtained from a number of sources, such as: trade associations and their publications; periodicals directed to personnel officers; newspaper ads; and executive recruiters and employment agencies. Today's figures are essential. Ignore the tables of comparable salaries prepared by tax publications — they will be based on cases decided years ago, involving compensation paid years before that. While the principles used in these cases may sometimes be relevant to your situation, pay no attention to the dollar amounts which were found reasonable (or unreasonable) in those cases.

Second, establish the executive's qualifications for the job. If the executive's qualifications are about standard for the position, and the pay is about what comparable executives of comparable firms are paid, it is virtually certain that the compensation will be considered reasonable.[2]

But suppose the executive will draw a larger than normal salary. This could be justified by showing the executive has superior qualifications (more than usual experience or training, for example), or responsibility greater than counterparts in other companies usually have, or that this business is larger than is typical in the industry, or that the executive has shown outstanding performance. Any

---

[2] But if the executive is also a stockholder, there is a danger that, regardless of reasonableness, the payments may be considered dividends, not deductible for tax purposes. See page 26.

one of these factors could support a higher-than-usual salary, though it would be impossible to specify just how much higher. But where it is essential or important to pay an executive substantially more than would clearly be justified under the above considerations, it may be wise to use a bonus arrangement.

Paying an executive substantially more this year than last is especially likely to excite Revenue Service suspicions that an overpayment is being made. Therefore, be prepared to justify the raise; for example, by citing new or widened duties, or specific individual or company achievements. Making up for past undercompensation is one justification for increased salary expressly approved by the U.S. Supreme Court.

Payments this year for services performed in past years can be reasonable even though the executive also drew salary in those past years. Reasonableness here would require a determination that the executive was underpaid in past years, and that current pay is to cover past undercompensation as well as to provide adequate pay for this year. It is comparatively easy to establish underpayment if the business was in its start-up phase, was caught by a general economic depression, or was subject to government pay ceilings. It is also wise to specify in advance of payment, in a board of directors' resolution or other company document, that this year's pay is intended to cover past undercompensation. A sample resolution appears at the end of this chapter.

This justification of high current pay on the grounds of past underpayment is a rule of tax law. It may prove harder to satisfy dissident stockholders than the Revenue Service that further payment for past services is in order. Advance planning can help, though. If the company is currently unable to pay what its directors consider an appropriate salary to its executives, the board can express its intention to make up for this when circumstances improve. This could prepare the ground and would tend to still complaints against salary increases from both stockholders and the Revenue Service.

Remember that if the justification for the current high rate of compensation is that the executive was underpaid in the past, that justification disappears once undercompensation is taken care of in the current year. To protect deductions in future years, future compensation should be reduced below the current level (though it can still be above levels in undercompensated years), or a new justification must be found.

Bonuses may be made to depend on an executive's performance, or on the performance of the company as a whole. Or they may be given more or less automatically, as further compensation—some Christmas bonuses, for example. When judging whether an executive's compensation is reasonable, reasonableness is determined on the basis of the entire compensation (salary, bonus, and any other taxable item). There is no separate inquiry as to whether any particular bonus is unreasonable. Thus, if a salary of $90,000 and a bonus of $10,000 is reasonable for a job, then a salary of $10,000 and a bonus of $90,000 is equally reasonable for that job.

Some reasonableness-of-compensation disputes are in fact something other than an argument over whether an amount is reasonable. Rather, they are quarrels over whether an amount described as compensation is really entirely compensation, or partly something else. The problem usually arises where the executive is also a stockholder (or a relative of a substantial stockholder) and the "something else" is usually a distribution of earnings (a dividend). Even an amount which would be reasonable if paid as compensation is not deductible for tax purposes, whatever label it is given by the company, if it is in fact a distribution of earnings. Also, a stockholder who is not an employee would be entitled to object to a distribution to stockholder-employees of company earnings in the guise of compensation.

PREPARING FOR IRS CHALLENGE

It is understood that Revenue agents, when checking whether compensation is reasonable, are especially alert to:

1. Salary for the current year which is substantially more than the executive was paid in the preceding year.
2. Bonuses paid close to the end of the company's taxable year.
3. The fact that no dividends, or only a small amount of dividends, were paid in recent years.
4. Salary in proportion to stockholdings.

While no particular step is necessary to protect against an IRS challenge that salary is unreasonable, and no particular step guarantees success against such a challenge, the authors suggest these measures:

1. Fix a specific dollar amount of salary, before the year begins. (If the salary is to be contingent, or there is a contingent bonus, the *formula* should be fixed in advance.)
2. Set forth a complete explanation of why the salary is what it is. Where the salary corresponds to what other companies are paying, reflect this fact and use the most recent salaries. If this year's compensation includes an element making up for past undercompensation, say so. Recite the executive's qualifications and achievements, and so forth. Note the fringe benefits which this executive *does not* get which executives elsewhere may enjoy. Point out that he or she is expected to do some unreimbursed busi-

ness entertaining (if that is the case), which would tend to support a higher compensation level.

3. Put this in writing, as part of an employment contract or board of directors' resolution. If too bulky for inclusion in a contract or resolution, reflect key points there and make the complete documentation a part of company records.

Forestalling stockholders' challenges

The reasonableness of corporate officers' salaries may occasionally have to be established against stockholders' suits under state corporate law. The principles and standards for determining reasonableness here are comparable to those under federal tax law.

One consideration occasionally used under state law—the effect of income tax on salary—is *not* used for federal tax purposes.

THE PART-TIME EXECUTIVE

Many small companies have executives who divide their time among several enterprises. Also, in some companies, a veteran executive may with age cut down time put in at the office. As a general proposition, part-time services cannot be as liberally compensated as full-time services. But courts face reality here. They recognize that a part-time executive may be worth more to the company than a full-time clerk. And they do not seek to make an hour-by-hour proration of pay. That is, assuming that one company's president who works a 50-hour week draws $50,000, the president of another comparable company who puts in a 20-hour week there could be worth much more than $20,000. In language that should be welcomed by every executive, Federal Circuit Judge Mahoney said, "It is well accepted in the business world that an executive's salary is not dependent upon the amount of time spent on the job. An executive may do some of his most creative work while relaxing at home."[3] But be ready to show the part-time executive's grasp of his or her duties, and satisfactory results from efforts made.

PAYMENTS FOR FUTURE SERVICES

It is comparatively rare for a company to pay sizable cash compensation substantially before the services are rendered. However, the employment bonus is more frequently being used by major corporations to entice needed executive talent (for example, the $1.5 million bonus paid to the chief executive of International Harvester). While prepayment for services would sometimes be criticized by stockholders, it may be a necessary element in today's competitive climate for outstanding executives.

From a tax standpoint, a company can deduct only the compensation paid for services which were actually rendered by the end of the taxable year for which deduction is claimed. Amounts paid before services are rendered are deductible pro rata over the period in which they are rendered. Thus, if a calendar year corporation paid $44,000 in 1979 for services to be rendered in 1980, it could not deduct anything until 1980, but the entire amount would be deducted in 1980 if the services were actually rendered then. If it paid $44,000 in February 1979 for services rendered April 1979 through March 1980, it could deduct $33,000 in 1979 and $11,000 in

---

[3] *Lydia E. Pinkham Medicine Co.* v. *Commissioner of Internal Revenue*, 128 F. 2d 986.

1980. This rule applies whether the company uses the cash or the accrual accounting method, and regardless of stockholder approval of the prepayment or any contractual obligation to prepay.

An executive on the cash method (as virtually all are) reports the payment when it is received, even though it has not yet been earned and even though the company cannot yet deduct it.

BOARD OF DIRECTORS' RESOLUTION TO MAKE UP FOR PAST UNDERCOMPENSATION OF CORPORATE OFFICER

This meeting having been called for the purpose of acting upon the proposal for a grant of further compensation to _____ for past services to the company,

It is the determination of this Board that said _____'s services were not adequately compensated for in past years because *(reason)*, and it is hereby

RESOLVED, that this Board authorize and direct the payment of _____ dollars ($_____) to _____, as further compensation for past services to this company as an officer thereof and in any other capacity.

4

Planning the
cash bonus

Bonuses and other incentive awards have long been a feature of executive compensation planning. The legendary bonuses of the early 1900s are still being echoed, if not exactly duplicated, in the 1970s—the top three executives at Ford Motor Company each received bonuses for 1977 of $615,000 or more.

Incentive pay is a practical form of stimulus and reward for the smaller company as well as for the giants. And with the smaller firm, it is often easier to tailor incentive pay to the performance of particular executives. The incentive awards we will consider in this chapter are those which are decided on before they are earned. Usually they will be expressly covered in a plan, an employment contract, or board of directors' resolution. If the incentive pay arrangement is not worked out beforehand, the amount paid is simply additional compensation for past services, and will risk difficulties with the Revenue Service and the stockholders.

There are two differing views on what to cover under an incentive compensation arrangement with any particular executive. Under one theory, the regular salary is set at a fairly high, or at any rate, competitive, level, and the incentive is geared so that bonuses are not earned unless company performance is outstanding. Here the thought is that regular salary is compensation enough for a workman-like job and that bonuses should be paid only for extraordinary achievement.

The other theory is that the executive should be paid a basic minimum salary plus a bonus which varies directly with the performance of the company for that year. In this case, the executive's total compensation will more or less follow the year-to-year rise and fall in the company's fortunes.

Practice often departs from theory when a bonus program is adopted. Directors and management may take the approach that when an incentive plan is added, regular salary should therefore be reduced. In practice, however, many companies with bonus plans eventually come to pay higher than normal salaries as well as bonuses.

Either view of the salary-bonus relationship is acceptable from a legal standpoint. The selection of either depends on what the company prefers and what its executives insist on or will settle for. The company and the executive must of course agree on what should be the proper measure of the executive's performance under an incentive plan. In most cases, the test is profits. Thus, the bonus might be some percentage of profits. Alternatively it might be a percentage of profits above some predetermined dollar amount, or a percentage which varies with the amount of profit. It might also be a percentage of the profits in excess of some predetermined rate of return on invested capital.

Occasionally, the award can depend on other items, such as dividends, sales (especially for sales, marketing or advertising managers) or costs (for production managers or comptrollers). And executives charged with special, short-run tasks may be rewarded on some basis connected with that task. For example, an executive negotiating an acquisition may receive a bonus related to the purchase price and terms of the agreement. These alternatives are discussed later in this chapter, under "Target bonuses."

Usually, though, the incentive award depends on profits. This raises the danger that payment of such an award might be considered a distribution of profits rather than compensation for services. Distributions of profits are not deductible by the company. Nonetheless, the Revenue Service is willing to recognize an incentive bonus based on profits as compensation. As such, it can be deducted by the company if it is reasonable pay for the services rendered. Furthermore, the high-bracket executive can make use of the 50-percent tax ceiling on personal service income.

But what is reasonable pay? Standards of reasonableness may be stretched a bit when incentive or contingent compensation is involved, but the basic rules covered in Chapter 3 remain applicable. The principal factor is that determination of reasonableness requires consideration of all the executive's pay—regular salary, incentive or contingent award, and any other compensation received from that employer. A base salary of $50,000 and a $20,000 bonus is no more or no less reasonable than a base salary of $20,000 and a bonus of $50,000. In either case, compensation is $70,000.

Management's problem here is to design a plan calling for an incentive bonus which will be accounted reasonable (as part of the executive's overall compensation) whatever that amount may prove to be. Suppose the company will pay its executive vice president a salary of $60,000 plus 2 percent of profits in excess of $500,000. When drawing this plan, the company cannot know how much the incentive will generate because it cannot be sure whether profits will be $400,000 or $4 million. The resulting compensation could be $60,000, or $130,000, or something else. The company therefore may be foreclosed from using the strongest argument that pay is reasonable, the claim that its executive got no more than comparable executives in comparable companies. Instead, its main argument would have to be that the executive contributed so much to profits that whatever was earned under this arrangement represented fair reward for the services rendered. Company profits reflect the value of the services; the higher those profits, the more the executive must have done to produce them.

The Revenue Service accepts this argument in principle. The fact that the contingent deal may result in a higher compensation than would ordinarily be paid does not prevent treating it as reasonable compensation. The IRS will honor the arrangement if it represents what amounts to an arm's length and fair bargain, agreed to before the services are performed. In determining what is reasonable, the IRS looks to the circumstances at the time the agreement was made, not those at the time it may be questioning reasonableness on a tax audit.

The exact portion of profits to be paid the executive may be a matter for negotiation with the company, just as regular cash salary may be. (Indeed, the definition of profits may be a matter for negotiation.) But the following approach should be considered where there is concern that the compensation might be considered unreasonable.

Suppose it is planned to pay an executive a regular salary of, say, $50,000, plus an unspecified percentage of the profits. Check the salaries of executives in comparable companies. Assuming their salaries exceed $50,000, compute what percentage of the profits of their companies that excess represents. The percentage to use for your executive might represent an average of the percentages from those companies which most resemble yours, or those executives whose work most resembles your executive's work.

But those executives will be drawing straight salary.[1] Since your executive's compensation is to some extent at risk, the percentage of profits decided on could be slightly inflated to compensate for this risk. Courts have recognized that if compensation is contingent or partly contingent, it is reasonable to pay a little more than persons with fixed salaries receive for the same work.

Deduction for incentive compensation to stockholder-executives in close corporations has been challenged on this theory: Incentive pay based on profits to someone who has a sizable stock interest is unnecessary—and therefore not a business expense—because the stock interest in itself provides incentive enough. While this theory has been endorsed by a court decision, it has not been widely adopted, even by the Revenue Service, and need not at this time be considered a major threat to deduction for incentive pay to stockholder-executives.

DEFINING PROFITS

We should recognize that when an incentive agreement is being drafted, "profits" needs to be carefully defined. They can be defined in any way the executive and the company may choose, but definition there must be. Profits could be defined as the amount shown as profits under the method of accounting currently being used by the company in its financial statements. But if accounting principles are changed, this could require the company to keep a

---

[1] Some may be drawing salary plus incentive pay. If their incentive arrangement is known, it may serve as a guide to your own.

special set of books just for the bonus plan or, if the contract permits, redefine the bonus arrangement to fit the revised accounting principles. Profits could be defined as taxable income for federal income tax purposes, before or after federal income taxes. Here, compensation might have to be adjusted (additional amounts paid, or amounts refunded by, the executive) if tax liability is later changed following IRS audit. Also, the profit picture could change in future years as Congress changes the rules on what items are income or deductions.

If the company has corporate affiliates, the parties must decide whether profits are to be this particular company's profits or consolidated profits (usually preferable). If other executives will also participate in the incentive bonus, will profits be computed before or after their bonuses? Will profits include or exclude extraordinary gains and losses?

No method of determining profits for this particular purpose is wrong. But the parties should realize that profits is a flexible concept and should be careful to design a definition they can live with. A sample incentive plan, employing its own definition of profits, appears at the end of this chapter.

BONUS ARRANGEMENT NEEDS TIME LIMIT, PERIODIC REVIEW

Now suppose that the parties have agreed on a plan to pay incentive compensation for 1979 and after. The plan clearly defines the basis on which the incentive pay is to be computed (profits, sales, or whatever). And suppose that the compensation to be paid the executive under this plan is reasonable according to standards prevailing in 1979. Does this mean that compensation paid under this plan in 1980, 1981, and thereafter will be accounted reasonable?

Not necessarily. Circumstances may change, so that a

payment under the agreement in 1981 may be unreasonable even though payments in 1979 were reasonable and fully deductible. For example, if the executive worked full time in 1979 but part time in 1981, the 1981 pay clearly could be excessive. And a number of court cases from World War II developed the point that if the economy or the market sharply changes after the agreement was written, incentive pay can become unreasonable. During the war, some of a particular company's profits could still have been produced by executive efforts, but other profits were simply the result of wartime scarcities. The executive did not produce these profits and compensation based on them was not reasonable or deductible.

Of course, the employment contract may oblige the company to make payments based on profits, regardless of what causes the profits. This, however, does not make company payments deductible. The company deducts reasonable compensation and no more; it does not matter that larger amounts are legally required to be paid to the executive.

This suggests that incentive plans should last only a year or two. Where a longer term arrangement is desirable, the plan should leave some opportunity for renegotiation, so that the company need not continue paying amounts it cannot deduct. The contract might be made to terminate, or to bar further increases in pay, upon the occurrence of war, national emergency, disaster (for federal disaster relief purposes), consumer or commodity price rises of more than a stated percentage, or other events which could affect profits but which the executive did not cause or contribute to.

In some companies the bonus is negotiated on an annual basis. This is particularly true where company performance may be heavily influenced by factors outside the company's control. Such companies may want an incentive arrangement that will motivate its executives to achieve certain financial goals in response to changing external circumstances. In such situations, choosing a bonus formula related to profits can be very difficult. In fact, it is sometimes impossible to set a profit formula that will be appropriate beyond the current year. Therfore, the *incentive* would fail because the executive would not have a consistent opportunity to earn a bonus as the external conditions changed from year to year.

TARGET BONUSES—AN ALTERNATE APPROACH

In order to provide a more even incentive opportunity, reinforcing the motivational aspect, companies have developed so-called target bonus plans. Specific performance goals are established for the company's calendar year, and a bonus is earned if the desired goals are met. The bonus is a dollar amount (sometimes set as a percent of base salary) agreed to in advance as a suitable reward for meeting the goals. Thus, the incentive amount is not directly generated by the performance criteria (such as the percent of profits described above) but is an agreed-upon amount that will be paid if the performance criteria are fully met.

Such target plans generally are negotiated between the executives and the chief executive officer of a company on a year-to-year basis. This establishes the normal bonus to be earned for meeting the agreed-upon goals. And, the goals can be focused on the operating environment and particular company opportunities for the coming year. Obviously, the company would want these goals to represent successful management of the business in light of the circumstances it faces.

The performance goals could be profits, return on investment, sales targets, product introductions, consummation of an acquisition, or special tasks identified as priority projects. Performance criteria can reinforce and reward any aspect of the business that management wants to emphasize. Thus, it goes beyond the pure profit measures typical of most formula bonus plans.

Once the target bonus amount and performance criteria are determined, a scale of achievement must be set. Typically, this would involve identifying the lowest level of accomplishment for which any part of the award would be paid. Then, several intermediate steps should be identified that will serve as a guide to judging the *degree* to which the goal has been achieved. Typically, the minimally acceptable level would provide for payment of 25 percent of the target amount, intermediate steps might then be developed where 50 percent, 75 percent, and 90 percent of the award would be earned.

Similar benchmarks should be developed for payments of more than 100 percent of the target bonus amount when performance exceeds the established goal. Plans of this type generally have an upper limit equal to 150 percent (or in some cases 200 percent) of the target bonus amount. In most instances, these upper limits would be paid if performance exceeded goal by 20 percent to 35 percent. This is most easily measured with quantifiable goals such as profits. However, benchmarks can be established for less quantifiable goals or ones that require judgmental evaluation of the success of a particular project.

Example: Suppose Keefer, the executive vice president of Global, is paid a salary of $60,000. For 1979 he has a target bonus of $25,000. This amount will be paid to Keefer if Global's profits (as defined in the agreement) are $1,500,000. The minimum acceptable level to start earning the bonus is set at $1,250,000 and the maximum profit to be included in the bonus calculation is set at $1,875,000 (125 percent of goal). The exact bonus earned will be determined by the following schedule:

Profit level attained ($000)		Percent of goal	Bonus amount earned ($000)		Percent of target bonus
	Below $1,250 . . .	83	No award.		0
	$1,250	83	$12.5		50
	1,350	90	20		80
Goal	1,500	100	Target	25	100
	1,650	110	30		120
	1,725	115	35		140
	1,800	120	40		160
	1,875	125 and above	45		180

If Global's profits for 1979 reach $1,500,000, Keefer would earn the full $25,000 target bonus.

If Global's profits only reach $1,400,000, Keefer would earn $21,667 (interpolation from the above table).

If Global's profits exceed goal and reach $1,700,000, Keefer would earn $33,335 (interpolation from the above table).

For 1980 and each year thereafter, a similar process would be followed. The relation of the minimum and maximum profits to goal could be changed to fit actual experience and anticipated profit opportunities. Or, the goal itself might be something other than profits. It could be profits combined with one or two special tasks. In any event, the basic bonus framework remains but the goals are reset each year.[2]

In the target bonus approach, the reasonableness of the

---

[2] In one target bonus plan carrying a ceiling amount, executives reportedly sought to put a lid on current profits, at the ceiling level used in the bonus plan. Their aim was to shift any further profits to next year, when the bonus plan would resume. This practice, though very rare in the authors' experience, underscores the need to target the bonus ceiling at a level which truly tests executive capacities.

targeted compensation becomes even more important. Because the bonus is set in advance (instead of resulting from a formula applied to unknown future profits), the *target* bonus amount must itself meet the test of reasonableness. A direct comparison of the salary plus target bonus should be in line with the pay levels of similar organizations for similar executive positions (using the techniques discussed in Chapter 3). Also, the level of performance required to qualify for the target award must be defensible. If both the target amount and required level of performance to earn the full award are defensible, payments greater than the target amount should have as great a chance of meeting tests of reasonableness as do the formula bonuses. The authors suggest that full records of goals and their accomplishment be maintained.

This approach to developing a bonus plan can be very effective in tying the incentive award to individual contribution to the company results. On the other hand, its flexibility requires careful management attention to assure that the company receives a fair return on the incentive compensation investment. Use of this approach without a full commitment to planning and measuring performance would most likely fail.

Such target plans rely more heavily on management evaluation. Because performance will be evaluated and a rating assigned, the plan does not provide as strong a guarantee to the participant as does the direct formula bonus. On the positive side, this approach can relate more directly to solving business problems that strengthen the financial results. This is particularly useful when management must take actions that may dampen current profits to build for the future. The authors recommend the target approach when special projects need emphasis and when the operating environment requires year to year flexibility.

In the authors' experience, bonuses which are a percentage of profits are not very effective incentives except where the executive is a substantial stockholder of a close corporation. In other settings, it is the *targeted* bonus that is the influential incentive, where the amount of the bonus is determined by appraisal of the executive's contribution and success in meeting predetermined goals. The degree of incentive provided by a bonus program is directly related to the way the company designs and administers the plan.

EARLY DEDUCTION

If the company is on the accrual method of accounting, it can deduct the incentive compensation for the year the bonus is earned, even though it is not paid or even computed until the following year. Incentive compensation will normally be related to company profits for a particular year. The exact amount of these profits will not be known until the year ends. Thus, the bonus cannot be computed until after the year is over. Yet the company can deduct the bonus on the return for the year the profits in question were made.

Example: Company and executive both report on the calendar year. The executive's incentive compensation is 1 percent of company profits. On February 14, 1980, company accountants determine that its 1979 profits were $2,000,000, and the executive is paid the $20,000 of 1979 incentive compensation on February 27, 1980. The company deducts the $20,000 of incentive compensation on its 1979 return, if it is on the accrual method. The executive reports the compensation as income for the year received, in this instance, 1980.

To qualify to take the deduction for the year before it

is computed, the accrual method corporation must be committed to make the payment; committed, that is, to pay a bonus under some particular bonus computation method or formula. The commitment must be made before the end of that year. Also, the company must make the payment reasonably promptly in the following year. (If the executive is a controlling stockholder or a close family member, the payment must be made in the first 2½ months of that following year.)

In this chapter we have assumed that the incentive arrangement was worked out before the start of the year. Thus, the requirement of a bonus commitment is met automatically.

But deduction is available even if the bonus is not a contractual arrangement with the executive, but is decided on by the company as additional compensation only well after the year began. If so, the bonus commitment should be put in writing. This is usually done at a board of directors' meeting, and the commitment is written into the minutes.

The commitment need not be to make incentive payments to any particular individual. The company could commit itself to a bonus formula in, say, 1979, and decide in 1980 which executives will receive a bonus. Bonuses distributed in 1980 would still be deductible on the 1979 return if distribution is reasonably prompt in 1980.

Remember that an incentive arrangement worked out before the year begins is somewhat more likely to be deductible as reasonable compensation than a bonus decided upon late in the year, after the profit picture for the year becomes discernible. When the bonus decision comes late in the year, there is a somewhat greater tendency to treat the bonus as a distribution of profits rather than as compensation for services.

THE BONUS FUND

Incentive bonuses need not be separately designed for or negotiated with each individual executive who will receive a bonus. Instead, some companies have a bonus fund, based on profits or other stated goals in which each executive, or selected executives, will share. For example, a company could agree to contribute to the fund an amount equal to 2 percent of company profits. The executives who will share in this fund would normally be determined in advance, though this is not always so. The portion of the fund each executive will receive could also be determined in advance. Thus, each executive's share could be made proportionate to salary, or his or her share could be decided only after the year is over, based on individual performance. Here, the bonus share might be determined by a compensation committee, which would base the award on what committee members think each executive contributed to profits or achievement of goals that year. Such a committee would typically include nonemployee directors or others not eligible for the plan.

Bonuses paid out of a bonus fund can be deductible as part of reasonable compensation, just as separately negotiated bonuses may be. There is some danger, of course, that a bonus award based on an appraisal of the executive's performance for the year can look like a nondeductible distribution of profits, rather than compensation for services. But this danger is lessened when the award is made by a committee which is not subordinate to the executive in question. Further, evaluation against specific goals set with the executive before the beginning of the year (or at least early in the year) with accomplishment documented in a year-end appraisal will greatly strengthen the company's position that compensation is reasonable.

REPORTING BONUSES RECEIVED

The executive reports the bonus award in the year it is received (or in the year it is made available so it can be withdrawn at will, if this is earlier).

Suppose Euclid Company and Stewart, its president, both use the calendar year. And suppose that at the start of 1979 they agree to a salary of $55,000 a year, plus an incentive bonus of 2 percent of profits, to be determined and paid in the first 60 days of 1980. For 1979, Stewart receives only $55,000, all salary, and reports only that amount. Profits in 1979 were determined to be $2 million. Stewart's bonus of $40,000 is paid February 26, 1980. For 1980, Stewart reports his $55,000 of 1980 salary plus the $40,000 bonus received that year. The company deducts 1979 salary in 1979 and 1980 salary in 1980. If it uses the accrual method, it deducts the bonus in 1979; if the cash method, it deducts the bonus in 1980.

The executive's maximum tax rate on compensation cannot exceed 50 percent under the personal service income rules discussed in Chapter 2. The Revenue Service may occasionally seek to deny personal service income benefits to stockholder-executives, on the claim that some of the compensation is actually a dividend. While no pattern of IRS attack using this theory has yet been developed (because the personal service income rule is still comparatively new), it is probable that the executive's personal service income benefit will be attacked only after the corporation's deduction has been attacked.

BONUS ADVANCES

Companies occasionally make advance payments during the year of a bonus based on the year's profits, before the year's profits have been determined. These advances are treated like the executive drawing accounts discussed in Chapter 2. That is, if the executive must repay any bonus not earned, the advance is not taxable until the amount of the bonus is finally determined, and then only to the extent of the amount the executive may retain.

SAMPLE INCENTIVE COMPENSATION AGREEMENT

AGREEMENT made this _____ day of _____ between _____ (hereinafter, "the company") and _____ (hereinafter, "the employee").

WITNESSETH

1. [Employee's duties, term of contract, etc.]

2. As compensation for the employee's services hereunder, the company agrees to pay the employee: (a) a salary of $_____, per annum, payable semimonthly, and (b) an additional amount (hereinafter, "incentive compensation") equal to _____ percent of the amount of consolidated net earnings of the company and its subsidiaries, except that in no event shall incentive compensation exceed _____ percent of salary.

Consolidated net earnings of the company shall be such earnings as are determined by the independent accounting firm employed by the company as its auditors, and shall reflect deduction for federal income taxes, compensation of all kinds paid to the employee, and all other proper charges. The determination of consolidated net earnings made by such accounting firm shall be final and binding on company and employee, and no adjustments in incentive compensation shall subsequently be made because of adjustments in federal income taxes or other items.* The consolidated net earnings for purposes of this incentive computation shall be computed not later than 60 days after the end of the company's fiscal year

---

*Instead, it might be desirable to insert a clause providing for binding arbitration if either party to the agreement takes exception to the determination of profits by the accounting firm.

and distribution of any incentive compensation shall be made
not later than 75 days after the end of that fiscal year.
3. et seq. [Clauses unrelated to incentive compensation.]
IN WITNESS WHEREOF the company and the employee
have executed this agreement as of the day and year first
written above.

[company]

by _____   _____
[title]   [employee]

Alternative clauses based on profits. Below are alternative clauses which may be substituted in the Sample
Incentive Compensation Agreement above.

A. _____ percent of the first _____ of profits [consolidated
   net earnings or other definition].
   _____ percent of the next _____ of profits.
   _____ percent of the next _____ of profits.
   And so on.

In some agreements, the percentage of profits to be paid
drops as profits rise; in others, the percentage rises—for
example, 2 percent of the first $500,000, 3 percent of the
next $1 million, and so on.

B. _____ percent of the profits in excess of _____ percent of
   the sum of the company's average amount of capital stock
   outstanding during the year.

This bases the award on profits which exceed some predetermined rate of return on invested capital.

C. _____ percent of profits in excess of $_____.

This is somewhat similar to the preceding clause, basing
the award on profits which exceed a predetermined dollar
amount.

Special considerations in compensating the stockholder-executive

The need to establish that compensation for an executive is reasonable, and techniques for doing so, are covered in Chapters 3 and 4. This chapter will cover other problems peculiar to the cash compensation of the stockholder-executive.

PROTECTION AGAINST IRS DISALLOWANCE

Suppose that in 1979 Bell Corporation pays a salary of $100,000 to Carlisle, who is Bell's president and 15-percent stockholder. An IRS agent, on auditing the company's 1979 return in 1981, decides that only $80,000 of Carlisle's salary is reasonable compensation for his services; the $20,000 balance is not deductible. Bell might challenge this determination administratively within the IRS, in court, or in both ways. But assuming it accepts the agent's finding (or loses any challenge), the result is that Carlisle actually collects $100,000 but the company can deduct only $80,000, and is fully taxable on the $20,000 balance.

A solution to this problem, from the company's standpoint, is to require the stockholder-executive to repay any amount paid as compensation for which it cannot take a tax deduction. The foresighted company would make this requirement a condition of Carlisle's employment, and impose it before the services are performed. If the stockholder-executive has a binding legal obligation to repay, the Revenue Service will allow a business expense deduction for the repayment. If such a repayment obligation had existed in the Bell-Carlisle situation, and Carlisle had repaid the $20,000 in 1981, the tax picture would be: For 1979, Carlisle would be taxable on $100,000, of which $20,000 is later determined to be not reasonable compensation; if considered a dividend it would not qualify for the maximum tax relief discussed in Chapter 2. Bell Corporation would be taxed in 1979 on the nondeductible $20,000 (plus its other 1979 income). For 1981, Carlisle could deduct the $20,000 repayment he makes that year against his other income. The company is not taxed in 1981 on receipt of the $20,000 on which it was already taxed.

This repayment arrangement is widely known among professional practitioners, and they often recommend it. But these points should be noted to put such arrangements in perspective:

1. They are practical only for stockholder-employees and, for the most part, only for those with substantial holdings. An executive derives no benefit from repaying compensation. He or she is worse off economically by repaying and taking a tax deduction than by keeping the money. Thus, an executive is not likely to agree to such a repayment arrangement unless he or she will continue to have an interest in the amount repaid, as a stockholder.

2. The repayment arrangement was first recognized (allowing an executive to deduct repayment) in a court case in which the repayment requirement was set forth in

a board of directors resolution. Some practitioners therefore recommend that the repayment requirement be put in a board resolution. The authors instead recommend putting the repayment requirement in an employment contract. In the authors' view, a board of directors' resolution will not always be effective as a binding obligation to repay. (A legally binding obligation is not always a prerequisite to a business expense deduction, but it seems advisable to try for one in this area.) A sample employment contract clause is shown at the end of this chapter.

3. Even stockholder-officers may be reluctant to agree to repay excessive compensation. They may fear that the company's knowledge that it will recover any excessive amount from the executive may weaken its will to fight for the deduction in IRS negotiations. An amount treated as excessive compensation may not get maximum tax benefits in the executive's hands. Thus, before agreeing to repay, some stockholder-executives might insist that the repayment agreement oblige the company to contest the reasonableness issue in good faith through all levels of the IRS, or allow the executive to do so on its behalf.

4. Some practitioners are nervous about using such repayment arrangements, fearing that the Revenue Service is especially likely to attack compensation deductions once it knows that a repayment arrangement exists. The thought here is that the mere existence of a repayment arrangement tends to show, in the revenue agent's mind, that compensation is excessive. To this attitude, the authors have these comments:

Some agents do conclude that if a repayment arrangement exists, compensation is probably excessive. Thus, where the agent learns of the arrangement, deduction is somewhat more likely to be challenged than where no such arrangement is made.

The agent sometimes will not learn of the arrangement. This will depend on the agent's work routine. Some agents make it a practice to examine board of directors' minutes as part of their tax audit.

This way, they can learn of repayment arrangements reflected in directors' resolutions. This approach would not necessarily disclose repayment requirements in employment contracts, though, of course, the agent might ask to see those as well. Agents who don't approach their corporate tax audits in this manner might not learn of the repayment arrangement for the year the deduction was taken. But if some compensation is ruled nondeductible anyway, they may learn about the repayment arrangement in a later year, when auditing for the year the excessive amount is repaid. This may then prompt a challenge to company deductions in other years.

Moreover, courts as well as revenue agents can be influenced by the presence of a repayment arrangement. That is, courts in a few cases have treated such repayment agreements as weakening a company's claim that compensation was reasonable.

5. All the negative features of repayment arrangements work towards the company's *economic benefit.* Should repayment be required, the company winds up with more funds than without repayment. Thus, where the existence of a repayment arrangement is taken to indicate that compensation is excessive, this is *favorable* to the company's financial position.

Example: Thule Corp. paid Stevens $150,000 in 1978, under a repayment arrangement. Deduction for this amount saved $72,000 in 1978 tax. On audit in 1980, the revenue agent denies $40,000 of this deduction, which Stevens therefore repays in 1980. The denial of the 1978 deduction for $40,000 increased Thule's tax bill by $19,200 plus interest, but this was more than offset by Thule's cash recovery of $40,000.

"BEST SALARY" CONSIDERATIONS

The "best salary" concept contemplates setting the salaries of stockholder-executives at that amount which results in the lowest *total* tax on compensation income paid and on corporate income retained. It is a *tax saving* concept, with no compensation planning or incentive aspects.

A plan to set the salary of stockholder-executives at that exact level which will minimize tax collections is possible only in limited situations. It presupposes that any amount stockholder-executives forego as current compensation can be later withdrawn, by them or their heirs, in some tax-favored way.[1] Such a "best salary" plan therefore requires that the stockholder-executives be substantial stockholders and that they be prepared to act in concert. In fact, the "best salary" plan works best (assuming it works at all) where the stockholder-executive is effectively the principal or sole stockholder.

Just which amount of salary is "best" under this theory will depend on the amount of the corporation's income before compensation to the stockholder-executive. For simplicity, we will assume that only one stockholder-executive is involved, and that he or she will file a joint return. Some of the corporate income will be paid as compensation, and some will be retained by and taxed to the corporation. The tax advisor will determine the exact amount of salary which produces the lowest total tax on stockholder-executive salary paid and corporate income retained.

For example, if corporate income (before the stockholder-executive's salary) is $32,600, the best salary would be $7,600,[2] with the corporation retaining the $25,000 balance. This produces the lowest total tax take since the corporate tax bracket is 17 percent and the stockholder's tax bracket is 18 percent. Increasing the stockholder's pay would increase the total tax paid, since he or she would be

---

[1] Tax-favored ways to withdraw corporate funds would include tax-free merger with a larger firm or sale of stock at capital gains rates.

[2] More precisely, a salary which with other income and deductions would produce a taxable income of this amount.

in a higher bracket on every dollar over $7,600, while the corporation's bracket would not decline correspondingly. Decreasing the pay would not save tax.

On corporate income of $135,200, there would be a best salary range between $35,200 and $45,800, with the balance retained by the company. Within this range, the tax cost to the executive and the tax saved by the company would be the same.

The "best salary" concept requires a major adjustment where large amounts are involved. There is slight difference between the maximum corporate income tax (46 percent) and the maximum individual income tax on compensation income (50 percent, with some qualifications, see Chapter 2). Even though the immediate individual tax cost of salary over $45,800 may be a bit more than the corporate tax cost of retaining those added salary dollars, it is wiser on the whole to pay the extra salary (assuming it will be considered reasonable compensation). This way, the stockholder-employee will have the immediate use of the aftertax salary, without having to wait until some tax-favored withdrawal can be structured. Also, withdrawal may involve some additional tax cost (capital gains tax, for example), which immediate salary payment avoids. Thus, where corporate income (before stockholder-executive salary) is substantial, the best salary can be one in which the corporation retains $75,000 (taxed at a maximum 30 percent) and pays the rest as salary (taxed at up to 50 percent or so, assuming it is reasonable compensation). The reasoning here would be that the last $25,000 retained in the corporation would bear a tax of $7,500. The $17,500 aftertax balance (disregarding capital appreciation) could be extracted later at a long-term capital gains tax cost of no more than $4,900 (assuming no alternative minimum tax) and probably less. Thus, the tax cost of retaining that $25,000 in the corporation and then extracting it at capital gains rates would be less than the tax cost of paying it as salary (despite the 50 percent ceiling).

Should the corporation retain *more than* $75,000? Probably not. The tax cost of retention and later extraction is more likely to exceed the cost of paying it as salary for amounts retained in excess of $75,000, which are taxed at 40 percent or more.

The same principles apply, though the corporate income figures would be different (higher), if there are two or more stockholder-employees to be covered.

Though the "best salary" concept is fairly widely known among tax practitioners, the authors consider it of limited value in practice. It can occasionally suit the small business. It works best for the entrepreneur conducting two or more businesses, who does not currently need much income from one or more of those businesses and therefore can tailor withdrawals from the business to suit his or her tax advantage.

"Best salary" is not necessarily deductible salary. In fact, deductibility is an especially serious problem here. For most corporations, it is impossible to know in advance what the year's income will be. Thus, the exact salary for the year can be set only during the year, and often only late in the year. Also, since corporate income may fluctuate from one year to another, salary may fluctuate as well. Revenue agents auditing corporate tax returns are trained to notice these factors. To the IRS, salary fluctuations tend to indicate that at least part of the amount designated as salary is in fact a nondeductible dividend. Another factor with the same tendency arises where two or more stockholder-employees are paid salaries proportionate to their stockholdings. The "best salary" concept suffered still another setback in a court case in which the judge concluded that the fact that a stockholder-employee was paid the "best" salary, the salary that resulted in the least overall tax cost, tended to show that part of what he received was not reasonable compensation.

A tax difficulty of a different sort arises with respect to the earnings the company retains. If the company economizes on salary (maybe thereby avoiding reasonable compensation problems), it increases its profit which could be distributed as dividends. A dividend distribution would bear a much heavier total tax burden than paying the same amount out as salary would: The company has no deduction for the dividend payment, and so pays full corporate tax on it. The stockholder-executive's dividend is taxable income and it does not qualify for maximum tax relief.

Yet if the company does not distribute profits as dividends, it can risk the penalty tax on accumulated earnings. This tax is in addition to regular corporate tax. It is imposed where corporate earnings are retained instead of distributed as dividends and the motive is to save stockholders the income tax they would pay on their dividends. The penalty tax is excused if accumulated earnings don't exceed $150,000. Tax is also excused on accumulations in excess of $150,000 if the company can show a business reason—such as a specific expansion program—for such accumulation.

This means that a company which follows a best salary policy under which substantial amounts are retained rather than distributed should be prepared to show a business reason for these retentions.

THE DEPARTING STOCKHOLDER-EXECUTIVE

A number of complex factors arise when a company decides to buy out a particular stockholder or group of stockholders.[3] These factors aren't properly part of a book on executive compensation. But one important factor worth considering here arises when buying out a stockholder who is also an executive with an employment contract. If the corporation wants to buy an executive out, it ordinarily wants to terminate his or her services; the stock buy-out is subordinate to that.

In any buy-out involving an employment contract, the corporation and the stockholder-executive will have conflicting interests from a tax standpoint as well as an economic standpoint. The executive of course will want to collect as much as possible whereas the company wants to pay as little as possible. But besides differing over amounts, they have a tax incentive to differ over what the payments are for. The executive has two things to sell: a stock holding, which will go to the corporation, and an employment contract, which will be cancelled. Anything he or she collects for cancelling the employment contract would be fully taxable ordinary income. What is collected for the stock would be tax free as return of capital, with any excess treated as capital gain. The executive therefore wants most of the amount received treated as for stock (tax free and capital gain) and only a small amount treated as for the employment contract (ordinary income).

The company, however, wants most of what it pays treated as for the employment contract, since such a payment is deductible as a business expense. Any amount it pays for the executive's stock is a nondeductible capital expenditure. Ordinarily, the tax treatment of the payment will be determined by the way the company and the stockholder-executive allocate the total payment in the buy-out arrangement.

---

[3] The *company* decides because there are tax advantages in having the company do the buying. The initial decision is, of course, made by the board of directors acting for the other stockholders.

Example: Suppose Redgrave is the president of Hewitt Corporation and owns 15 percent of its stock, which cost him $150,000 six years ago. He also has an employment contract paying him $80,000 a year, which still has four years to run. Following a policy dispute with other stockholders, it is decided that he will sell all his stock and agree to cancel his employment contract for a total payment of $450,000. The buy-out deal might allocate, say, $350,000 of this to the stock and $100,000 to the employment contract. Or it might allocate $200,000 to the stock and $250,000 to the contract. Which allocation is chosen makes a sizable difference to each party. In the first method, Redgrave has $200,000 capital gain and $100,000 ordinary income, and the company deducts $100,000. In the second method he has $50,000 capital gain and $250,000 ordinary income, and the company deducts $250,000.

Redgrave is much worse off—he gets to keep much less of the $450,000 paid him—with the second allocation than with the first. But one party's detriment is the other's benefit. The deal is much less costly to Hewitt under the second allocation. Thus, if one party is tax-conscious and the other is not, a benefit approaching a windfall can result, to the tax-wise side.

This is not to say that the party who is aware of the tax factors should be silent about those factors, and design a wholly selfish allocation of the agreed amount. It sometimes happens that the other side (for instance, the executive) later realizes the tax detriment in the allocation and refuses to abide by it. The executive reports the allocation for tax purposes as he or she would like it to be. For example, though the agreement may have allocated $300,000 to the employment contract and $150,000 to stock, the executive might report it for tax purposes as $400,000 for stock and $50,000 for the employment contract. This maneuver is usually unsuccessful. That is, the parties generally are held for tax purposes to their agreement as written. But this is not always so. The IRS is not a party to such agreements and is not obliged to follow them. It can provide its own interpretation of the deal, or deny tax benefits to both parties, forcing them into court. Thus, even if the tax-conscious party's allocation is upheld, this may only happen after extensive tax audits and expensive litigation.

Some practitioners therefore prefer to spell out the tax costs and consequences to their less-informed adversaries, to reduce chances of reneging later. This can still leave some room to design the transaction to meet the parties' tax and financial convenience. For example, if deduction is especially important to the company this year, the executive might agree to a heavy allocation to the employment contract but might insist on a higher overall settlement amount.

The final agreement might include a clause requiring each party to report the deal for tax purposes as it is set forth in the contract. The IRS is not bound by this either. Thus, one party who deviates from the agreement could be upheld for tax purposes, but the other party would then have a claim for damages resulting from the former's breach of contract.

POSTPONING PAYMENT OF CONTROLLING STOCKHOLDER

A tax technique involving corporations using the accrual method deserves examination here. An executive who controls such a corporation sometimes notices that it can take a tax deduction for compensation owing to the executive which he or she need not yet report as income. A corporation on the accrual method can deduct compensation it owes but has not yet paid. The stockholder-executive, on the cash method, is not taxable on compensation owed until it is received. The apparent result is a tax deduction with no corresponding taxable income.

But the tax law strictly limits this technique. The corporation is allowed the accrual deduction for compensation to a more-than-50-percent stockholder only if the compensation is actually paid within 2½ months after the end of its taxable year. Thus, if corporation and executive are both on the calendar year, the corporation can deduct compensation due but unpaid for 1979 only if it pays that amount by March 15, 1980, and the executive is taxable when it is received, in 1980. If payment is not made within that 2½ month period, the corporation's deduction is denied forever.

But deduction is still allowed if the amount, though not actually pocketed by the executive, is made available to him or her *(constructively received)* during the year or within 2½ months thereafter. The executive is taxed in the year he or she constructively receives it. So a corporation may take the deduction and then, when subjected to a tax audit, claim that the compensation was constructively received. One difficulty with this is that the IRS may not accept a constructive receipt claim unless the corporation withheld tax on the amount in issue. At current withholding rates, up to 36 percent, and under today's rules requiring speedy deposit of tax withheld, a sizable part of the amount being deducted must be parted with promptly, in cash, in any case. This withholding requirement therefore effectively undermines reliance on constructive receipt as a means to avoid actual collection by the controlling stockholder-executive.

SUBCHAPTER S STOCKHOLDER-EXECUTIVES

The *Subchapter S* corporation is a tax-saving mechanism for closely held corporate business.[4] A Subchapter S corporation is in every respect a real, legal corporation under state corporate law. But it is exempt from U.S. corporate income tax, except in rare cases. Its stockholders are taxable directly on their share of corporate income whether or not it is actually distributed to them as dividends. And they can deduct their share of corporate operating losses.

There is an important tax-saving consideration for stockholder-executives of such corporations. They should be advised to maximize the amount of corporate income which is paid out as salary, minimizing the amount retained as undistributed income or distributed as dividends.

The tax motivation for such a move lies in the tax ceiling—50 percent—on personal service income. Personal service income includes salaries and bonuses. It *excludes* dividends and undistributed corporate income, which are taxable at rates up to 70 percent.

This, with some oversimplification, means that a Subchapter S stockholder in the top tax bracket shelters from tax 20 cents of every dollar converted from dividends into salary.

Take the case of Barnes, a stockholder-executive who now collects $60,000 in salary and $35,600 in dividends from his Subchapter S corporation. Barnes could reduce his tax bill by up to $1,024 if he instead collected $85,600 in salary and $10,000 in dividends, though both represent a $95,600 income.

Increasing compensation (and decreasing other income from the corporation) is a practical consideration only if executive employees (or some of them) hold or control

---

[4] The term refers to Subchapter S of the Internal Revenue Code, specifically 26 U.S. Code sections 1371-1379.

substantially all the stock. Stockholders who are not employees would not benefit from this arrangement, and might either block it outright or sue to undo it later. Also, the arrangement produces no benefit unless corporation income is such that the corporation could pay salaries large enough to qualify for maximum tax relief. Thus, for a married stockholder-executive filing a joint return, increased salary would have to be somewhat above $60,000.

The possibility that the Revenue Service may treat some or all of the increase as excessive (unreasonable) compensation should not deter the stockholder-employee from seeking the salary increase. There is nothing to lose by this move. If the increased amount is not deductible as compensation, the executive may be taxable on that amount at ordinary rates, up to 70 percent. If it had not been taken as compensation but as a dividend, or had been left in the corporation, he or she would have been taxable on it at ordinary rates, up to the same 70 percent.

Of course, increased compensation saves taxes only if at least some of the increased amount is reasonable. The company should take all available steps to establish that the amounts paid are reasonable. For suggestions on this, see Chapters 3 and 4.

CLAUSE COVERING REPAYMENT OF
EXCESSIVE COMPENSATION

Any payment made to _____ [the executive] as salary, commission, bonus or other compensation for personal services, which shall be disallowed in whole or in part as a deductible expense by the Internal Revenue Service, shall be reimbursed by _____ to _____ [the company] to the full extent of such disallowance, not later than _____ days after demand for reimbursement is made by _____ [the company]. In lieu of such reimbursement by _____, the Board of Directors of _____ [the company] may at its discretion direct that amounts be withheld and deducted from _____'s compensation until the amount owed to _____ shall be recovered.

6

The role of deferred compensation

Actor William Holden reportedly was paid $1 million for starring in the movie *The Bridge on the River Kwai*. For tax reasons, he chose to take this sum in annual $50,000 installments over a 20-year period. Texas attorney and politician John Connally's fee for serving as executor to the Sid Richardson estate came to $750,000. For tax reasons, he arranged to receive this in installments of varying amounts over 11 years.

Tax savings are the motivation behind virtually all deferred compensation arrangements. The scale of compensation, and of tax saving, when dealing with company executives will seldom approach that for movie stars or high-powered Houston lawyers. But deferring compensation is to some degree easier to arrange for executive employees than it is for self-employed persons.

The simplest deferred compensation arrangements are products of progressive tax rates. The higher a person's taxable income, the larger the proportion of that income which must be paid in taxes. Deferred compensation plans are designed to postpone payment of some of an executive's compensation from the year earned, in a high tax bracket, to some later year, when the executive is expected to be in a lower bracket. They are not the same as pension or profit-sharing plans (analyzed in Chapter 14). For one thing, deferred compensation normally is tailored to fit one particular executive or a few executives. Unlike pension or profit-sharing plans, rank-and-file employees are never covered by deferred compensation plans.

Deferred compensation arrangements have declined in importance in recent years. Today, compensation cannot be taxed at more than 50 percent (with some qualifications, see Chapter 2). Formerly, when compensation was taxable at rates up to 70 percent, it seemed wise to postpone a certain amount of that income into retirement years. The advisability diminishes when the 70 percent rate is reduced to about 50 percent. Also, there are the income averaging rules. These rules permit taxpayers with windfall income or sharply rising income to compute tax somewhat as if all income for a five-year period were received in equal annual installments over that period. Such averaging, an alternative to maximum tax relief, is another way to reduce the tax on current pay.

Still another factor has been the increase during an inflationary era in the dollar amounts of executives' pension income, investment income, and other post-retirement income. Since this increase has occurred without any major reduction in income tax rates, many executives should expect to be—after retirement—in tax brackets not far below the 50 percent ceiling that applied to their salaries during their active years.

These factors reduce the tax advantage of deferred compensation arrangements by reducing the tax cost of current compensation. There is less to lose by maximizing current cash pay than by deferring some.

Because of these factors, the tax saving from simple

deferred compensation—in which the executive receives over future years the exact dollar amount that could be received currently—is therefore usually too slight to justify deferral. But deferral becomes a worthwhile alternative to current compensation if there is added a prospect of collecting *more* than the amount deferred, through "investing" deferred amounts. This will be discussed below.

TYPES OF DEFERRED COMPENSATION

Compensation planners recognize two basic types of deferred compensation arrangement.[1] In the first and much more common type, the company is willing to pay a high cash salary now, but the executive for tax reasons prefers to postpone receipt of part of this amount until a later year. This type is often called an "unfunded" plan, for reasons which will appear later.

In the second type, the executive will be paid an amount at some future time if certain conditions are met. These conditions usually relate in some way to services to be performed by the executive in the future. This type is called a "forfeitable" plan.

In both situations, the executive wants to avoid being taxed now on amounts to be received in future years. The obstacle to this is the tax concept of constructive receipt of income, the rule that if income is set aside for a taxpayer so he can collect it at will, it is taxable to him when set aside for him, regardless of when he actually collects it. Successful deferred compensation plans are those that

---

[1] Pension and profit-sharing plans, though often referred to as deferred compensation plans, qualify for many special benefits, are subject to many complex limitations, and are covered in Chapter 14. However, one occasional use for an unfunded deferred compensation plan such as is described in this chapter is to provide additional postretirement income to an executive whose pension benefit is subject to the dollar ceilings described in Chapter 14. Such deferred compensation is, in essence, a supplemental pension.

avoid constructive receipt. The discussion that follows shows how to draw up successful deferred compensation plans—what features they must have, may have, and cannot have. A sample plan appears at the end of this chapter.

Unfunded plan

Two requirements must be met in designing this type of deferred compensation plan:

1. The company's obligation to pay the deferred amount must be no more than its contractual promise to pay. The executive cannot have a right in or claim to any specific fund or property, but just a contract right to be paid. The company must not be obliged to pay any amount into a trust for the executive's benefit, set up an escrow account for the executive, or acquire any particular item of property out of which the future payment must be made. The company's promise is therefore said to be unfunded.[2] If it were funded, so that the executive had a claim to particular property or to any fund, he or she would be taxable on it in the current year (unless it was a forfeitable plan, discussed later in this chapter).

2. The deferral of compensation must be agreed to before the compensation being deferred is earned. But would this rule prevent reducing future pay and deferring *that* amount? For example, why not amend a present employment contract calling for $75,000 currently, and instead pay $55,000 currently and a deferred $20,000? While there is no express rule against this, an arrangement which results in an increase in total pay, for example,

---

[2] Companies often in fact set up funds or buy property (insurance or annuity policies) to cover liability to pay deferred compensation in the future. This is acceptable and maybe even desirable (see pp. 71-72) as long as it is not required. These are sometimes called informally funded plans. For our purposes, they are unfunded.

$56,000 currently and $20,000 deferred, or $55,000 currently and $21,000 deferred, seems safer.

The Revenue Service has accepted deferral agreements made after the amounts deferred were earned, where they were not yet due to be paid. This situation seldom arises in executive compensation planning. One setting where it could be used arises when the executive is to receive, say next July, a bonus based on this year's profits. Company and executive could agree, after the bonus is earned but before it is due, that instead of paying the bonus in a lump sum, it would be paid in equal installments over, say, five years. (They could, of course, have made this arrangement in the first place.)

How deferral works

Example: Grumble Corporation contracts to employ Blake in an executive capacity for five years. Compensation will be at the rate of $55,000 a year, plus $10,000 a year credited to a bookkeeping reserve. Amounts so credited will be distributed in annual installments of one-fifth of the total, starting with the year Blake's employment is terminated, or the year of her death or disability if earlier. On these facts, the $10,000 a year qualifies as deferred compensation. It will not be taxable until Blake receives it, which presumably will be when she retires. (If she died before then, it would be taxed to her heirs.) The agreement was made before the monies were earned, and no funding is provided; there is only a contractual promise and a bookkeeping entry.

Deferred compensation when received is subject to income tax just as salary would be. It qualifies as personal service income for purposes of the maximum tax on earned income (see Chapter 2 and the discussion below of "invested" deferred compensation). It is also subject to wage withholding and social security tax, except that a social security tax exemption is granted for amounts received after a retirement which occurred at or after the retirement age specified in the company's pension plan.

Typically, deferred compensation is paid out in installments over a period of years (normally, between three and ten years). This is done to avoid the high tax rates that apply to bunched income, though with maximum tax relief this is less important today than in the past.

Note that for unfunded plans there is no requirement that amounts being deferred be subject to forfeiture by the executive at any time. Also, it doesn't matter that the company may have been willing to pay the entire $65,000 currently. The amount to be deferred need not be known in advance. It could, for example, be a percentage of the profits for the year the services are performed.

Deferral payout mistakes

A practical mistake in deferred compensation planning arises in designating when the deferred amounts should be received. Almost every executive wants the deferred amounts to be paid in installments after retirement, when the tax bracket will be lower. Yet the deferred amounts often are paid before retirement, in high-income years, so that the reduced tax rate advantage of deferral is lost.

The mistake is the contract clause which calls for payment of the deferred amount after the executive terminates his employment with the company. Many an executive will terminate employment with the company, not by retirement, but by taking a job with another firm at a higher salary. This new salary could in itself result in higher taxes; the deferred amount from the former employer could produce still higher taxes.[3]

Another, more obvious, trap, but one some executives fall into, is the deferral for a specified number of years, where the executive is still working when that deferral period has expired.

A properly drafted deferral agreement can avoid these mistakes. The deferred payments could become payable only after the executive has reached the age at which he or she expects to retire, for example, age 65.

Some executives may not be sure of the age at which they will want to stop work. In this case, deferral could be until such time as the executive "ceases substantially full-time gainful employment, but for a period of not less than _____ years."

Another possibility for reducing the impact of timing mistakes is this: Suppose an executive is scheduled to receive $20,000 next year, earned for services performed in past years, but he does not want to collect this next year, since he will still be working at a high-salaried job. Presumably, the Revenue Service would accept as valid an agreement made now which defers the $20,000 until after retirement. The problem is that this further deferral requires a new contract (at least as to these amounts). The company might not be willing to accommodate the execu-

---

[3] Some technical explanation is in order here. Because of maximum tax relief, *compensation* normally is not taxed at more than 50 percent, regardless of its amount. Thus, a highly paid executive's tax rate on *compensation* (personal service income) does not rise simply because some of it is being collected prematurely. But a larger amount of compensation pushes up the tax rate on the executive's *investment* income, which does not qualify for maximum tax relief. For example, an additional $20,000 of compensation could add, say, 5 percentage points to the tax rate on the executive's dividend income.

And if maximum tax relief is unavailable in the year the deferred amounts are collected because of tax preferences (see Chapter 2), they would be subject to full rates, up to 70 percent.

tive with a further deferral if, for example, the deferred amounts are becoming due because the executive is leaving to join a competitor. In this case the executive would take the deferred $20,000 next year as scheduled, and defer a corresponding amount out of next year's salary until retirement.

Assuming deferred amounts are not due until after retirement, a further technical point should be checked. It can be wise to make sure that deferred amounts do not become payable until the year *after* retirement has occurred. This will avoid receipt of this amount during the executive's final year of employment, when he could still be in a high tax bracket. This postponement might not be necessary if he will work only a few weeks during the year in which he retires. Thus, payout could be made to begin in the year following retirement except that it would begin within a month after retirement if retirement occurred in, say, the first four months of the year.

For executives, timing of deferral payout normally would not have to take account of the fact that the executive may want to make a lump-sum withdrawal of the amount standing to his credit in a company pension or profit-sharing plan. Arrange for the payout to occur when it is otherwise desirable to receive it, without regard to the lump-sum pension opportunity. Executives would often elect ten-year averaging of lump sums withdrawn (see Chapter 14), even where long-term capital gains treatment is available for part of the withdrawn amounts. Under ten-year averaging (unlike capital gain treatment), tax is computed as though the recipient had no other income that year. For executives, this can produce a lower tax liability than capital gain treatment and the averaged income (again unlike capital gain) is not a tax preference subject to the minimum tax or the alternative minimum tax.

Other planning aspects

Deferred compensation agreements often run for long periods. Every effort should therefore be made to foresee the future, for both executive and company, and to cover anticipatable events in the agreement, perhaps with provision for independent arbitration of disputes.

The deferred compensation agreement typically requires the company to make one or more payments of deferred amounts already earned if the executive's employment is terminated by death or disability. Payments to the estate or heirs of a deceased executive are taxed as follows: The commuted or present value (as of the date of the executive's death) of the right to deferred payments is included in the estate for estate tax purposes. (For estate tax considerations in general, see Chapter 17.) Amounts received by the executive's estate or heirs under an unfunded plan are also subject to income tax at ordinary rates subject to maximum tax relief. But any estate tax attributable to deferred amounts can be deducted against the amounts included in income.

Funding for company convenience: Insurance

There is no rule barring the company from buying property out of which it intends to fund any obligation it might have under the deferred compensation agreement. But deferral is lost if the company is *required* to obtain such property, and it is unwise to hint that the company ought to obtain it.

In practice, companies sometimes do acquire property to fund their deferred compensation obligations. This may be stock or other investments, but is often an insurance policy. Funding through insurance would work this way:

The company would take out a policy on the executive's life to cover its deferred compensation liability, naming itself as the beneficiary. The executive would have no rights in the policy, and would not be taxable on company payments of premiums. The company could not deduct the premiums since it is the beneficiary.

If the executive dies before becoming eligible to receive the deferred compensation installments, the company would collect the insurance proceeds. These proceeds are tax-free to the company. Many deferred compensation arrangements require the company to pay any earned deferred amounts to named heirs of the executive if death occurs before installments are fully paid. Where this happens, the company would deduct its payments for tax purposes (assuming they are reasonable compensation).

If the executive survives to receive the deferred compensation in installments, the company normally would cash in the policy. Any profit the company received on the policy (that is, surrender value less premiums) is ordinary income; loss, if any, is not deductible. The company may deduct amounts it pays the executive (assuming they are reasonable), and the executive pays tax at ordinary rates (subject to maximum tax relief) on what he collects. To summarize, funding with insurance means: (*a*) no company deduction for insurance premiums, (*b*) no tax to company on insurance proceeds, (*c*) ordinary income (or nondeductible loss) to company on policy cashed in before death, and (*d*) company deduction (to the extent reasonable) for payments to executive or heirs.

The executive's receipts are ordinary income; so are receipts by heirs, and there is also an estate tax.

Company deduction for deferred compensation

Deferred unfunded compensation is deductible by the company, just as other compensation is. The company deducts only when the compensation is paid, and not when it is earned by the executive, even if the company uses the accrual method of accounting.[4] Only reasonable compensation for the executive's services is deductible.

In practice, few questions have arisen about the reasonableness of deferred compensation paid an executive under a plan. But the problem might arise in this way: Coleman's contract calls for $70,000 this year plus another $20,000 to be paid five years hence. The company will deduct only $70,000 this year, so this year's deduction might not be questioned. Five years from now, the company will pay and deduct an additional $20,000. This additional $20,000 might be challenged as unreasonable. If Coleman has retired, any payment would seem unreasonable at first glance because Coleman rendered no services that year. If Coleman is still an employee, the $20,000 on top of his other salary could seem excessive.

To counter IRS challenges, the company must show that the payment represents compensation for services performed in the past. It should therefore have ascertained in the year the services were rendered that the current pay plus the deferred compensation was reasonable. That is, it should have applied the tests for determining reasonableness set forth in Chapters 3 and 4, and it should have retained full documentation as part of company records to support its claim of reasonableness.

Inflation has probably tended to protect deferred compensation arrangements from challenge. For example, $90,000 of compensation for 1979 might seem excessive if looked at in 1980. But if looked at in 1985, after the compensation had been paid in installments of $70,000 in 1979 and $20,000 in 1984, it might well seem reasonable. This may help to explain why the reasonableness of

---

[4] For financial accounting purposes, deferred compensation reduces current earnings of accrual method companies.

deferred compensation has not yet become a serious issue in executive compensation planning.

Phantom stock and other "investments" of deferred amounts

For some executives, deferral *alone* has little or no tax benefit (see page 64). For them, deferral's attraction lies in the opportunity to "invest" deferred amounts and the "earnings" thereon free of tax until these investments and earnings are withdrawn. The advantage here—as with contributory pension and profit-sharing plans (see Chapter 14)—is that investments grow faster if earnings are tax-free until withdrawn even if they are fully taxed when withdrawal occurs.

"Investment" of deferred amounts first gained popularity through the device called *phantom* or *shadow* stock. Suppose an executive's employment contract calls for $60,000 this year and an additional $10,000 in ten years. This $10,000, deferred for ten years, is worth much less than a present payment would be. The executive loses ten years of investment increment by opting for deferral. He or she would prefer to have that $10,000 put into some income-producing or growth investment. Yet if the company were obliged to put the deferred $10,000 into some investment in which the executive had an ownership interest, it would not qualify as deferred compensation but would be taxable currently, when earned.

The solution here is the phantom stock plan or similar "investment" arrangement. The $10,000 is considered for purposes of the deferred compensation agreement as if it were put into some particular investment, designated in the agreement. At the end of the deferral period, the executive is paid the value of that "as if" investment. Deferral is not jeopardized because the company is not obliged to make that investment, or any investment. It is just that the value of that "as if" investment becomes the measure of the amount to be paid when deferral ends. The make-believe investment could be in a bank account, an annuity, stock of any company, or any bond. This arrangement was given the name phantom or shadow stock because usually the deferred amount was treated "as if" invested in stock of the company paying the deferred compensation.

Example: Cowell, president of Hedake Corporation, is paid $60,000 this year, and an additional $10,000 is credited to a deferred compensation account. This $10,000 is considered under the employment contract as if invested in Hedake shares. When deferral ends, ten years hence, Cowell will receive an amount of cash equal to the value at that time of the number of shares which the deferred amount would have bought when deferral began.

Assume Hedake Corporation shares are currently selling at $50. Thus, it is as if Hedake invested the deferred $10,000 in 200 Hedake shares. Ten years from now, Hedake shares are at $225 each. Cowell therefore is entitled to $45,000 (200 × $225). Cowell has no right to the Hedake *shares,* just their cash equivalent.

The amount Cowell collects is ordinary income and qualifies for maximum tax relief. The company's payment is deductible as compensation, to the extent that it, coupled with regular salary, is reasonable (a point we will further examine below).

If Hedake stock stood at $40 when deferral ended, Cowell's $8,000 would have been treated the same way: ordinary income, and company deduction if reasonable.

In the simple phantom stock plan described here, deferred compensation is "invested" in stock and the executive is paid the market value of those phantom shares when deferral ends. A variation of this arrangement would pay at the end of the deferral period an amount equal to the dividends earned on the phantom stock. This may include or exclude paying the value of the stock itself. Also, "as if" interest might be accrued on "as if" dividends, during the deferral period. Or accumulated "as if" dividends might be converted into additional phantom shares.

So far, we have been considering phantom stock arrangements simply as a way of investing deferred amounts for the executive's benefit, so that investment increments are not lost during the deferral period. Here, company and executive can agree on what kind of investment shall be the measure of the payout. Thus, they could agree that the deferred amount should be treated as if invested in IBM stock, a Bank of America savings account, or anything else. The executive might be entitled to receive an amount equal to any dividends on the make-believe investment, with or without the right to receive the value of the investment itself, and might also be given the right to alter the make-believe investment during the term of deferral. Thus, company and executive could consider the initial investment as if sold when the executive so elects, and the proceeds put into some new "as if" investment the executive designates.

Another practical use of the phantom stock plan is as a substitute for paying the executive in stock of the employer company. Paying an executive with stock may provide an incentive to improve company profits, in which the executive will share as stockholder. On the other hand, Chapter 8 points out that paying with stock can be more expensive to the company than paying with cash, without any greater financial benefit to the executive. A solution to this problem would be to pay in phantom stock. This way, he or she would benefit from any rise in value of the stock. (The arrangement could be to pay the value of the stock plus the value of all dividends in the interim, if this is desired.) The executive would therefore have a stockholder's incentive to improve company profits, yet would be paid in cash rather than in stock, so that the company would have full deduction for the amount paid (if reasonable), and not the limited deduction that arises if there is a payment in stock which the executive later sells at a capital gain. Of course, company deduction is taken only when the company pays. Deduction therefore comes later under phantom stock plans than under straight stock payment arrangements.

To assess the economic advantage of "as if" investment, assume it is made in *any* income-producing investment, and contrast the aftertax yield on this pretax investment with the yield from an *after*tax investment with no deferral.

Example: Ryan and Eliot are each entitled to a $20,000 bonus in each of five years (1979-83), and during these years each would be taxed on that bonus at 50 percent under maximum tax rules. Ryan takes the bonus in cash each year, invests it each year at 8 percent for ten years, and withdraws each year's investment in 1989-93. Eliot has each year's bonus deferred and "invested" in an "as if" investment at 8 percent for ten years, receiving each year's investment in 1989-93. Assume Ryan and Eliot are in a 50-percent bracket in 1989-93 (so there is no tax benefit from deferral alone).

Ryan's total aftertax collection—of a currently taxable bonus invested with a currently taxable yield—is $81,440. Eliot's total aftertax collection—of a currently nontaxable bonus invested with a currently nontaxable yield, but fully taxable when received—is $107,950, or $26,510 more.[5]

Any investment increment the company will owe when the deferral ends is funded by the corporation out of *after-tax* earnings. For example, suppose an "as if" investment of deferred compensation at 8 percent a year for 10 years. If the company actually bought a bond paying interest of 8 percent (and reinvested earnings at 8 percent), this interest income would be taxable to the company as earned, and so would total less than 8 percent compounded when deferral ends. The same result would occur if company earnings were reinvested in the business at an 8 percent yield.

If the "as if" investment were in stock of another company, and the employer actually bought such stock, it would be subject to capital gains tax on any appreciation when deferral ended and the executive was paid the stock or its value.

Will a payment equal to the value of the "as if" investment be considered reasonable compensation? For example, suppose the amounts deferred in 1979-83 total $80,000. At the end of the deferral period (say 1988) the "as if" investment is worth $270,000, so the executive is entitled to receive cash in that amount. Is the $270,000 reasonable compensation?

This question arises under tax law, for purposes of the company's deduction, and under state corporate law, as a possible dissipation of company assets against the interests of the stockholders. There are as yet no clear answers for either tax law or corporate law purposes.

---

[5] This example illustrates the saving involved, but the authors should not be understood as endorsing the arrangement. This is a plan for deferring compensation into the 1990s, which no practical executive would undertake lightly.

Remember that the phantom stock is used as a measure of an amount to be paid later. In tax law, we are used to arrangements which measure the executive's bonus by this year's or last year's profits, sales, and so forth. Such measuring rods will often directly reflect the value of the executive's services. The same could be said of a payment in stock which is subject to forfeiture by the executive until earned, maybe years later, through services. But basing compensation on the value which investment property may achieve several years after the right to receive this value has been earned is something quite different, even where that property is stock in the employer corporation.

To the authors it seems that reasonableness of compensation in a phantom stock plan would be hard to establish, for purposes of the company's compensation deduction. The difficulty is in establishing that the value of stock in, say, 1985, reflects the value of services rendered previously. Fortunately for deferred compensation planners, the IRS may not share the authors' concern on this matter. There is apparently no instance of an IRS challenge to reasonableness of phantom stock reaching the courts. (This also means, of course, that reasonableness has never been officially confirmed.)

In the authors' opinion, the absence of IRS challenge probably results from the fact that closely held companies—the usual targets of IRS attack—have seldom used phantom stock.

But as a matter of state corporate law, reasonableness is plainly in question. The authors have unearthed two court decisions asking whether phantom stock results in excessive compensation which the stockholders can recover on the company's behalf. One decision found it reasonable; the other found it unreasonable. In the authors' opinion, the decision finding unreasonableness made the stronger argument, though the issue is far from closed.

FORFEITABLE PLANS

Another form of deferred compensation, other than the unfunded variety discussed above, is the *forfeitable* kind. In this case, the executive is not taxable on deferred amounts because he or she has not yet fully earned them. In unfunded compensation, the amount being deferred has been earned but is not currently taxable because payment is postponed and there is no trust, escrow, or other specific fund to which the executive has a claim. In the forfeitable arrangement, there may be a trust fund or other property for the executive, but there is no current tax liability because the executive's interest may be forfeited by future action or inaction.

Forfeitable deferred cash compensation is rare. Where it exists, it serves company needs rather more than the executive's needs. That is, though it accomplishes a postponement of current salary, the delayed payment is intended as an incentive to continued executive performance rather than as a tax-saving move to delay income and tax until retirement age.

An example would be an arrangement to pay Johnson, the advertising manager, $70,000 for 1979 plus an additional $10,000 paid into a trust of which Johnson is beneficiary, to be distributed to him in 1983 if he performs executive duties on a substantially full-time basis from 1979 through 1983.

Such an arrangement is recognized as providing an effective deferral only if:

1. The executive's interest in the trust is subject to *substantial* risk that he or she will forfeit it.

2. Assuming the executive transfers the interest, that interest remains subject to substantial risk of forfeiture in the hands of the transferee.

At this writing, there is no official indication or example of any deferred compensation paid into a trust which satisfies this twofold requirement. In the authors' opinion, this is not because it is impossible or unusually difficult to satisfy the requirement, but because there has as yet been no significant interest in the matter in the business community.[6] This is another way of saying that achieving deferral through this device is technically possible, but in practice attracts no one.

Unfunded, forfeitable deferred compensation would be possible as well—and even less interesting to executives. In forfeitable arrangements, though the company may pay into the trust this year on an executive's behalf, it can't deduct for its payment until the executive is taxable on it—that is, when deferral ends. The notion that the company parts with funds now from which it gets no tax benefit for several years ought to discourage company interest in this device.

SUMMING UP

In the present tax climate, the authors would seldom recommend deferred compensation arrangements to executives, for these reasons:

1. Deferred compensation means surrendering economic gain now for possibly greater gain through tax saving in the fairly distant future. This involves a prediction that tax rules will remain about as they are far into the future,

---

[6] The requirement here is a modification of that for compensation paid in restricted stock, discussed in Chapter 9. Restricted stock can itself be viewed as a kind of deferred compensation under a forfeitable plan.

something extremely risky in the highly volatile area of taxation.[7]

2. Thanks to the maximum tax, income averaging, and high post-retirement income, there is relatively little tax saving from deferral alone, without an "as if" investment of deferred amounts.

3. The executive risks losing the deferred amounts and "as if" investment increments through the employer's failure or default or, if in a forfeitable plan, through occurrence of the substantial risk on which deferral was based.[8]

---

[7] The risk in such predictions is illustrated by the recent changes in qualified stock option rules. The exercise of the option was subjected to minimum tax, tax on capital gain (on sale of the stock) was increased, part of that gain was subjected to the minimum tax, the same part reduced the benefit of the maximum tax, then capital gains tax was reduced, capital gain was exempted from the minimum tax and subjected to a new alternative minimum tax, and ceased to reduce the benefit of the maximum tax.

[8] This reportedly happened to Penn-Central executives.

LETTER AGREEMENT FOR EMPLOYMENT AND DEFERRED COMPENSATION

Dear Mr. _____ ,

The following shall constitute the agreement between us regarding your employment by _____ (hereinafter, the company):

The company will employ you during the period _____ through _____ .

Your base salary during this period shall be at the annual rate of $_____ , payable in equal monthly installments.

In addition to this base salary and in further consideration for your services under this agreement, the company agrees to accrue as deferred compensation in each month during the period of this agreement, an amount equal to one twelfth of $_____ and to credit that sum to a special account on its books.

Neither you, nor any legal representative or beneficiary designated by you, shall have any right (except as an unsecured general creditor) against the company with respect to any portion of the account.

The deferred compensation due you, consisting of the total amounts so credited to the special account, shall be paid to you in ten equal annual installments, beginning on the _____th day of January following the year in which you shall have terminated your employment with the company on a substantially full-time basis [or, following the year in which you shall have attained age _____ or shall have ceased substantially full-time gainful employment, whichever is the later (earlier)], with further installments on the _____th of January of succeeding years.

If you should die before payment of the last installment, unpaid installments shall be paid on the due dates as above set forth to the beneficiaries designated by you in writing, or, failing such designation, to your estate.

. . . [Other clauses]

Your acceptance by signing in the space below will constitute our agreement with respect to your employment by the company.

Very truly yours

_____
[Company]

by _____
[title]

Accepted:

_____
[employee]

CLAUSES COVERING PHANTOM STOCK
PROVISION FOR INVESTMENT IN SECURITIES
SELECTED BY EXECUTIVE

[Certain amounts are credited periodically to deferred compensation account]

The amount in the account shall be deemed invested in such securities as you [executive] shall designate which are traded on a national securities exchange. You shall have the right, on the first business day of each quarter of the calendar year, to designate the securities deemed sold or purchased for the account on that date. The account shall further be credited with the dollar amounts equal to the amount of dividends or interest paid on securities deemed held by the account.

The company is not required to purchase or sell any securities designated by you. If it should purchase any such securities, they shall remain the sole property of the company and will not become part of the account, nor will you or any legal representative or beneficiary designated by you have any right (except as an unsecured general creditor) against the company with respect to any portion of the account.

As of the first date on which an installment of deferred compensation shall become due from the account, your right to designate investments shall cease. The account shall be valued by adding the fair market value of all securities deemed part of the account to the dollar amounts in the account which are not deemed invested in securities. The fair market value of securities shall be the mean between the high and low prices for the day on the largest national exchange on which such securities traded for that day, or absent any trade that day, on the first preceding business day on which trades occurred. As each installment shall be paid, the balance in the account shall be reduced by the amount paid. The balance in the account (less each installment payment as it occurs) shall be deemed invested at interest at an annual rate of _____ percent, and an amount equal to such interest shall be credited to the account.

7

Paying executives with stock or other property

The executive may be awarded property in addition to cash and fringe benefits for services rendered. Usually, this is stock of the company, but may be a car or some other asset. Or, the company may give the executive the opportunity to buy stock or other property from it at a bargain price.

This chapter will cover the basic rules governing payments of property and bargain sales of property to executives. The rules given here apply to all types of property paid over or sold—stock, real estate, or anything else. But a number of special legal, accounting, and other considerations arise when the property involved is stock of the corporation the executive works for. These special considerations are explored in Chapter 8. Thus, both this chapter and Chapter 8 should be consulted by the compensation planner who is contemplating a payment or bargain sale of company stock, or is choosing between a payment (or a sale) of stock or, on the other hand, of some other property.

Additional special considerations are involved if the

company plans to pay for or sell stock or other property but with strings attached. This is the situation where the executive actually receives the property now, but will not get complete legal or practical ownership of it until some months or years in the future. These special considerations are covered in Chapter 9 on restricted property.

An executive is subject to tax when property is received for services rendered. This is true regardless of the nature of the property received: stock of the employer corporation, stock of another corporation, land, or whatever (with a minor exception for items of nominal value, see below). And it is true whether the company pays the executive in both cash and property or in property only.

Usually, the executive is taxable on property in the year it is received (for exceptions to this rule, see Chapter 9). This is important. Tax ordinarily is imposed when the property is received and is not postponed until it is converted into cash. The amount taxed is the fair market value of the property, regardless of what the property may have cost the company making the payment.

Example: Suppose Williams, Globe Corporation's production manager, received a $36,000 salary during 1979 and, in addition, a bonus of 50 Globe shares worth $125 each. Williams' compensation income for the year is $42,250 ($36,000 plus $6,250).

The taxable amount is the property's *fair market value.* This may occasionally be hard to determine. These are the guidelines to apply in determining the amount on which the executive will be taxable:

1. In most cases, the property is stock. If the stock paid as compensation is traded in an established market (including over-the-counter), the value of the stock generally is the mean between the high and low price of the stock in that market on the date payment is made. This is true

whether the stock paid as compensation is stock of the employer corporation or of some other corporation.

But if the trades in the market are infrequent, or in very small quantities, or the amount of stock being paid exceeds the amount usually traded, or if, as often happens, there is no established market in the shares, determination of their fair market value is a complex task. The company should first check whether any determination of the shares' value has been made recently for some other purpose—for example, determinations for purposes of personal property tax, gift tax, estate tax, or inheritance tax. The value as so determined may be used if realistic and recent enough, and assuming the number of shares in question does not involve a major or controlling interest. If no such recent determinations have been made, a professional specialist should be consulted. The specialist will consider a number of factors, such as book value, earning power and earnings history, and size of the block of stock in question and its effect on corporate control.

2. For other types of property, fair market value may be easier to determine. Thus, for such items as automobiles, boats, and TV sets, the prevailing retail price (including the used price if the item isn't new) should be used. If in doubt, have the property appraised (cost of appraisal is deductible). If large amounts are involved, the careful taxpayer may seek several appraisals and use the average of the appraisals. Real estate usually should be professionally appraised to determine its value. Valuations for real property tax purposes are seldom acceptable.

Bonds traded on an established market would be valued the same way stock so traded is valued. Otherwise, bonds or notes usually are considered to be worth their face amount, but may be assigned some other value, higher or lower than face amount, if justified by the facts (chiefly, the credit rating and the interest rate).

If a payment is received in stock or other property, the executive reports the fair market value of the property as compensation income in the year the property is received. The value of any property received as compensation from the company is personal service income. It therefore generally can't be taxed at *more* than 50 percent. (For details on this personal service income ceiling see Chapter 2.)

Where a company distributes turkeys, hams and other holiday gifts of nominal value to its employees, such gifts are tax-exempt—if the distributions are made to employees generally, to promote employee goodwill. Limiting such gifts to executives would make them taxable. Therefore they are not an element of executive compensation planning.

Bargain purchase. Another compensation device, closely related to the payment of compensation in stock or other property, is the grant to the executive of an opportunity to buy stock or other property at a bargain. Bargain purchases should be distinguished from options to buy property. As used in compensation settings, an option means the right or privilege to buy the stock or other property under an offer continuing for a stated period of time. A bargain purchase offer would be one without a stated duration which the executive could count on, one which might be withdrawn or modified at the company's discretion or to reflect changes such as rises or falls in the value of the offered property.

Sometimes there may be no practical distinction between bargain purchase opportunities and nonstatutory options. It would be unlikely that an employer would offer an executive a bargain purchase opportunity without allowing a few days or weeks for the executive to think it over; this could be the practical equivalent of an option extending for that period. But most compensation planners, and all executive optionees, prefer to see some substantial exercise period, months or years, written into the option. Chiefly for that reason—the need to provide for events and contingencies months or years hence—stock option arrangements are more likely to involve corporate documentation and formality.

The tax rules for an executive's bargain purchase of property from the employer are in essence the same as those for payment received in property. The only change in the picture is that something is paid for the property, and the only tax difference this makes is a dollar for dollar reduction in the amount that is taxed.

If the executive buys stock or other property from the company at a bargain—which means for any amount less than its fair market value—the property is taxable in the year it is received, at its fair market value less the amount paid for it. Thus, if in 1979 an executive is given the opportunity to buy 100 shares worth $90 each for $75 each, he or she has compensation income of $1,500 in the year the purchase is made ($9,000 value minus the $7,500 purchase price paid).

If an employer offers stock or other property at a bargain price and the executive chooses not to accept the offer, there is no compensation and no tax liability.

Courtesy discounts.   Employees are not taxed on their bargain purchases of goods from the company under a company policy of granting courtesy discounts on purchases of items of relatively small value, to employees generally, to promote employee goodwill, health or efficiency. Limiting such discounts to executives would make them taxable. They therefore are not elements of executive compensation planning.

SALE BY THE EXECUTIVE

Stock or other property which the executive received as compensation or bought in a bargain sale from the company normally is a capital asset to the executive. Any profit or loss on a later sale of the item is capital gain or loss. Gain is tax-favored *long-term* capital gain if it is held for more than twelve months from the day following receipt of the stock or other property to the day it is sold. *Receipt of the stock* refers here to the day the executive becomes legal owner of the stock, regardless of any delay in delivering the stock certificates, and even if such certificates are never delivered.

For tax purposes, gain (or loss) is the amount by which the sales proceeds in an arm's length sale exceed (or fall below) the amount on which the executive is taxed as compensation. Thus, if Broder received 100 shares worth $100 each in 1976 which he sold for $14,000 in 1979, he would have had $10,000 of ordinary compensation income in 1976 and would have $4,000 of capital gain in 1979. If he had sold them for $10,000 immediately upon receipt in 1976, he would have had $10,000 of compensation income in 1976 and no capital gain would occur at any time.

If the executive had bought the property at a bargain, the gain (or loss) is the amount by which the sales proceeds in an arm's length sale exceed (or are less than) the sum of the amount paid and the amount the executive was taxed on at the time of receipt.

WITHHOLDING ON PROPERTY PAYMENTS

The company must withhold income tax on property it pays as compensation. Just how withholding is to be handled is left to the company's own ingenuity. The Revenue Service provides no rules or suggestions. The authors suggest the following alternatives, from which the company can choose the one which best suits the circumstances:

1. Pay out a smaller amount of property and use the balance to satisfy the withholding amount. For example, suppose Wales Company intends to pay Bowker, its presi-

dent, a bonus of 200 shares worth $100 each, or $20,000. If Bowker's withholding bracket (not the same as the tax bracket) is 36 percent, Wales could simply award 128 shares and deposit $7,200 as the tax withheld on $20,000. Bowker would report a bonus of $20,000 and claim a $7,200 withholding credit against tax due. Better still, Wales could use the alternative withholding rate of a flat 20 percent of the value allowed for bonuses and other special payments. Here, Wales would withhold $4,000 and pay 160 shares; Bowker would have a $20,000 bonus and a $4,000 withholding credit.

This method for meeting the company's withholding obligation works best where the property is readily divisible, with each unit of equal value, as in the case of shares of stock.

2. Reduce the executive's cash salary by an additional amount (in addition, that is, to regular tax withholding on salary) representing the tax to be withheld on the property. For example, if an executive is paid $4,000 a month regular salary and is also paid a bonus of stock worth $2,000, the regular income tax withholding on salary could be increased by $400, representing the withholding on $2,000 at the alternate 20 percent withholding rate.

3. Where the executive intends to sell all the stock or a substantial part of it immediately after acquisition, the sale proceeds can provide the funds needed to cover the withholding obligation. Thus, if the executive is paid 100 shares worth $100 each and immediately sells 40 shares for $4,000, the proceeds can be used to cover the withholding, paying over to the company the amount required to be withheld (assume it is $2,000).

The immediate sale would normally eliminate any problem of valuing the property received. It would be worth what the executive got for it, unless the sale were not at arm's length (e.g., a sale to a family member or nominee).

4. Where the executive will keep the entire property, the cash equivalent of the withholding amount can be paid over to the company out of personal funds. This may require borrowing.

THE COMPANY'S VIEWPOINT

A company takes a compensation expense deduction for the compensation it pays in stock or other property, just as it does for compensation paid in cash. It deducts the amount the executive is taxed on, the property's fair market value, except that, as with cash compensation, it can't deduct any unreasonable or excessive part of compensation paid.

Thus, if Wye Corporation pays its vice president Bonner 150 shares of Wye Corporation stock worth $80 a share, Wye Corporation would deduct $12,000 (subject to reasonable compensation limits) regardless of its basis for the stock. The same deduction rule applies if Wye Corporation pays in shares of some other corporation, or in some other property such as land, a boat or a car.

The company deducts on its tax return for the year in which the executive's taxable year ends. If company and executive both use the calendar year, the executive reports a 1979 payment on the 1979 return and the company deducts on *its* 1979 return. But if the company uses a fiscal year, this rule is a bookkeeping nuisance. Suppose the company has a fiscal year ending September 30 and pays the executive in property on July 1, 1979. The executive reports it on his or her 1979 return, but the company cannot deduct until its return for October 1, 1979–September 30, 1980 is filed, since this is the year in which the *executive's* tax year ends.

Where the corporation pays compensation in property other than its own stock, it will also have gain or loss for tax purposes. This is because the delivery of property to satisfy a debt, including a debt for compensation, is a taxable sale of the property. (It is treated as a debt for compensation even though there was no preexisting obligation to pay the property—no contract requirement or other arrangement.) Gain or loss is usually capital gain or loss, but is ordinary income or loss if the property involved is in the nature of the corporation's stock in trade. Loss is not deductible if the executive to whom the loss property is paid, or the executive's family (parents, brothers or sisters, children, spouse, etc.), owns more than half the corporation's stock.

The amount of the company's gain or loss is the property's fair market value less the company's basis for it. To determine that value, follow the guidelines on pages 86-87. (Occasionally, the property is paid for services which were rendered at a stipulated price. Here, the fair market value of the property can be treated as equivalent to that price, absent better evidence of value.)

Example: Crown Corporation pays 50 shares of duPont stock to its president, Koenig, as a bonus. Crown bought the stock at $140 a share two years ago, but it was worth $200 a share when paid to Koenig.

With respect to this payment, Koenig has $10,000 of compensation income. Crown has $10,000 of compensation expense deduction (assuming total compensation to Koenig is reasonable) and $3,000 of long-term capital gain ($10,000 less $7,000) on the "sale" to Koenig.

For the company as well as for the executive, the bargain sale rules are essentially the same as for a payment in property. Its compensation expense is the fair market value of the stock or other property transferred to the executive reduced by the amount paid for it. This amount is deductible, assuming that, when added to the executive's other compensation from the company, it is reasonable compensation. Deduction is taken on the company's returns for the year in which the executive's tax year ends.

If the property subject to the bargain purchase is company stock, the company has no taxable gain or deductible loss from the transaction. If it is property other than company stock, the company's gain or loss is the property's fair market value less the company's basis for it. The amount the executive pays is not relevant in figuring the company's gain or loss but only in computing the compensation deduction.

Property is sometimes paid *now* for services to be rendered in the future. Technically, a company can only deduct compensation for services already rendered. Thus, if services to earn the property are to be rendered over a period of years in the future, the company theoretically must prorate its deduction over the period the services are rendered.[1] While it does not clearly appear that this deduction limitation is actually enforced, companies for which a full, present compensation deduction is an important element in the decision to pay in property should consider one of these alternatives:

1. Ask the Revenue Service for a ruling on when the company may deduct for its payment.
2. Set up a forfeitable, nontransferable arrangement to pay restricted property which will give full deduction when restrictions lift (see Chapter 9).

---

[1] This assumes the property is not forfeitable *and* nontransferable under the rules for restricted property.

BARGAIN SALE TO EXECUTIVE OF PROPERTY OTHER THAN COMPANY STOCK

EXAMPLES OF TAX TREATMENT

Example 1

Assume:

Property's value		$10,000
Selling price		$ 6,000
Company's basis		$ 2,000
Executive's income	$10,000 − $6,000 =	$ 4,000
Company's deduction (if reasonable).	$10,000 − $6,000 =	$ 4,000
Company's gain (or loss).	$10,000 − $2,000 =	$ 8,000 gain

Example 2

Assume:

Property's value		$10,000
Selling price		$ 6,000
Company's basis		$12,000
Executive's income	$10,000 − $ 6,000 =	$ 4,000
Company's deduction (if reasonable).	$10,000 − $ 6,000 =	$ 4,000
Company's gain (or loss).	$12,000 − $10,000 =	$ 2,000 loss

8

Special rules for payments in company stock

The rules in Chapter 7, on paying executives in property or selling them property at a bargain price, are fully applicable when the property in question is the stock of the employer. But there are additional tax, legal, accounting and practical considerations when paying or selling stock in stock bonus, stock award, stock purchase, or stock thrift or savings plans. These considerations are discussed in this chapter.

The rules are not significantly different. The executive who receives or buys stock is subjected to exactly the same tax rules as apply on receipt or purchase of other property. However, there is one important difference affecting the *company:* It has no taxable gain or deductible loss on its stock (see below). In other respects, it is additional rather than different rules that come into play when payment or purchase is in the company's stock.

Stock of the employer corporation has a twofold use in compensation planning. It can be a payment or reward for services already performed, and in this respect does not differ from payment in cash or in other property of equal value. But it also operates as an incentive to further productive work for the company. It gives the executive a stake in the company; the increases in company profits or net worth will benefit the executive shareholder over and above the other compensation received.

Executive incentive plans are generally structured to pay out bonuses in stock in direct response to particular executive achievements, much in the manner of cash bonuses discussed in Chapter 4. The type of plan discussed here contemplates that the executive is paid the stock after performance is shown. In such a plan, the executive reports the value of the stock as income when it is received. (Plans in which the executive is currently paid in stock which can later be forfeited if performance is not shown may seem similar in concept but are subject to differing rules, discussed in Chapter 9.)

Incentive plans for paying stock as a bonus are often designed to make half the payment in stock and the other half in cash. The executive could use the cash part to pay the tax on the award, and it would also provide the funds to cover any withholding obligation. Half in cash would seldom be too little, since the executive's federal tax on the stock generally couldn't exceed 50 percent. For executives in brackets below the 50 percent bracket (less than $60,000 of taxable income for married executives), some smaller cash proportion could be preferred, with a larger proportion of stock. But where state or local income tax is imposed, it may be desirable to pay half in cash in any case, to cover state or local tax obligations in addition to the federal take.

Company tax and cost factors. When a company pays an executive in company stock, it takes a compensation expense deduction for the fair market value of the stock, assuming compensation is reasonable. It has no taxable gain or deductible loss on the payment in stock, unlike the case where the payment is in property other than its stock. (If it had sold the stock to the executive at less than its market value, it would deduct the difference between value and what the executive paid, if compensation is reasonable, but still would have no taxable gain or deductible loss.) Thus a company can pay with its own stock worth $10,000, and take a $10,000 deduction, without any capital gains tax even though it has little or no basis for the stock.

But this is no free deduction. When a company pays stock with a $10,000 market value to an executive, it is thereby surrendering $10,000 which it could have collected on a sale of that stock to an outsider.[1]

Moreover, any amount collected on sale of its own stock to an outsider is tax free, just as its payment of compensation using such stock is tax free. Thus, a company's payment of compensation in its own stock costs the company (before taxes) an amount equal to the stock's fair market value, since it could collect that amount tax free by selling it instead. This cost is reduced by the tax value of the company's deduction for the compensation payment, so that the aftertax cost of payment in stock usually is 54 percent of the stock's value.

In deciding whether to make such a payment, the corporation will weigh whether the aftertax value of the stock payment to the executive justifies the aftertax cost to the company. In most cases, payment in company stock meets this condition. Aftertax value depends on the executive's tax bracket. But he or she cannot be taxed at more than

---

[1] As a practical matter, in smaller or closely held companies, the market value used for tax purposes sometimes differs from the amount an outsider would actually be willing to pay for the stock. It may be worth more to an executive who has a continuing intimate involvement with the corporation than to an outside portfolio investor. The corporation might not actually be able to collect as much on sale of the stock as the figure it uses to compute its deduction.

50 percent, so cost will never greatly outrun value. If the tax bracket were 43 percent (taxable income between $35,200 and $45,800 on a joint return), a $4,000 stock bonus could cost the company $2,160 but would be worth $2,280 ($120 more) to the executive.

But the cost-value balance may shift against the payment-in-stock device if the executive's capital gains on the sale of the stock are considered. For example, suppose an executive receives stock worth $10,000 this year and sells it two years hence for $22,000. This year, the stock's value to the executive may well exceed its cost to the company, thus making it a worthwhile compensation device. But if the sale two years later is also considered, the picture changes. Then the executive will pay a capital gains tax, of $2,400 or thereabouts. The company, of course, has no income or deduction from the executive's sale. But if the company had held on to the stock and had itself made the sale then, the $22,000 it collected would have been completely tax free. Thus, it has surrendered $12,000 of capital gain to the executive which is worth more to it than to the executive.

Example: Whelp, Inc. pays Brown 100 shares of Whelp stock worth $10,000. Whelp's deduction reduces its after-tax cost to $5,400. Assume Brown's tax on the 100 shares is $5,000 (aftertax value is therefore $5,000) which he pays out of his own pocket and without selling his shares. Two years later Brown sells all 100 shares for $22,000, keeping $19,600 after $2,400 of capital gains tax.

Brown's total take after taxes is $14,600 ($22,000 minus the sum of $5,000 and $2,400). Whelp's true aftertax cost (since it could have taken the $12,000 gain free of tax) is $17,400—that is, $5,400 plus $12,000. In this case, a $22,000 outlay costs the company $2,800 more than the outlay is worth to the executive.

Where a capital gain is foreseen, payment in cash instead of stock will give the executive the same amount as with stock, at less cost to the company. A cash payment of $29,000 would be needed to yield $14,500 after taxes to an executive in the 50-percent bracket; $25,439 in the 43-percent bracket.[2] The aftertax cost to the company of a $29,000 cash outlay is $15,660 ($13,737 after taxes on a $25,439 outlay), which is less, obviously, than the $17,400 cost of the $22,000 outlay of stock and capital gain in the above example.

Nonetheless, paying more cash instead of stock is not always a satisfactory solution from either a tax or a business standpoint. First, a payment of $10,000 in stock (plus regular salary) this year could be fully deductible as reasonable compensation. A payment of $29,000 or $25,439 in cash (plus regular salary) might be partly nondeductible as unreasonable. This might be so even if the payment were spread out over two or three years. The aftertax cost to the company increases by 46 cents for each nondeductible dollar of cash compensation. Thus, the company that prefers to pay increased cash compensation should be especially well prepared to prove that compensation is not unreasonably large. (See Chapter 3 for how to prove that compensation is reasonable.)

While the cost/value relationship is important, the psychological value to the executive of equity ownership may overshadow the cost analysis. The executive who receives compensation in stock may be largely responsible for the appreciation in stock values. As a stockholder (or larger stockholder), his or her contributions to the corporation may be greater than if only cash payments were being

---

[2] The terms 50-percent bracket and 43-percent bracket are technically inaccurate in this context. Read them to mean that the effective tax rate on the amount involved is 50 percent or 43 percent.

made.[3] This is a factor which only corporate management can judge. But despite a higher cost potential to the corporation, payment in stock instead of cash may be suggested where stock ownership would substantially stimulate productivity, cost consciousness, or retention of the executive.

INSTALLMENT SALE PLANS

From the company's standpoint, the sale of company stock to the executive for a price payable in installments can have benefits not found in stock options. From the first installment payment, the executive begins to feel a stake in the business and an incentive to improve its performance. Also, the installment obligation, while it lasts, tends to tie the executive to the company. Furthermore, the privilege to pay for the stock in installments rather than all at once is, from the executive's viewpoint, an economic advantage in itself. It may not be necessary to include any bargain element in addition (as it is with stock options).

The price the executive must pay is pegged when the installment purchase arrangement is agreed to. The executive pays this price, in installments, even though the stock's market value rises (but it could also fall, leaving the executive paying more than the stock's then current value). Assuming a bona fide purchase, the spread between the price agreed to and the value when the stock is fully paid

---

[3] Shadow stock will sometimes be an attractive substitute for actual stock. The company would treat the executive as if he or she owned 100 shares, agreeing to pay in, say, two years, what 100 shares would be worth at that time. The executive would have an incentive to cause company stock to rise in value. And the company could deduct the stock's value when it makes the payment two years hence. For details on shadow or phantom stock arrangements, see Chapter 6.

for is not compensation income, and it is not taxable until the stock is disposed of. At that point, the executive has capital gain (capital loss, if the stock declined in price) equal to the difference between the amount paid for the stock and its selling price. (From the company's standpoint, surrendering to the executive capital gain on its stock is an economic disadvantage, as discussed above in connection with stock paid as compensation.) An installment purchase plan, therefore, need not result in any compensation income to the executive, or in tax consequences of any kind until the stock is sold. What causes earlier tax to the executive, and generates a deduction opportunity to the company, is the company's action in selling the stock at a bargain, or letting an executive buy it without an absolute personal commitment to pay for it. That is:

a. If the stock will be sold to the executive at a bargain, the rules for bargain purchase of company stock will apply. The executive will be taxable on the market value of the stock at the time a binding commitment is made to buy it (less the amount of the payment agreed to). The executive is taxable in the year the stock is transferred, though it isn't yet paid for (assuming it is not restricted as described in Chapter 9).

b. The Revenue Service considers the arrangement a genuine installment purchase only if the executive is personally obligated to pay the purchase price. If the individual can cancel out (say, because the stock's market value falls), or if the purchase price is paid only out of dividends, the IRS treats the arrangement as an option. For the executive, this means that ownership of stock for tax purposes does not occur until it is paid for. Of course, the holding period for long-term capital gain purposes does not start to run until the executive becomes the owner. This sharply limits the chance at capital gain benefits.

Worse, if the market value has risen between the time the agreement is entered into and the time the stock is paid for, the spread between the stock's value at the time it is paid for and the amount actually paid for it is compensation income at that time. (For the rule where the executive does not acquire full ownership rights even after paying all installments, see Chapter 9 on restricted stock.)

Many companies setting up installment purchase arrangements today want a plan which avoids tax consequences until the executive disposes of the stock. Most of the remaining companies are willing to grant a bargain purchase opportunity which has tax consequences, but do not want an arrangement which the executive can back out of. Such an arrangement leaves both the individual's and the company's situations unsettled until the installment price (which the IRS would call the option price) is paid. In the authors' view, the company that wants a clear, bona fide predictable installment arrangement should make sure the plan meets each of the following requirements:

1. The executive is obligated to pay the full installment purchase price. This, however, does not preclude a provision that the debt to the company for the unpaid installment balance is to be satisfied first out of the stock itself, and it does not prevent requiring the stock to be pledged with the company as collateral.

2. The executive has full rights over the stock immediately upon agreement to buy it. This means the executive has the right to receive dividends on the stock. (This is not an absolute IRS requirement, but is advisable.) But check for possible state corporate law limits on the right to receive dividends on stock not fully paid for.

3. A substantial down payment should be required, with payment of the balance over a reasonable period. *Substantial* and *reasonable period* will depend on the amounts involved. But the authors incline toward a down payment

(or first year's payment) of not less than 20 percent, with payment completed within five years.

4. Interest should be required on the unpaid balance. This interest will be interest income to the company, and deductible by the executive. If the interest rate is less than 6-percent simple interest, the company normally will be treated for tax purposes as if it received interest at a 7-percent rate, and the executive will be allowed an interest deduction at that 7-percent rate, even though a lower rate was actually paid, and even if *no* interest was provided.

If these tests are met, the executive becomes the owner of the stock when a binding contract of purchase is entered into. The holding period for long-term capital gain purposes begins then, and any appreciation over the price at that time becomes a capital gain on sale. (If the installment price is a bargain, below the stock's value at that time, the spread between price and that value is compensation income in the year the executive contracts to buy.)

Example: Caleb is granted the opportunity to buy 100 shares of stock of Pfalz Corporation, his employer. Present value of Pfalz Corporation shares is $60 each and Caleb buys at that price, which is payable 25 percent down and the balance in installments—25 percent in each of the following three years—for which he signs a binding promissory note. By the time Caleb makes the final payment, the stock is worth $150 a share and he sells his shares at that price. He has a profit on the sale of $9,000, that is, $15,000 sales proceeds less his $6,000 cost. This profit is capital gain, and is all long term, since his holding period began when he entered into the installment purchase contract. Caleb has no taxable compensation income, and there is no compensation expense deduction for Pfalz Corporation.

If the executive should be taxable on the installment purchase, either because the initial price was set below value at that time or because there was no personal obligation to buy, the company is allowed a compensation expense deduction. This deduction is taken in the year the executive realizes taxable income (that is, in the company's tax year in which the executive's year ends), and in an amount equal to that income (but deduction for that amount plus other compensation to the executive cannot exceed reasonable compensation).

The company has no taxable gain or deductible loss with respect to its installment sale of its stock.

Installment purchases of stock are in some instances subject to federal margin limitations. These are rules designed to limit purchase of stock on credit. They apply only to stock traded on a national securities exchange and to certain stock traded over the counter (called OTC margin stock). This OTC stock is stock which the Governors of the Federal Reserve System have determined to have a degree of national investor interest. Thus, the limits don't apply to closely held companies. A list of OTC margin stock can be obtained from any Federal Reserve Bank.

The margin rules would require the executive to make a substantial minimum down payment for the stock and meet certain repayment schedules over the following three years. The rules are eased for certain plans. For full details and applicability, Regulation G of the Federal Reserve Board should be reviewed.

STATE LAW OBSTACLES

Issuance of stock for services occasionally poses problems for the employer under state corporate law. While issuance of stock for services already performed presents little difficulty, issuance of stock for services to be performed in the future may violate state law. Three possible solutions to this problem are:

1. Issuance of shares which are not transferable by the

employee until fully paid for through performance of services could satisfy local law requirements, but would be restricted stock, see Chapter 9.

2. A present contract calling for delivery of shares in the future, after the services have been performed, could also meet local law requirements. This would be a deferred compensation arrangement, covered in Chapter 6.

3. Payment of compensation with treasury stock (stock which was lawfully issued and later repurchased by the corporation) would not violate local law.

In practice, stock is issued or paid for future services in practically every case, in the sense that the transfer of stock would not be made unless the company expected that the executive would continue to perform services for the company.

A company should seek professional advice on compliance with local corporate law requirements before adopting a plan to pay or sell stock to executives.

ACCOUNTING FOR STOCK PLANS

Stockholders and management occasionally voice concern about how plans for paying compensation in stock, or making bargain sales of stock, may affect the stock's earnings per share. Normally, the immediate tendency is to decrease earnings from an accounting standpoint. The value of the stock is an expense (decreasing earnings), unless the executive will pay an amount for the stock which equals its fair value (or its quoted market price if available) at the time the stock is offered.[4] Thus, it is an expense factor in direct payments and bargain sales of stock, but not in noncompensatory installment sales (or

---

[4] Such plans also reduce earnings per share by increasing the number of shares. This is also true of stock options and noncompensatory installment sales.

in the stock options discussed in Chapter 11). This expense factor is somewhat offset by reduction of income tax expense, to reflect the compensation deduction for a stock payment or bargain sale. Still, the immediate net effect is an increase in expense and therefore a decrease in earnings.

STOCKHOLDER PAYS EXECUTIVE IN STOCK

It sometimes happens that stock is paid or sold to the executive at a bargain by a controlling or substantial stockholder rather than by the corporation itself. From a practical standpoint, it may be necessary to arrange this payment outside the corporation, because the corporation has no treasury or unissued stock, or because other stockholders will not agree to the payment, or because of some private agreement between executive and stockholder.

But payment of stock by a stockholder should be avoided wherever possible. It is of no tax benefit to the executive that he or she receives the stock from a stockholder rather than from the corporation. It is fully taxable ordinary income to the executive. It is not tax exempt as a gift, because the stockholder expects value in return—the executive's services, enhancing the value of the stockholder's stock.

Stock received from a stockholder qualifies for the benefit of the 50-percent tax ceiling, described in Chapter 2.

The stockholder is not allowed a compensation expense deduction for the value of stock paid the executive, since the executive's services are not rendered to the stockholder. The stockholder is treated as having made a contribution to the corporation's capital.

The corporation is allowed to deduct the payment, in the amount the executive must report as income, to the extent compensation to the executive is reasonable.

Any stockholder who intends to pay stock to an executive should inform company management of this fact so that the company will know when and how much it can deduct. The company would not necessarily learn of its deduction opportunity simply by learning that stock was transferred from stockholder to executive, since that could have been an ordinary sale. It can also be wise for stockholder and management to confer before the amount of stock to be paid is decided upon, to be sure that the executive's total compensation won't exceed reasonable limits.

The rules described here would also extend to cases where the stockholder is the parent corporation of the employer corporation, paying the executive in its own (parent) stock or in stock of the subsidiary (employer) corporation.

If the company lacks stock, it could purchase (redeem) some of the stockholder's stock. This ordinarily would result in capital gain (sometimes capital loss) to the stockholder, but cash would also be collected from the corporation, which does not happen, of course, if the stockholder is simply paying stock to the executive. There is a danger that the stockholder's redemption will be taxable as a dividend instead of as a gain or loss. But the danger is slight if the only purpose for the redemption is to provide the corporation with needed stock, and especially if there are other large stockholders.

If the stockholder sells stock to the executive at a bargain (instead of simply paying it over to the executive), the executive has taxable compensation income equal to the amount of the bargain and the company deducts that amount, subject to reasonable compensation limits. The amount paid by the executive is treated as paid by the corporation in redemption of the stockholder's stock.

It can occasionally happen that an executive will buy without suspecting there will be a tax liability—without knowing there is a compensatory bargain, in other words. For all these reasons, a sale of stock from stockholder to executive is risky from a tax standpoint and should be avoided wherever possible.

STOCK PURCHASE PLAN

_____ (hereinafter, the company), to encourage the purchase of common shares of its stock by selected employees, hereby adopts the following stock purchase plan:

1. Officers and other executive personnel (hereinafter, "executives") of this company, as designated by a committee consisting of the company's president and two other members of its board of directors, shall be eligible to participate in the plan. The number of shares to be issued to any executive under the plan shall be determined by the committee, but not more than _____ shares in all may be issued and not more than _____ to any individual.

2. The price at which the shares may be purchased shall not be less than the fair market value of such shares on the date the contract of purchase between executive and company shall be executed. The committee shall exercise due diligence in determining that value, and is hereby authorized to engage the services of professional appraisers and consultants in this effort, all reasonable costs of determining value to be borne by the company.

3. Each executive selected for participation in the plan shall be notified of his selection and of the number of shares which he may purchase under the plan. The executive may refuse to participate, or may agree to participate in full or as to a lesser number of shares (but not less than _____ shares). An executive choosing to participate shall enter into a purchase contract for his shares.

4. Payment for shares shall be made concurrently with the execution of the purchase contract, as follows: A check payable to the company representing not less than _____ percent of the purchase price, and a promissory note for the balance of the price, payable in quarterly installments (commenc-

STOCK PURCHASE PLAN *(continued)*

ing _____ months after execution of the contract) of not less than _____ percent of such price at each installment date, with interest on any unpaid balance at the rate of 6 percent per annum.

5. Immediately upon receipt of payment of the purchase price as described above, title to the purchased stock shall pass to and vest in the executive purchaser. The executive shall have all voting rights with respect to such stock, and the right to all dividends thereon. However, certificates representing purchased stock may be retained by the company as security for payment of the note.

6. The rights and obligations of executive and company under the purchase contract shall not be affected by termination of the executive's employment, for whatever reason, following execution of the contract.

9

Restricted stock and other restricted property

Companies often want to make strings-attached payments or sales to their executives. Thus, a company may want to give (or sell) stock to an executive now, but withhold the right to sell or vote the stock until some future date. In the usual case, full rights in the property are withheld as hostage for further performance of services. That is, the executive might be denied full rights to the property until he or she has worked an additional number of years, or until some level of profits, sales, and so forth have been achieved. Failure to reach the desired goal could cause the executive to forfeit the stock or other property in question. Where the executive receives or buys stock or other property from the employer but acquires less than complete ownership of it at that time, the executive is said to have *restricted stock* or *restricted property*.[1]

There are no legal barriers to the use of restricted stock

---

[1] The practical effect of restricted property can be somewhat similar to the effect of deferred compensation discussed in another chapter. But the motivations behind the two devices differ: Restricted plans usually are designed to suit company business needs; deferred compensation plans are designed to suit the executive's tax situation.

or other property as a compensation device. Legally, it is no more alarming to make the executive's right to full ownership of property depend on satisfactory performance of job duties—as the company or the employment contract defines "satisfactory"—than it is to make cash compensation depend on satisfactory performance. There is no legal objection to the fact that the stock or other property in the executive's name or possession on restricted terms is taken away if requirements for full ownership are not met. In fact, this forfeitability device is a sound arrangement to avoid complaints by stockholders against the board's sale or transfer of stock for an inadequate consideration. Issuance of stock for future services may violate state law. Issuance of restricted stock, to be earned in the future by performance of valuable services and which will be forfeited if such services are not performed, is more widely accepted, though still sometimes barred. Here, when the executive acquires full rights to the stock, the full value will have been "paid" through the services performed (plus the cash paid, if any).

Immediate taxation of restricted property

Restricted stock can be an unattractive compensation device from the executive's standpoint. Depending on how the deal is drawn, the executive can be subject to tax on the full, current value of the restricted stock or other property in the year it is received, even though the executive is legally prevented from selling any of it to raise money to pay the tax. The executive may therefore have to borrow on or sell other assets to pay tax on stock which might be forfeited in a later year anyway.

For example, suppose Hesburg receives a bonus of 100 shares of her employer, Global Corporation. She cannot vote or collect dividends on these shares for three years.

Global shares are currently selling at $120 on the market. Hesburg can be currently taxed on $12,000 (100 × $120), even though the shares are not worth $12,000 because she cannot vote or receive dividends on them. Or suppose she was given the opportunity to buy the shares at $40 and did so. She would be taxable on $8,000 (100 × $120 minus 100 × $40) even though to her the bargain is less than that amount because she cannot vote or collect dividends on the shares.

Global can take a compensation expense deduction for the amount Hesberg is taxable on when she receives the stock, assuming Hesburg's total compensation is reasonable.

Deferred taxation

On the other hand, the company can design a payment or bargain sale of restricted stock or other restricted property so that the executive is not subject to tax on it until the stock becomes "substantially vested." (If so, the company won't be able to take a deduction for the stock or other property until then.) To do this, it must make the executive's rights to the stock or property: (1) *Forfeitable,* that is, subject to a substantial risk of forfeiture (explained below) *and* (2) *not transferable* by the executive free of such risk. That is, if the executive sells or gives the restricted item away, there must be a substantial risk that the recipient of the item will also forfeit the property because of the executive's failure to meet the conditions for full ownership.

Substantial risk of forfeiture

When a risk of forfeiture is substantial depends on the circumstances of the case. Certainty is difficult in this area.

But the company that wants an arrangement which will let its executives postpone tax would insert one of the following requirements:

a. Oblige the executive to return the property if the executive does not complete some additional period of substantial services, for example, three years' full-time future services in an executive capacity. A requirement that the stock be returned if the executive commits a crime would not be a substantial risk of forfeiture, nor would a requirement that the stock be resold at book value or other reasonable price on termination of employment.

In addition to the requirement of forfeiture if the executive fails to work for a particular period, there could be a forfeiture of the stock if the company fails to attain certain earnings goals or if the stock fails to reach a certain market or book value. Whether this particular risk is substantial will depend on whether, when the agreement is made, the possibility of forfeiture is significant or negligible.

b. Forfeiture if the executive joins a competing firm. In the authors' view, this is often a distinct possibility, especially in certain industries, and so the risk of forfeiture could be substantial. But the Revenue Service is a bit more cautious here. Its position is that the risk generally is not substantial, but can become so in certain circumstances. The executive's age, skills and health are factors in determining how substantial the risk is.

In judging whether a risk is substantial, the terms of the contract are important but not decisive. The contract may reflect a substantial risk and yet the risk may in fact be slight, because of the relationship between executive and company. The Revenue Service is aware of this. It says that if an executive owns more than 5 percent of the company's stock, this will be a factor in deciding whether the risk is really substantial. In other words, where the executive is a more-than-5 percent stockholder, there is a somewhat larger danger that the risk will be considered insubstantial and the executive taxed immediately.

Transferability

Besides providing the substantial risk of forfeiture, the company which wants to postpone tax for its executives must arrange that the stock or other property is not transferable by the executive free of the risk that the transferee will forfeit it. *This* risk of forfeiture would be tested under state law, not tax law. The requirement is met if the company has the right under local law to reclaim the property from the transferee because it was forfeited by the executive. This requirement is not hard to satisfy in practice where the restricted property is company stock, as it usually is. The company may simply type the relevant restrictions or provisions of the employment contract on the share certificate itself, or type a legend on it that refers to the contract and bars or limits transfer.

If both requirements—substantial risk of forfeiture and nontransferability free of risk—are met in the company's plan, the executive is not taxed when the property is received (unless the executive elects to be taxed). And the tax exemption continues until the property first becomes nonforfeitable (no substantial risk of forfeiture), or becomes transferable (free of risk of forfeiture) if that happens earlier. In normal practice, this will mean the executive continues to be tax-exempt until full rights to the property are acquired, and part or all of it can be sold to raise the funds to pay the tax. But the executive could be subject to tax earlier if, for example, the company cancelled some requirement that had made the risk substantial, or cancelled some limitation on transfer of the stock.

Example: Muncie is allowed to buy 100 restricted shares of his company's stock July 1, 1979. The shares are subject to substantial risk of forfeiture—they would be forfeited by him if he failed to serve full time for the next three years. The shares are also designed to be nontaxable, that is, the share certificates are stamped with evidence of the restrictions. In addition, no dividends are payable on the shares until the restrictions are lifted.

Unrestricted shares of the company are selling for $100 each, but Muncie is allowed to buy them at $10 each. Muncie is not taxable on his acquisition of the shares on July 1, 1979.

On July 1, 1982, the substantial risk of forfeiture terminates and Muncie acquires full rights to the stock. On that date, unrestricted shares are selling for $250 a share. Muncie therefore has $24,000 of compensation income at that time, that is, the value when restrictions end ($25,000) minus the amount he paid ($1,000).

Example: Torres is paid a bonus of 100 shares of his company's stock on November 1, 1979. He must return these shares if he leaves the company's employ. But for each year he remains employed by the company, he ceases to be obliged to return ten shares.

The payment of 100 shares on November 1, 1979 is subject to substantial risk of forfeiture. But on November 1, 1980, ten shares are not subject to substantial risk of forfeiture and the fair market value of ten shares on that date is taxable to him then. On November 1, 1981, he is taxable on another ten shares, at their 1981 value, and so on.

Taxation of income on restricted property

Any dividend or other income the executive receives on the property while it is forfeitable and nontransferable is taxable as compensation income (not as dividends, rent, etc.). This means it is personal service income and cannot be taxed at more than 50 percent. Once the restrictions lapse, however, the dividends would be taxable as ordinary income, not protected by the personal service income maximum rate of 50 percent.

When stock or other property is taxable, the amount on which the executive is taxed is the market value of the property, less the amount paid, if any. In determining market value in any restricted property situation, disregard all restrictions except those which by their terms will never lapse. Thus, even though stock may be subject to restrictions which affect its value, the value of stock which is not subject to restrictions is used to figure the taxable amount, unless those restrictions are nonlapse restrictions.

For example, if a company's shares are trading on the market at $80, but the executive can only get $76 for shares held because of the restrictions on it, the executive is still taxable on $80. A value of $76 could be used instead only if the restriction, which reduces its value, is one which by its terms will never lapse.

A nonlapse restriction is given a narrow definition by the Revenue Service. To qualify, the IRS says each of the following tests must be met:

1. The restriction must limit the executive's right to transfer the property—for example, it must require the stock to be resold to the company upon a certain event.
2. It must set a price for property which the executive would collect on resale, or a formula for determining the price.
3. The restriction must apply to and be enforceable against any person to whom the executive transfers the property, except the company itself.

Thus, if the executive is required to offer the stock for resale to the company upon termination of employment, at its book value on the date it was received, and the executor of the executive's estate must offer it for resale at that value if the executive dies while employed, the stock is subject to a nonlapse restriction. Furthermore, the value to be used in computing tax on the executive is the price at which the stock is to be sold—here, the book value.

An obligation to resell the property at its market value at the time of the resale is not a nonlapse restriction; it would not affect the stock's value.

The authors agree with the IRS that tests 1 and 3 must be met, but not that test 2 (formula price) must be met. That is, a formula price would qualify, but other restrictions (instead of formula price) would also qualify. These would include: restrictions on the executive's rights to dividends on the stock and limits on the class of persons to whom stock can be transferred—such as members of the executive's family (to keep stock ownership within the family), individuals who are U.S. citizens or residents (to avoid loss of status as a Subchapter S corporation), or, in the case of professional service corporations, persons licensed to practice that profession (which in any case could be a requirement of state professional corporation law). The Revenue Service does not at present agree that any of these is a nonlapse restriction.

The executive who manages to obtain a reduction in present tax because a nonlapse restriction cuts the tax value of property received may be subject to another tax if that restriction should be cancelled by the company. For example, if the company should later cancel the executive's duty to resell at book value, the executive would then (with some exceptions) be taxable on the market value after the cancellation less its value immediately before the cancellation.

Under federal law, stock in many cases cannot be offered for sale to the public unless the stock issue is registered with the Securities and Exchange Commission. Registration involves detailed public disclosure and is a costly and lengthy process. But the shares can be transferred to private investors or other holders free of registration if these holders do not sell them to the public. In such private issues, the company typically requires the holder to represent in writing that he holds stock for investment and not for resale. The practical effect of such a representation (the investment letter) and the other circumstances is that stock subject to the letter can't be sold to the public for a prolonged (though unspecified) period, but only to other private investors, unless the issue should at some time be registered. Investment letter stock is therefore valued in the marketplace at large discounts below the price of registered stock of the same company. The IRS has taken the position that such investment letter stock is not subject to a nonlapse restriction. Therefore, the discount from market value must be ignored when valuing the stock for tax purposes. That IRS stand has been sharply criticized by tax practitioners. In the authors' opinion, however, the IRS here is justified, in the sense that its position appears to reflect the will of Congress.

In the authors' view, then, investment letter stock is at present a highly unfavorable compensation device from the executive's standpoint, since the stock will be taxed currently on much more than the true or realizable market value of what the executive receives.

The executive whose tax is postponed because of risk-of-forfeiture and nontransferability clauses can elect to be taxed at the time the property is received instead of when the restrictions lapse, *if the executive wishes.* Such an election would be made if the executive thought the property (usually, company stock) would be worth a lot more when the restrictions end. If that estimate proves correct, the election can save substantial tax. The executive will be taxed on a low value now, and will not be taxed again when restrictions end. If the executive decides to elect immediate taxation, the election must be filed with the IRS within 30 days of the receipt of the restricted property.

Example: Casey is paid 1,000 shares of restricted stock worth $20 a share, which Casey believes will be worth $200 a share when restrictions go off five years hence. If his estimate is correct, he will have $200,000 of fully taxable compensation income at that time. If he instead elects to be taxed now, he is taxed on $20,000 and avoids the additional potential tax at ordinary (compensation) rates on the $180,000 increase in value. Of course, he would be taxed on the appreciation over the $20,000 tax basis at capital gains rates when he sells the stock (e.g., if he sold the stock for $200,000 when the restrictions lapsed, he would be taxed on $180,000 of capital gains income).

There is the obvious economic risk that the stock may have dropped in value by the time the restrictions lapse. There is also an important tax risk. If for some reason the executive should forfeit the stock, the tax paid on it cannot be recouped. The executive cannot get a refund or claim a tax credit or deduction for this tax.

Thus, the decision to elect immediate taxation calls for close calculation, weighing the possibility of forfeiture against the prospect of capital gain. Forfeiture will be a serious possibility. Remember that the election opportunity does not arise unless there is already a substantial risk of forfeiture.

Usually, the executive is the best judge of the extent of that risk. The election decision cannot be made as well by tax, investment or other professional advisers. However, when making the decision the executive should remember that besides the tax and economic risks just mentioned, the election involves a prepayment of tax, which may prove to be a hardship.

SELLING RESTRICTED STOCK OR PROPERTY

Once the executive has been taxed on the restricted property, capital gains treatment applies if the stock is sold at a profit, and a capital loss occurs if it is sold at a loss. Capital gain is tax-favored long-term gain if the stock is held for more than 12 months from the time it is received to the date of sale. The gain is the amount received less the sum of the amount paid for the property (if any) and the amount on which the executive was taxed.

Example: Crawford's company sold her 200 restricted shares for $80 a share when the market value was $110 a share. Since there was no substantial risk of forfeiting her shares, Crawford was taxable when she got them. And since there was no nonlapse restriction on the shares, they were valued for tax purposes at their market value of $110. Crawford therefore was taxed on a bargain of $30 a share ($110 minus $80), or $6,000.

Two years later, when the restrictions are lifted, Crawford's stock is worth $195 a share, and she sells them all at that price. She has a long-term capital gain of $17,000, that is, $39,000 less the sum of the $16,000 purchase price and $6,000 of compensation income.

If an executive forfeits property after being taxable on it, a capital loss deduction would be allowed for the amount that had been taxed and the amount paid for it, if any. However, this does not hold true if the tax were paid through the voluntary election discussed above and the shares are forfeited while substantially nonvested. In that instance, the loss would be limited to the amount that had actually been paid for the restricted property, without regard for the amount included in compensation.

The executive may find a buyer for restricted property even though it is still subject to substantial risk of forfeiture and is not transferable free of such risk. Here, the executive has not already been taxed on receipt of the property (unless the voluntary election to be taxed has been made). Thus, on sale of the property the executive is taxed on the sale proceeds less the amount paid for the property, if any. This amount is compensation income, not capital gain. If the sale is made to a relative or otherwise is not an arm's length sale, the executive would be subjected to tax again when forfeitability or nontransferability ends (or if there is an arm's length sale of the property), on the value (or selling price) of the property at that time minus the proceeds of the non-arm's-length sale. (If the non-arm's-length sale had been for more than the stock's fair market value at that time, which rarely happens, the executive would have been taxable then only on its fair market value less any amount he or she paid for it, and this market value would be treated as the sale proceeds in figuring the second tax.)

For long-term capital gain purposes, an executive's holding period generally begins when he or she becomes taxable on the property. But if the executive has elected to be taxed currently, the holding period begins when the property is transferred to the executive free of restrictions.

COMPANY'S TAX TREATMENT

The company is entitled to a compensation expense deduction for restricted property in the amount the executive is taxed on, assuming that amount represents reasonableness. The authors believe that reasonableness should be judged as of the time the property was transferred subject to restrictions, and not as of the time the restrictions end. Thus, full deduction should be available even though the value ultimately realized by the executive may be much greater than when the property was transferred. But the Revenue Service has not yet taken a public stand on the point.

The company takes its deduction for the year the executive becomes taxable (technically, the company's taxable year in which the executive's year ends). Thus, if the company intends to postpone tax on the executive, it must be willing to accept postponement of its deduction. The postponed deduction will be a larger deduction if the stock or other property goes up in value meanwhile. Any dividend or other income collected on the property which is compensation income to the executive (see above) is deductible as compensation by the company. But once the dividend income ceases to be compensation to the executive—because he or she has become taxable on the underlying property (which is now "substantially vested")—it ceases to be deductible by the company.

An executive who elects to be taxed currently on a restricted item is required by Revenue Service regulations to notify the employer. This is so the employer will know when to take its deduction.

The Revenue Service doesn't require such notification in other settings. Therefore, the company should require the executive to notify it if the executive should sell property while it is still forfeitable and nontransferable and, if that sale was not at arm's length, of any later arm's-length sale. Without this notification, the company would not know the executive realized compensation income (for which the company can take a deduction).

Deduction is not allowed unless the company withholds tax on the amount the executive must include in income. Since the executive already has the asset itself, this means the company withholds against other compensation it pays the executive. This is easy enough in most cases where the company controls or monitors the point at which restrictions lift. Occasionally, there can be problems, such as:

a. Where the executive is no longer employed by the company when he or she becomes taxable—the company then has nothing to withhold against. The authors have heard privately that IRS will allow deduction in this situation if the executive has reported the income, but this is *un*official.

b. Where the executive sells the property while it is still forfeitable in, say, 1979, or makes an election in 1979 to be taxed early, and the company, also on the calendar year, learns about this in 1980. It may be that IRS will allow the deduction on an amended return for 1979 if the company withholds in 1980, though this is not yet official.

If the company takes a deduction with respect to stock or other property which the executive later forfeits, the company would then (when forfeiture occurs) report as income the lesser of:

1. The property's market value when forfeited less any amount paid at forfeiture; or
2. If it was the company's own stock, the amount it deducted.

The company's gain or loss from transactions in restricted stock or other restricted property is computed under the rules in Chapters 7 and 8.

The company's accounting treatment

Restricted stock and its accounting treatment have been carefully defined by the accounting profession. Where restrictions are related solely to the passage of time (performance of future services for a specified period of years), the market value of the stock (minus the amount, if any, received for it)—without regard to the restrictions—is charged to book income as a compensation expense. The amount charged is the market value at the time the stock or property is transferred to the executive subject to restrictions. The amount would normally be accrued over the period covered by the restrictions. This practice is consistent with most other forms of compensation. Note, however, that it will differ from the amount the company can deduct on its tax return (see above).

If the restrictions relate to company performance, such as growth in the company's earnings or stock price, the authors believe the accounting will be determined according to the standards set for performance plans as discussed in Chapter 11. Following that approach, the stock or property would still be charged to book income as a compensation expense and accrued over the period of restrictions. However, the amount to be charged would not be the market value at the time of *transfer*, but would be the value at the time the restrictions lapse (i.e., when the performance requirements are met). When the restricted property is stock traded on an exchange, the company will have to adjust its accrual each quarter to reflect the current market value of the stock.

The problem that this latter approach presents is that the full impact of future appreciation in the value of the stock must be charged to book income. And, of course, that amount cannot be accurately predicted at the time the stock is awarded. Thus, the cost (or risk) cannot be fully evaluated. This could be particularly important to closely held companies that might contemplate a public offering. Although the initial value of the award might be

relatively small, the value several years in the future—
potentially after a public offering—could be substantial,
resulting in a heavy charge to book income to reflect the
appreciation in the stock's value in the very year that the
company would be trying to put its best foot forward.

How to use stock options and related stock appreciation rights

Economic and tax developments in the past few years have muted corporate boardroom enthusiasm for the stock option as a compensation device. For decades, it offered an unmatched fortune-building opportunity for executive personnel. The business press regularly reported stock option profits in the hundreds of thousands of dollars going to executives of well-known companies, such as Chrysler or CBS.

Even today, many executives can benefit handsomely from stock options. But the tax and financial climate has changed. The executive's profit potential is less, both before and after taxes. Further, companies have come to recognize the cost of stock options in considering their appropriateness. The reappraisal of stock option policy during the 1970s has resulted in a somewhat diminished role for this executive incentive device.

Despite the problems, the stock option continues to be a mainstay of the executive compensation programs of many companies. This chapter explores the nature and use of the stock option, as well as its tax and accounting implications. The use of stock appreciation rights in conjunction with options is also explored.

WHAT A STOCK OPTION IS

A stock option is an opportunity to buy stock at a set price, some time in the future. It must be distinguished from an opportunity to buy stock directly and immediately (at a bargain or in installments, or both) under some form of stock purchase plan. The term *stock option* means the right or privilege to buy stock under an offer continuing for a stated period of time. Stock purchases not involving options are analyzed in Chapters 7 through 9.

As stock options are typically used in executive compensation planning, the company grants its executive employee an option to buy stock in that company. Both company and executive expect—or at any rate, hope—that the value of the stock will rise. If it does, the executive exercises the option and acquires the stock. The executive profits from the deal because the price paid for the stock under the option is less than the stock's current market value. If instead of rising in value the stock drops in value after the option is granted, the executive declines to buy the stock and allows the option to lapse. Thus, if this were all there was to it, a stock option would give the executive a chance at a stock profit, with no risk of loss.

This simple example is enough to show why executives might want stock options. (There are other reasons, as we will soon see.) But why did companies give stock options? There are several answers: For one thing, they were often felt to have little or no cost. The stock may have cost the company nothing to create, or at least management could have looked at it that way. Yet the company could collect something for it on a sale to the executive. Second, the executives prized stock options above other forms of noncash compensation, because of their tax advantages under prior tax laws. Third, it gave the executive a stake in the company. Stock ownership tied the executive more firmly to the company and increased the incentive to produce profits for the company which would be shared with the executive through stock ownership.

Each of these reasons served to encourage management to grant stock options to executive personnel. *And each of these reasons has been undermined by recent developments.* The combined effect of these developments has been to reduce, though not eliminate, the use of stock options. Executive enthusiasm for stock options has lessened as tax advantages have narrowed and stock market profits languished. Worse, executives have not hesitated to sell their stock as profit opportunities arose, thereby cutting this particular tie with their companies, uprooting one more executive stake in the company's success and prosperity. Further, company examination of the cost of options reveals a pattern very similar to a cash payment—that is, the aftertax cost to the company about equals the aftertax gain to the executive.

For example, suppose a company lets an executive buy stock for $50,000 which the executive later sells for $120,000. The company collects the $50,000 paid by its executive plus a reduction in taxes of about $35,000 (the effect of the compensation deduction the company realizes on the option spread which is taxable to the executive). The executive's profit on the deal, after taxes, will be at least $35,000. If there had been no stock option, and the company had sold the stock for $120,000, it would have kept the entire amount, free of tax.[1] The stock option arrangement therefore had a true cost to the company of $35,000 ($120,000 minus $85,000). Of course, if

---

[1] A company pays no federal income tax on profits on its own stock.

the executive were in a lower tax bracket, the aftertax gain would be greater, increasing the cost effectiveness for the company.

Generally speaking, stock options are worthwhile from a company's standpoint in the following situations:

1. Where the option is needed to retain the services of a valued executive who would resign unless given the chance to acquire a share of the business.

2. Where the option is needed to stimulate an executive's productivity or cost consciousness by providing a share of the profits.

3. Where the option is a device to generate new equity capital from employees, thus avoiding underwriting costs.

4. Where the special accounting for stock option costs makes it possible to offer an executive additional income opportunity that the company could not otherwise afford.

Today's typical stock option (sometimes called a nonstatutory option) can be tailored by the company to achieve practically any desired balance of company versus executive benefit. The company has complete freedom to decide who can be given nonstatutory options and the conditions under which they are granted (assuming stockholders and state law impose no special obstacles).

TYPICAL STOCK OPTION

According to current practice, the typical stock option runs for ten years and is granted at a price equal to the fair market value of the stock on the date that it is granted. Many companies impose limitations on how soon the option can be exercised by stating a waiting period (usually one year) and then permitting the option to become exercisable in installments (e.g., up to 25 percent during the second year, 50 percent—less any previously exercised portion—during the third year, until the full option is exercisable). Of course, the company is free to determine any option period and terms for exercise. To illustrate the workings of a typical option, we have assumed a fully exercisable option and a decision to exercise relatively early in the option term.

Example: Acme Corporation grants a stock option to select executive employees, including Freeman, one of its vice presidents. Freeman is given the opportunity to buy 1,000 shares at $95 a share, the price at which the stock is selling publicly when the option is granted. Freeman exercises the option when the stock is selling for $120 a share. Thus, she pays $95,000 and receives stock worth $120,000 (a profit of $25,000). She sells the stock the following year for $135 a share for a total profit of $40,000 ($135,000 minus $95,000).

In the usual situation, Freeman would be subject to tax on her purchase of the stock. The taxable amount in the year of purchase would be $25,000 ($120,000 minus $95,000), and it would be fully taxable at ordinary rates up to the 50 percent maximum rate for personal service income.

Freeman would also be subject to capital gains tax on her sale of the stock in the following year. Since she paid a tax on $25,000 of profit at the time of exercise, she is not again hit with a tax on that $25,000. Her taxable profit in the year of sale is $15,000 ($135,000 minus $120,000). Capital gains tax on this would be about $3,000.[2] In a transaction which yields an overall gross profit of $40,000, Freeman would keep about $24,500.

Acme Corporation would normally be allowed to take a tax deduction in the year of exercise of $25,000, equal

---

[2] Capital gains tax is assumed to be imposed at a 20-percent rate throughout.

to the amount which Freeman must report as ordinary income. With this deduction, Acme's true cost of Freeman's first $25,000 of profit is about $12,500. This should be compared to Freeman's gain of at least $12,500 after taxes. Most compensation planners would consider this a reasonable balance of company cost to executive benefit. Further, most planners would stop the cost to benefit analysis at this point. Freeman's decision to hold the stock for a long-term capital gain more than 12 months later is a personal investment decision on her part.

Because the long-term capital gain ultimately realized in this example is in fact an investment result rather than compensation, there is no further deduction allowed Acme.

The company has the duty to withhold tax with respect to the bargain element in a stock option at the time of exercise, just as it must withhold tax on salary. The government has not prescribed any particular method for withholding in this situation. One method would be to reduce the dollar amount of salary to be paid the executive (after regular tax withholding on that salary) by an additional amount representing the tax to be withheld on the bargain element of the option. Another method, where large amounts are involved, would be to have the executive pay the company the required withholding amount out of personal funds, which the company would use to cover its withholding liability. If the executive will sell the stock immediately after exercising the option, the sales proceeds will provide the funds needed to cover the withholding obligation. But if the executive intends to keep the stock, or is *required* to keep it at least six months under "insider's rules" of the Securities Exchange Act (which apply to officers, directors and more-than-10-percent shareholders of listed corporations and other corporations required to file reports annually with the SEC), the executive may have to borrow needed withholding funds.[3] Under one arrangement, called a stock appreciation right (SAR), an executive may surrender options to the company for a cash amount equal to the value of the option (the stock's market value less the option price). Such SARs are typically paid half in cash and half in stock. The cash and the value of the stock received are taxable income just as the gain on the exercise of the option would have been. However, the cash provides funds out of which to satisfy the tax liability (withholding as well as the tax at the 50 percent personal service income rate). The result is identical to an option exercise where stock is sold to cover cash needed to exercise the option and meet the tax liability on the option. The stock appreciation right (discussed in detail later in this chapter) merely bypasses the intermediate steps.

OTHER VARIATIONS ON THE TYPICAL STOCK OPTION

Stock options can be designed in ways which can increase or decrease the relative attractiveness of the option to either the company or the executive. These include options with a value at grant, discounted stock options, and options for restricted stock.

Options with a value at grant

In some instances the executive might prefer to have an option with a specific, determinable value at the time of grant. In that instance, the bargain element in the option

---

[3] The executive is not technically forbidden to sell, but must turn over to the company any profits realized on trades within this six-month period.

would be taxable at the time of grant, and not later when the option is exercised. Where the executive expects that the stock will appreciate in value over the period of the option, he or she should prefer tax at grant to tax at exercise. Payment of tax at grant would normally mean a smaller total tax—that is, less tax at ordinary rate and larger capital gains.

This can be seen in the Acme/Freeman example above. If the option to Freeman had a value of, say, $6 a share when it was granted, recognizing the value of a future call on the stock at the fixed $95-per-share price, Freeman would have $6,000 of ordinary compensation income at that point, and would pay a tax of $3,000 then. She would not be taxed at exercise of the option, and her additional $34,000 profit on sale ($135,000 minus the sum of $95,000 and $6,000) would be subject to a capital gains tax of about $6,800. Thus, she would keep $30,200 of her profit, or $5,700 more than if the typical nonstatutory option rules were followed.

Congress has asked the Revenue Service to provide for valuing options when they are granted, for persons who want to elect to be taxed on the option's value at grant instead of at exercise. This would replace the stricter Revenue Service requirements of "readily ascertainable fair market value," which at this writing are still in effect. To have such readily ascertainable value, an option must be transferable. The executive must be allowed to sell it and the company must be willing to recognize any purchaser of the option as entitled to buy the underlying stock. It will help if there is a fairly active market in the stock, on a local or national exchange or over the counter.

For so long as the stricter "readily ascertainable rules" apply, the company increases the capital gain potential to the executive by having the option meet the "readily ascertainable" requirements—assuming this can be done.

Discounted stock options

Another way to make the option more attractive to the executive is to offer a discounted stock option—one that has an exercise price less than the fair market value of the stock on the date the option is granted. Use of a discount provides the potential for immediate gain by the executive (assuming there is no waiting period before exercise). It also provides some protection against short-term variation in the market price. Although the percentage discount can vary to meet specific situations, most plans provide for a discount of 25 percent or less. A lower discount from market price would most likely include restrictions on the stock as discussed in Chapter 9.

Applying the discounted option approach to the Acme/Freeman example illustrates the approach. Suppose Freeman had been granted the 1,000-share option at $70 per share at a time when the stock was selling for $95 (approximately a 25-percent discount). Freeman would not have a tax liability at the time of grant for the $25,000 bargain element in the option at that time. When Freeman later exercises the option when its fair market value has risen to $120,000, she is taxable on $50,000 ($120,000 minus $70,000). Her gain would be taxable as ordinary income up to the 50-percent maximum rate on personal service income.

At the time of exercise, Freeman would have an aftertax gain of at least $25,000. The company's aftertax cost would also approximate $25,000 ($120,000 minus the $70,000 paid by Freeman and the $25,000 tax reduction).

Following the earlier example, if Freeman sold the stock a year later at $135 a share, her capital gain would still be $15,000 ($135,000 minus the $70,000 paid for the stock and minus the $50,000 previously taxed as income). The company, of course, would not realize any further tax deduction at the time of sale by Freeman. Using the discounted option, Freeman would have realized a total aftertax gain of approximately $37,000. This gain is $12,500 more than under the typical stock option. Actually, this is the aftertax value of the $25,000 discount at the time the option was granted

Options for restricted stock

Stock options can also be tilted to favor the company. This is most often done by some provision that prevents the executive from acquiring full rights to the stock even after exercising the option and paying the price for the stock. One such provision would cause the executive to lose rights to the stock if he or she quit or were fired before some specified future date. The usual consequence of such a restriction is to increase the tax on the executive (as compared to other nonstatutory options) and to decrease the true cost of the option to the company. In many cases, the executive will pay no tax until the year full rights to the stock are acquired, but at that point all profit is fully taxable as ordinary income. There is no capital gain, and the company takes a tax deduction for the entire profit. (Details of restricted stock transactions are covered in Chapter 9.)

Applying this result to the Acme-Freeman illustration, Freeman's tax would be about $20,000 and she would keep $20,000 of her $40,000 profit. The company's true cost also would be about $20,000.

ESTABLISHING A STOCK OPTION PLAN

The stock option is comparatively easy to establish, though the authors recommend that a professional practi-

tioner be consulted beforehand. The key features of typical stock options are noted below.[4]

1. An option may be granted to anyone the company
chooses. It can thus be granted to selected executives; it
need not be made available to employees generally. It does
not matter how much or how little stock an executive
already owns.

2. Tax rules do not require that stockholder approval
be obtained. (Of course, company by-laws, company
policy, stock exchange rules, state laws, SEC rules, or
ordinary prudence may require such consent.)

3. The executive may be given or denied the right to
sell the option. This right must be given under present
Revenue Service regulations if the company intends the
option to have a readily ascertainable fair market value at
grant.

4. Federal tax law sets no maximum or minimum price
for the stock. Stock worth $100 a share can be optioned
at $1 a share or less, if the company chooses.

5. The property subject to the option need not be stock
in the company, but could be stock in some other company, or other property. Executives of a small company
would especially welcome an option to buy nationally
traded stock at a bargain. The chief drawback from the
company's standpoint is that it will often be obliged to
pay a tax on transactions involving stock other than its
own stock.

6. The company may prevent the executive from enjoying full rights to optioned stock, by imposing any restrictions it pleases (local law and by-laws permitting) on the
executive's right to sell, pledge or vote the stock or to
share in dividends. These restrictions will often postpone

---

[4] A sample stock option agreement appears at the end of this chapter.

tax on the executive until the restrictions are lifted, but in so doing will reduce the capital gain opportunities for the executive and increase the company's deduction.

7. There is no minimum period the executive must hold the stock, but to qualify for favorable capital gains rates on the stock it must be held for more than 12 months. (An executive who sells the option must have held it more than 12 months to get capital gain benefits.) Capital gains may occasionally be subject to the alternative minimum tax discussed in Chapter 2, but this tax does not apply to any other profit or bargain element of stock options.

8. The option device can be fully effective as an executive inducement even during stock price doldrums. For example, suppose Clifford was granted a five-year non-statutory option to buy 500 shares at $95 when the stock was selling at $98, but before he acted on it the price fell to $89. Clifford, of course, has no incentive to pay $95 for stock selling at $89. But the company could grant a new option, to buy at any lower price, say, $86, thus restoring the effectiveness of the option program.

9. With an option, the executive has the power to choose when to realize compensation income under the option. For example, if the option price for 200 shares is $80 a share and the stock is selling at $150 in December 1979, the executive can choose to exercise the option and take the $14,000 of compensation income either in December of 1979 or January of 1980 (assuming no drop in market price). The power to control the timing of income is unavailable in some other executive compensation situations, such as current bonuses or deferred compensation. Assuming the stock price increase has generated a gain, this flexibility favors options over the other compensation devices from the executive's standpoint. (The company, of course, has no deduction until the executive exercises the option—which puts the timing of

this significant deduction item outside company control.)

For interest-free or low-interest company loans to enable executives to exercise their stock options, see Chapter 15.

QUALIFIED STOCK OPTIONS

It is no longer possible for companies to *adopt* so-called qualified stock option plans. Companies that adopted such plans before May 21, 1976, however, can still grant options under those plans to their executives. Executives with such options will still be allowed to exercise them and apply the special tax provisions until May 20, 1980. Any such qualified options exercised after that date will then be taxed as the typical options discussed earlier in this chapter, usually referred to as nonstatutory options to distinguish them from the "statutory" qualified stock option.

The executive's tax treatment

The *grant* of the option is not taxable to the executive. *Exercise* of the option does not generate taxable income, but can still have a heavy adverse tax impact. The bargain element in a qualified stock option at the time the option is exercised—that is, the value of the stock acquired minus the option price (cost of the stock)—is treated as "tax preference." This can make the bargain subject to the minimum tax on tax preferences, imposed at a rate of 15 percent. This *could* mean that an executive who paid $50,000 for stock worth $120,000 would owe a minimum tax of $10,500 (15 percent of $70,000). But the minimum tax applies only to the amount by which a person's tax preferences exceed the greater of (*a*) half the income tax liability or (*b*) $10,000. Thus, depending on tax liability and the amount of other tax preferences, the minimum tax burden can prove to be less than 15 percent of the stock option preference income.

Somewhat more serious is the provision which limits the use of the 50-percent maximum tax on personal service income where the executive has tax preferences, including the bargain element on exercise of a qualified stock option. The personal service income which can benefit from this 50-percent tax ceiling is reduced by one dollar for each dollar of tax preference. Thus, if the executive exercised a qualified option at a $40,000 bargain, $40,000 of personal service income, which would otherwise be taxable at no more than 50 percent, becomes taxable at the ordinary rates, up to 70 percent. This is a more severe tax detriment than the minimum tax because the tax here can be an additional 20 percent, instead of the 15 percent of the minimum tax, and because here (unlike the minimum tax situation) there is no floor (greater of $10,000 or half the income tax liability). This affects executives whose earnings put them substantially above the 50-percent tax bracket. For example, a married executive filing a joint return is unaffected unless salary and bonus exceed $60,000 after reduction for deductible job-connected expenses and a proportion of other deductions (based on outside income).

An added practical problem here is that the executive may be caught in a three-way cash squeeze. The executive is already parting with cash to buy the stock, is hit with a minimum tax on an income item (the bargain) which isn't realized in cash and can't be sold to raise cash, and the tax burden increases by up to 20 percentage points on other compensation actually realized in cash.

When and if the executive should decide to sell the stock, the profit on the sale can qualify for favorable long-term capital gains treatment. While a portion of the capital gains is subject to the alternative minimum tax, this tax seldom applies to highly-paid executives. The capital gains preference does not affect the maximum tax benefit.

For the high-salaried executive who must sell stock within three years after it is acquired, the tax cost of a qualified option can become higher than a nonstatutory option with the same terms. The minimum tax and lost maximum tax benefit on other compensation caused by the bargain at exercise of the option may have already been paid, and the executive must now also pay full tax (and not just capital gains tax) on the profit when it is sold. There is no credit, refund or other tax relief in the year of sale for the tax burdens borne in the year of exercise.[5]

Additionally there is no offset for the year-of-exercise burden where the executive holds the stock for the required period but the stock declines in value after exercise. In other words, there is no relief for the executive who paid tax on a bargain amount never realized because it diminished or disappeared by the time the stock was sold.

The company's position

The company must pay a high price, in real economic terms, to make capital gains benefits available to its executive. The company cannot take a tax deduction for an amount which the executive can treat as a capital gain. This means the company may not take any deduction with respect to the option. Furthermore, the company would be exempt from tax on its profits on its own stock. Thus, if it makes $8,000 of stock profits available to its em-

---

[5] One exception: No minimum tax or loss of maximum tax benefit occurs with respect to the bargain if exercise of option and sale of stock occur in the same year. The tax result in this case is the same as with a nonstatutory option.

ployee through a qualified option, the true cost to the company is the full $8,000, even though the true value to the employee is only approximately $6,400. Looked at another way, surrendering $8,000 of profits on its own stock is equivalent to surrendering $14,815 in typical company operating profits.

How to keep the option qualified

Suppose the company adopted the qualified option plan before May 21, 1976 and now intends to grant options pursuant to the plan to selected executives. The option granted must meet all these conditions:

1. The price the employee is to pay for the stock cannot intentionally be set at less than the stock's market value at the time the option is granted. For example, if the stock is selling on the market at $100 a share when the option is granted, the executive cannot be given the right to buy it for less than $100 a share. (He or she may accidentally be given the right to buy for less than $100. This could happen where the company is unaware of the true value of the stock when it grants the option. The executive does not lose all the benefit of a stock option in this case, but must pay a tax penalty which increases the true cost of the stock. If the price to the executive was intentionally set below the stock's value when the option was granted, status as a qualified option would be forfeited.) This rule means that the executive will benefit from the option only if the stock's value rises after the option is granted.

2. The executive may not own more than 10 percent of the company's stock, including the stock acquired under the option. If the company's equity capital exceeds $1 million, the amount an executive is permitted to own may be reduced to 5 percent of the stock.

3. The executive cannot have the right to transfer the option to another person during his or her lifetime.

4. Once the executive exercises the option and pays for the stock, the executive must be given all substantial rights of ownership over the stock. The company may not impose special limits on the right to sell it, or to receive dividends on it.

5. The executive loses the right to capital gain treatment unless the stock is held for at least three years before sale. If the stock is sold within three years of acquisition, the profit is fully taxable ordinary income in the year of sale and the corporation is allowed a tax deduction for that amount in that year. This is the only situation in which the company is allowed a deduction with respect to a qualified stock option. Unfortunately for the company, its deduction depends solely on the executive's decision to realize a present profit rather than risk a future drop in price. The company has no control over whether it will be allowed a deduction, or the amount of the deduction. The company should require the executive to inform it of any sale of company stock made within three years after acquiring it under the option, and the selling price, so the company will know when and how much it can deduct.

6. The qualified stock option device can be rendered practically unusable where the market price of the stock under option has fallen. For example, suppose on March 1, 1979 a corporation grants an executive an option, exercisable any time in 1979, to buy 200 shares at $80 a share (the market value of the stock on that date). If the price should rise above $80, the executive will consider exercising the option; if not, there will be no reason to exercise.

Suppose the price should drop to $70. The company might want to cut the option price to, say, $72. But such a modification of the option would forfeit the special tax treatment (for the executive) of status as a qualified stock option, and it would be treated as a nonstatutory option.

Also, the company would be unable to make a new qualified option available to the executive during the period that any unexercised part of a previously granted qualified option remains outstanding. Thus, so long as the March 1, 1979 option remains unexercised—because the market price of the stock is below the option price and there is therefore no profit in exercising the option—qualified stock option benefits aren't available to that executive under any new option, until the March 1, 1979 option expires. Exercise of a new option while the prior unexercised qualified option is still outstanding is subject to the rules governing nonstatutory options.

ACCOUNTING FOR STOCK OPTIONS

The typical, nonstatutory stock option is the only compensation device that does not result in a direct charge to the company's income statement. All the costs associated with the typical option are accounted for on the balance sheet.

For example, in the earlier Freeman/Acme illustration, Freeman was given an option to buy 1,000 shares at $95 a share which she exercised when the stock had a market value of $120 a share. Under current accounting procedures, Acme does not charge earnings or make any accounting entry at the time the option is granted. The only impact the option has on Acme prior to its exercise is that the 1,000 shares must be included in computing fully diluted earnings per share.

At the time Freeman exercises the option, Acme is entitled to a tax deduction equal to the $25,000 on which Freeman pays ordinary income tax. However, since Acme has not recorded a compensation expense on its income statement to reflect the option, it is not permitted to reflect the tax savings on the income statement, either. The savings in tax is accounted for as a contribution to Capital Surplus (capital in excess of par value) in the shareholders' equity portion of the balance sheet. In the case of Freeman's exercise of the option, the accounting would be as follows:

Acme issues 1,000 shares with par value of $1.00.

Acme receives $95,000 from Freeman. Of that amount, $1,000 is recorded as par value for the additional 1,000 shares outstanding, and $94,000 is shown as Capital Surplus.

Acme's $25,000 tax deduction results in a tax savings of approximately $12,500, which is also recorded as Capital Surplus.

The remaining $12,500 of Acme's true cost of the option becomes a dilution in equity spread among all stockholders. (Had Acme sold the stock for the full $120,000 market value at the time of exercise, Par Value would have increased by $1,000 and Capital Surplus would have been increased by the remaining $119,000.)

If Freeman's option had been a qualified stock option, the same accounting treatment would have applied except that there would have been no tax deduction and Capital Surplus would not have been increased by the $12,500 tax reduction amount.

Thus the typical stock option—either the nonstatutory option granted at full market value or the qualified stock option—is the only mechanism for permitting an executive to receive income without an offsetting reduction in the corporation's income to reflect the compensation expense.

When variations in the option approach are employed, the accounting treatment will also vary. One factor, however, does remain constant—granting the option will always affect the calculation of fully diluted earnings. The accounting changes can be illustrated by continuing to follow the earlier Acme/Freeman transactions.

Options with a value at grant

The accounting treatment in this instance is similar to any other payment in property. The value of the option ($6 times 1,000 shares) at the time of grant would be charged against income as a compensation expense.

Options for restricted stock

With options for restricted stock there is no charge to income at the time of grant. At the time of exercise, however, the accounting conventions applicable to restricted stock (see Chapter 9) come into play. The value of the stock, less any amount paid for it, *at the time it is issued* (option exercise) is a compensation expense. It is charged to income, but may be accrued on an aftertax equivalent basis over the period of restrictions.

In the Freeman example, the charge to income would be $25,000 (the $120,000 market value at the time of exercise less the $95,000 Freeman paid for the stock). That amount would then be charged to income (most likely in equal installments) over the number of years covered by the restrictions. There is one further complicating factor: Although the charge to income is based on the market value of the stock at the time of *exercise,* the company's tax deduction is determined by the market value of the stock (less the amount Freeman paid) at the time the *restrictions lapse*—in this example, $40,000 ($135,000 minus the $95,000 purchase price). Since $25,000 of the actual tax deduction has already been charged to income based on the market value at exercise,

that portion of the tax deduction has already been accounted for. The remaining $15,000 tax deduction, worth
approximately $7,500 to Acme, would be accounted for
as a contribution to Capital Surplus.

Discounted stock options

Discounted stock options include an immediate benefit
or value for the executive. Thus, there is considered to be
a compensation expense equal to the discount. Since
Freeman was granted the option at $70 a share when its
market value was $95, compensation of $25,000 (the $25
discount times the 1,000 shares) must be accounted for in
the year the option is granted (on an aftertax equivalent
basis). When the company's actual tax deduction is determined at the time of exercise ($50,000 in the Freeman
example), the $25,000 previously accrued as a charge to
income is offset and the remaining $25,000 tax deduction
results in an approximate $12,500 contribution to Capital
Surplus.

IN SUMMARY

The stock option enjoys a favored position from the
accounting viewpoint. It could be argued that the true cost
of options are really hidden from the stockholder.

Stock appreciation rights

Stock Appreciation Rights (SARs) are long-term incentives which have some similarities to stock options (or to
restricted stock) and some to performance shares. They are
like stock options in that the executive's reward depends
on appreciation in stock values rather than on attainment
of a more specific individual or group objective. They are

like performance shares in that they don't require the executive to make a direct out-of-pocket investment in company stock.

SARs contemplate that the executive will be paid an amount (in cash, stock or both) equal to the increase in stock value occurring over a period.

Example: On September 1, 1979, Barclay, vice president of Vision Corporation, is granted 500 Vision SARs for a four-year period. On that date, Vision Corporation stock is worth $40 a share. On September 1, 1983, Vision Corporation stock is worth $110 a share. Each SAR is therefore worth $70 a share (the stock's appreciation), or a total $35,000 to Barclay.

In this example, the SARs "matured" and were cashed in at a specified time of four years. But the plan could instead have permitted Barclay to exercise his rights at any time within a specified period or during his employment.

Typically, when SARs are exercised or mature, the executive receives half the amount in cash and half in stock, though payments all in cash or all in stock are not unknown. The half-in-cash is to provide the executive with funds to pay the tax (more on this below). The required tax withholding is in effect satisfied out of the cash portion.

SARs may be granted alone or, as is somewhat more common, coupled with stock options. If the latter, there would be an exercise period generally comparable to that of the stock option. Exercise of an SAR for a stock share would cancel the corresponding option for a stock share; if the SAR is for a share of stock plus equivalent cash, its exercise would cancel an option for two shares.

Assuming the SAR is paid all in cash, or half-cash, half-stock, an executive who is short of cash would exercise the SAR, surrendering the corresponding stock option.

The cash would satisfy the tax on the SAR and any balance could be applied towards the purchase of stock (or the balance could be *paid* in stock). An executive who didn't need cash could exercise the option, paying any tax on the exercise of the option out of his or her own pocket.

The grant of an SAR is not taxable to the executive where exercise of the SAR entails loss of a corresponding stock option. Where there is no corresponding option but the SAR has a fixed maturity, the grant is also presumably not taxable. Where there is no option and the SAR has an exercise period, it can reasonably be argued that the grant still is not taxable (because exercise forfeits any later increase in value) though there appears to be no formal IRS position on this.

Exercise or maturity of the SAR is taxable. The executive is taxed on any cash received and the value of any stock received, at ordinary income rates qualifying for maximum tax relief.

The company deducts the amount of the cash and the value of any stock to the extent that the payment is reasonable compensation.

SARs were designed to meet the cash needs of corporate insiders in public companies who want to exercise stock options. Rule 16(b) of the Securities Exchange Act requires the recapture of any profits realized from matched stock transactions (sales and then purchases or purchases and then sales) occurring within a six-month period for all "insiders" of the corporation. Rule 16(b) is to prevent senior executives in the corporation from using inside information to gain (or avoid a loss) in dealings in company stock. Because of this 16(b) requirement, the insider is forced to hold stock that other participants in the option plan would be able to sell at their own discretion. Thus, the corporate insider can't borrow to exercise the option and then immediately sell sufficient stock to repay the loan and generate the cash necessary for the tax on the option gain. At best, the insider must wait for six months before making such a sale. The SAR grows out of this problem and was developed to circumvent this issue for corporate insiders. Thus, the SAR allowed them to realize stock option gains in the same manner as other option participants. Viewed from this perspective, the SAR becomes somewhat of a financing technique for realizing stock option gains.

For example, if Leeco had granted Smith an option for 1,000 shares at $20 a share and the value of the option had increased to $30 a share at exercise, Smith, upon the exercise of the SAR, would be entitled to $10,000 (the $10-per-share gain times 1,000 shares). This could be taken down as a $5,000 cash award and 167 shares of stock ($5,000 ÷ $30 per share).

There has been a dramatic increase in the number of companies offering SARs, due in large part to the SEC's recent clarification of its posture regarding SARs. Under the SEC's current guidelines, the granting of a SAR is not considered a purchase for insider trading purposes. At the time that the SAR is exercised, the receipt of any *stock* is deemed a purchase and the six-month restricted period for insider trading would apply. If a settlement of the SAR (that is, the executive's collection on the SAR), is made in cash *and* complies with SEC timing rules, the settlement is considered neither a purchase nor a sale. Obviously, the same principles apply to an SAR that is settled in a combination of cash and stock, as long as the timing rules are met.

With respect to the timing rules, the SEC has defined four periods during the year in which such elections to exercise may be made, if payment may be made in cash. These are so-called window periods and occur on the third through twelfth days following the release of the company's quarterly financial statements. In this way, the SEC believes that all material information affecting the company should be equally available to insiders and the general investing public. By limiting SAR exercise to these periods, it is hoped that all investors will be acting on full information about the company.

Accounting considerations

Because of the accounting considerations, SARs are frequently limited to the insiders. Unlike the stock option which is accounted for only on the balance sheet, an SAR leads to a direct charge to book income. All appreciation in the market value of the stock over the SAR's base price must be accrued as a compensation expense. Of course, if the stock price happens to drop in a later period, the decrease in market value offsets the SAR's expense and is a credit to the income statement. Also, if the SAR expires unexercised (such as in a termination of employment) the previously accrued charge to income would be added back. The major accounting difference between an option and an SAR is that if the SAR has value, its cost will have been charged to the book income of the company.

The addition of stock appreciation rights can be an important improvement in stock option plans. The SAR is the only mechanism that provides the opportunity to realize the option gain without facing significant cash flow needs—especially on the senior executive group (the corporate insiders).

SAMPLE NONSTATUTORY STOCK
OPTION AGREEMENT

AGREEMENT made and entered into as of the ____ day of ____, 19__, between _____, a _____ [state] corporation, hereinafter called the Company, and _____, hereinafter called the Employee.

Whereas the Company having determined that its interests will be advanced by enabling selected employees to acquire a proprietary interest in the company, and as a further incentive to such employees to promote the Company's interests,

Now, therefore, in consideration of the premises, the parties agree as follows;

1. The Company hereby grants to the Employee, as a separate inducement and not in lieu of salary or other compensation, the right and option to purchase _____ of its common shares at _____ a share, under the terms hereinafter provided.

2. This option may be exercised by the Employee, in whole or in part, at any time within a period of 10 years from the day and year first above written.

3. The Employee exercises the option by written notice to the Company, which notice shall specify the number of shares to be purchased, and which shall be accompanied by a check in full payment of the option price for such shares; and until such payment the Employee shall have no rights in the optioned stock.

4. The Employee agrees that all shares purchased by him under this option are acquired for investment and not for distribution, and that any notice of exercise of the option shall be accompanied by a written representation, signed by him, to that effect.

IN WITNESS WHEREOF, parties hereto have caused the agreement to be executed on the day and year first above written.

_____
Corporation

by _____ [title]

Attest:

_____   _____
Secretary   Employee

STOCK APPRECIATION RIGHTS PLAN

[Introduction and administrative provisions]

1. Participants shall be awarded Stock Appreciation Rights (hereinafter "Rights") in conjunction with the stock option grant dated _____ (the "reference stock option"). Any time after six months following the date of grant, the participant may exercise the Right in accordance with the exercisability of the reference stock option and receive an amount equal to the appreciation in market value of his or her Rights as determined in paragraph 2 below. Such amount shall be paid in cash or in shares of common stock of the Company or in a combination of the two as determined by the Compensation Committee of the Board of Directors.

2. The value of one Right on any date shall be the market value of one share of common stock of the Company on such valuation date less the option price of one share under the reference stock option. The value of all Rights exercised by a Participant shall be the number of Rights exercised by such Participants times the value of one Right on such date. The market value of the common stock of the Company shall be the mean between the high and low quotations for such stock based on composite transactions on the _____ Stock Exchange on such date or, if no trading occurred on such date, on the next trading day.

3. The maximum number of Rights which may be granted under the Plan is _____ and the maximum number of shares of common stock of the Company which may be issued under the Plan is _____.

4. No Rights may be transferred except by will or the laws of descent and distribution.

5. If a Participant leaves the employ of the Company, otherwise than by authorized early retirement, retirement after age 65, disability or death, he or she shall forfeit all Rights under the Plan.

6. Upon issuance of common stock of the Company, the recipient thereof shall represent that the shares of stock are taken for investment and not resale. The recipient shall also make such other representations as may be necessary to qualify the issuance of the shares as exempt from the Securities Act of 1933 or to permit registration of the shares

STOCK APPRECIATION RIGHTS PLAN *(continued)*

and shall further represent that he or she shall not dispose of such shares in violation of the Securities Act of 1933. The Company may place a legend on any stock certificate issued pursuant to the Plan to assure compliance with this requirement. The Company shall not be required to distribute any shares of common stock until it shall have taken any action required to comply with the provisions of the Securities Act of 1933 or any other then applicable securities law.

7. The Company shall deduct from each distribution under the Plan the amount of any tax required to be withheld and paid over to any governmental authority for the account of the person entitled to such distribution.

8. Upon exercise of Rights, a corresponding number of shares subject to option under the reference stock option shall be cancelled. Such cancelled option shares shall be charged against the shares reserved for the plan as if exercised and shall not be available for future option grants under the plan.

11

Alternative long-term incentives

While stock options continue to be the most popular form of long-term executive reward, alternative approaches have been developed in recent years. These plans (unlike the annual bonus plans discussed in Chapter 4) reward executive performance over a number of years. Their distinguishing features include:

Financial performance standards for the award period.

Less reliance on *market price appreciation* of the stock to produce a reward.

Substantial rewards when company financial performance meets or exceeds the established performance standards.

These awards, often referred to as performance awards, offer maximum flexibility in rewarding executives for meeting predefined corporate goals. Some approaches offer company stock as well. Such programs can provide a stronger executive incentive than stock options while meeting many of the same compensation goals (e.g., longer term focus, capital accumulation and estate building, with stock interest).

This chapter reviews the major issues in designing a performance plan. Additionally, the most popular performance plan alternatives to stock options are discussed in detail, including a description of their features, tax and accounting treatment, and discussion of advantages and disadvantages to their use.

PERFORMANCE STANDARDS—THE COMMON ELEMENT

Performance plans all involve performance targets established for a period of years. The performance targets provide the link between corporate objectives and rewards to executives, thereby creating the desired incentive element. The targets under a long-term plan should be generally related to *where* the organization wants to be at the end of the period, as opposed to *how* it intends to get there. This helps to reward executives for supporting decisions that may negatively affect current results but are necessary to long-term success.

There are many financial indicators of long-term corporate growth and success. Most programs, however, have focused on earnings growth as the key measure, and most companies express the earnings growth in per share terms. Some plans use other goals such as earnings on gross assets, dividend rates, or debt/equity ratios, to expand or replace an earnings per share goal. Some companies expand the financial goal with one or two strategic goals such as accomplishment of an acquisition, a change in the mix of the business, or successful introduction of a new product. These types of supporting goals, if they are defined so that their accomplishment can be determined reasonably by the board of directors, can be highly successful in directing attention both to solid financial performance and the achievement of the company's strategic plan.

The manner of stating the targets must also be considered. The goal should be stated in a way that will encourage an even flow of earnings without penalizing weakness in one period that is offset in the following period. That provides the necessary flexibility to make long-term decisions that might adversely affect profits in the current year, while building the foundation for future growth and earnings. The compensation planner may want to avoid a compounded growth rate approach which rewards the *swing* from the beginning of the period to the end, regardless of the performance in the intervening years.

The most appropriate approach is the use of a cumulative goal during the period. For example, assume SECO's goal is a 12 percent per year increase in earnings per share. The target for a performance period covering 1979 through 1981 and based on the 1978 earnings per share of $1.50 would be as follows:

    1979 earnings = $1.68
    1980 earnings = $1.88
    1981 earnings = $2.11
    Plan earnings
        objective = $5.67,   cumulative earnings
                             per share during
                             1979, 1980, and 1981

Once the performance target has been established, the portion of the award amount to be earned at various levels of achievement of the target must be identified. As a part of the target-setting process, the company will have to define some minimum level of performance, below which no award would be earned. Using SECO's 12 percent growth in earnings per share, the earnings schedule might follow the concept outlined below:

> No award would be earned until cumulative earnings per share reach some minimally acceptable level, such as an 8 percent increase which equals $5.26 cumulative earnings.
>
> When this minimum level is reached, the executives might "earn" 25 percent of their award for that cycle.
>
> If the cumulative growth rate exceeds the minimum level, the portion of the award considered to be earned would increase from 25 percent to 100 percent as the targeted 12 percent level is approached.

This relationship should be defined in an incremental earnings schedule similar to that suggested for target-oriented incentive plans in Chapter 4, once actual goals have been established.

No matter how carefully a company plans, there may be unanticipated extraordinary losses or windfall gains during a performance period. When an event does occur that causes the targeted level of achievement to become totally unrealistic—on either the high or low side—some adjustment of the plan targets should be made to keep the incentive impact of the plan. However, only unusual situations, clearly beyond the control of management, should be considered. Targets should never be adjusted to offset the effects of management action or to totally insulate management from normal business risks. On the other hand, it is important that participants understand the plan as a business management tool, and as such the board of directors should have the right to make modifications as required during the performance period to reflect sound business judgment.

OTHER DESIGN ISSUES

No matter what form the final performance plan might take, there are several key decision areas that will have to be covered.

Eligibility

Eligibility should be limited to officers and other key employees who are in positions which directly affect the profitability and success of the organization over the long term. This will be a much more restricted group than that established for the annual incentive program.

As with all incentives, the individual must perceive that he or she can control or at least significantly influence the result. This concept has even greater applicability in a performance plan than under an annual program, if any incentive value is to be realized. Stock options used by most companies do not really support this concept because the market price of the stock is too far removed from the work situation. That is, it does not closely reflect what one executive or a group of executives may do. Performance plans, however, can provide a direct link to company performance for a select group of participants.

Performance period

A long-term incentive program by definition focuses on more than one year's results. Among those companies presently using such programs, the performance periods range from three to six years. The relationship to the company's planning process, and the impact of the length of the period on an individual's award, must be considered in setting the award period.

Planning cycle. The farther the planning process moves

from the current year, the more unrealistic it becomes. Long-term plans typically project fairly reasonably through the second and third years, but periods beyond generally fall victim to "blue-sky" thinking and ultimately may bear little resemblance to reality. Thus, a three-year cycle would appear best from the planning aspect.

Individual incentive. Individual expectations regarding the frequency of payment under a performance incentive will vary, but they are most commonly related to expectations associated with stock option programs. While options typically have been exercised between the fourth and fifth years, overlapping option grants frequently result in potential for gains on a two- to three-year basis. There is no evidence to suggest that a shorter award period will increase the incentive impact, but an award period that is too prolonged can reduce the incentive impact.

The choice of an appropriate award period is also influenced by the frequency of subsequent cycles. Use of back-to-back periods (for example, 1979-1981, then 1982-1984) with no overlap provides a long-term balance to the annual incentive program. It also places full emphasis on achieving the desired results by the end of the award period. However, this approach may place too much weight on a single long-term plan. Since most companies revise and update their long-term plans annually, an award period tied to a now-outdated plan may be inappropriate.

An alternative to back-to-back award periods is starting a new award period as each new long-term plan is developed. For example, an award period might cover the long-term plan for 1979, 1980, and 1981. In 1980 a new plan would be set forth for 1980, 1981, and 1982, with a corresponding award period. Some companies believe that starting a new award period with each new plan reinforces their planning process better and relieves the pressure to adjust the performance targets as the company revises its plan.

Another aspect in the choice of back-to-back versus overlapping cycles involves executive retention. For example, if a new three-year award cycle were to begin every year, the executive would have a continuing stake in long-term incentives. If the executive quit at the end of the 1979 through 1981 cycle (having earned that award), the awards accruing for the periods 1980 through 1982 and 1981 through 1983 would be forfeited. This should provide incentive to remain with the company.

Although the proper award period may vary according to each company's planning process, most performance plans now focus on a three-year period. Further, the trend is to overlapping periods with a new award beginning each year.

Award size

The most difficult area in designing a viable long-term incentive program is determining how large an award to make. The payout from the program must be:

Competitive with the practices of other companies.

Large enough to motivate the desired performance.

Meet the test of reasonableness of compensation as discussed in Chapter 3.

A common body of knowledge on award size has not yet fully developed. Thus, most companies have referred back to prior stock option practices—the prior long-term incentive—and tried to develop similar reward opportunities.

PERFORMANCE SHARES

Performance share plans use stock value (as does a stock option). But performance shares also make it possible to earn a reward based on internal financial results (regardless of the market price of the stock). Under this arrangement, an executive is contingently credited with a number of performance shares, essentially equal to shares of the company's common stock. The individual earns the performance shares on the basis of performance against preestablished goals covering the performance period. (A sample performance share agreement appears at the end of this chapter.)

At the end of the period the executive receives the number of shares earned on the basis of the performance criteria. Thus, the executive has the opportunity to earn a fixed number of shares solely on the basis of absolute company results. The ultimate value of those shares depends upon the stock market's reaction to the company's performance. Through this approach the executive receives some reward (assuming good performance) even in periods of market depression when a stock option might be totally worthless. However, the executive is also tied to the shareholder's measure of success over the long term: the value of the stock.

Example: SECO awards Kelly, its executive vice president, a performance share award for 1,000 shares. The current value of the stock is $20 per share, the performance target is an increase in earnings per share of $5.67 (equivalent to an average increase of 12 percent per year), and the performance period is three years (covering 1979, 1980 and 1981).

At the time of the award in 1979, Kelly has only an opportunity to earn the 1,000 shares according to the company's financial performance during the three years covered by the award. The award has no immediate value to Kelly.

Suppose SECO's earnings per share for the three years were as follows:

$$1979:\ \$1.60$$
$$1980:\ \$1.93$$
$$1981:\ \$2.18$$

The total earnings during the period, $5.71, slightly exceeds the performance target. Kelly earns the full 1,000 shares which are then awarded early in 1982 (as soon as the 1981 results are finalized). No matter what may have happened to the market price of the stock, Kelly has earned and been *paid* 1,000 shares of SECO stock.

If the marketplace viewed SECO's performance favorably, the stock price would have risen from the value in 1979 to, let's say, $25 per share. The result is that Kelly has 1,000 shares with a total value when paid of $25,000.

Tax treatment

The executive is taxed on the fair market value of the stock at the time it is actually delivered. The amount will be eligible for personal service income tax treatment. At that same time, the company is permitted a compensation deduction for the market value of the shares delivered. In the above example, Kelly would have been taxable in 1982 on $25,000 of personal service income. Similarly, SECO would have been allowed a tax deduction for the $25,000 compensation expense.

Accounting for performance shares

Unlike the stock option, a performance share award is a direct charge to the company's book income. The value of the shares at the time paid is a compensation expense. That full amount must be charged to income by the time the award is paid. The compensation expense is allocated over the periods for which the service is performed, and current accounting standards require the amounts to be adjusted quarterly to reflect the likelihood that the award will be earned *and* the impact of changes in the market value of the stock during the quarter.

In the preceding example, SECO would have had to accrue the $25,000 compensation expense item during the company's fiscal years 1979, 1980, and 1981. In this instance, assuming the company felt there was a reasonable probability that the award would be earned, the first quarter of 1979 would have been charged with 1/12 of the value of the award when it was originally made (in this case, 1/12 of $20,000, or $1,667). Accruing that amount in each of the 12 quarters during the performance period would reflect the earning of the full 1,000 shares at the original $20 price.

Each quarter, however, the amount accrued would have to be adjusted to reflect changes in the price of the stock. For example, if the market price of the stock had increased to $23 at the close of the first quarter of 1979 the accrual might be approximately $1,917 (1/12 of the projected value of the 1,000 shares at $23 per share). If in the second quarter of 1979 the price of the stock dropped back to $21 per share, the accrual that quarter would have to equal the difference between 2/12 of the 1,000 shares at $21 per share less the $1,917 already accrued. In that instance, the second quarter charge would be $1,583.

As a long-term incentive, the performance share concept has much to recommend it. The concept establishes a reward mechanism that responds to the growth and success of the company. It also reduces the influence of an uncertain stock market that is buffeted by forces frequently far removed from company performance. At the same time, it recognizes the fact that stockholders look to market value (and dividends) for *their* reward. The performance share concept seems to encompass both aspects in a reasonable manner.

Despite the strong points of the concept, performance shares give rise to certain risks from an accounting viewpoint. The compensation expense that must be accounted for by the company, and also the basis of the tax deduction, are determined by the fair market value of the shares at the time of payment. Thus, when a company awards 1,000 performance shares, it does not know what the final cost of that award will be.

In theory, if the market value of the stock follows the increase in the earnings of the company, the planned compensation cost (controlled by the size of the award) will be reasonable and proper in light of the benefits realized by the company. However, if the market forces result in a significant increase in the price of the stock, the full amount of that increase must be absorbed by company earnings—whether or not the stock increase reflects company earnings. This feature could be important, particularly to a closely held company. If the company decided to make a public offering during the performance period, the leveraged increase in the stock value could cause a significant charge to earnings. This would occur at the very time the company would want to report solid earnings progress.

In the above example, SECO would have had a $25,000 compensation expense with an aftertax cost of approximately $13,500 (assuming a 46 percent company tax rate). Kelly would have received 1,000 shares of stock valued at $25,000, with an aftertax value of at least $12,500 (assuming the full 50 percent maximum tax rate for personal service income). If he had sold enough shares to meet his tax liability (assuming no appreciation in value between delivery and sale and, therefore, no capital gains tax), he would have held onto 500 shares of SECO stock.

PERFORMANCE CASH

In this approach, the executive is awarded a contingent cash bonus amount. The executive has no right to the cash until established performance standards are met. Typically, the standards relate to company financial results over a period of time (usually three or more years) and are expressed as a target or goal. The executive will earn none, some portion, or all of the contingent cash amount depending on the degree of achievement of the targeted financial results.

Example: Instead of the previous performance share award, SECO decides to give Kelly a performance cash award of $25,000 to be earned according to the performance criteria and time frame described above. The award is contingent on company performance and Kelly will not realize any part of the award until after the performance period. Assuming the same performance pattern for SECO, Kelly would be paid the $25,000 bonus early in 1982.

Tax treatment

The executive is taxed on the cash amount actually received in the year paid. Personal service income tax limits will apply. For the company, a tax deduction is allowed in the year the award is earned on the amount actually paid. For both the individual and the company there is no tax impact related to any part of the contingent amount that is not earned and, therefore, never awarded.

As before, Kelly would have been taxable in 1982 on $25,000 of personal service income. Similarly, SECO would have been allowed a tax deduction for the $25,000 compensation expense.

Accounting for performance cash

Like the performance share award, the performance cash award is a direct charge to the company's book income. The value of the award at the time paid is a compensation expense. That full amount must be charged to income by the time the award is paid. The compensation expense is allocated over the periods for which the service is performed, according to the likelihood that the award will be earned.

In the preceding example, SECO would have had to accrue the $25,000 compensation expense item during the company's fiscal years 1979, 1980, and 1981. In this instance, assuming the company felt there was a reasonable probability that the award would be earned, each quarter would have been charged with 1/12 of the $25,000 value of the award.

Planning for performance cash

Performance cash plans reward internal performance and totally avoid the ups and downs of the marketplace in determining the reward to the executives. Thus, their advantages are similar to the motivational advantages of the performance share.

Both the taxation and the accounting of performance cash plans are comparatively simple. Therefore, the company can structure the cost to coincide with the benefits received if the performance criteria are met. The risk of having that amount further affected (for example, increased) by the market price of the stock under a performance share plan is thus avoided.

Unfortunately, these cash plans lack any direct tie to company stock—a feature that is included in most other long-term incentive alternatives. For that reason, the most typical use of performance cash is in combination with at least a partial stock payment of the ultimate cash amount earned or used as a financing vehicle to accumulate cash to exercise a stock option.

The result of the $25,000 performance cash award described is the same as the earlier performance share award. Kelly would realize $12,500 at an aftertax cost to SECO of approximately $13,500. This comparison would change only if the stock price in the performance share example had been something other than $25 at the time of payment. If that had happened, Kelly's gain and SECO's cost[1] would have moved, correspondingly, up or down. But of course the performance cash approach avoids that by setting a fixed dollar amount at the time of the award.

COMBINATION APPROACH

The performance share places heavy emphasis on actual company financial performance, but it is also tied to market value of the stock. But it involves a financial risk, which is reflected in the accounting treatment. The cost is beyond the control of the company, since it depends on the market value of the stock at the time of the actual payment. By combining the fixed cost of the performance cash plan with the favorable accounting treatment of the stock option, a third approach can be developed. (For details of stock option accounting, which avoids the charge to book income, see Chapter 10.)

Under a typical combination performance cash/stock

---

[1] The question of a company's cost when it pays in stock as compared to payment in cash is considered in Chapter 8.

option approach, the executive is awarded a contingent cash amount that will be earned on the achievement of performance goals over a defined period of time (just like the performance cash plan described above).

The opportunity to realize any market price appreciation during the performance period is covered by granting a stock option at the beginning of the period. The two portions are coordinated so that if performance goals are met, the executive would be paid cash to finance the exercise of the option. This way, the executive would realize the market price appreciation, and net the same number of shares after taxes as would have been earned under a similar performance share award.

From the company point of view, the performance cash portion fixes the company's cost and charge to income in accordance with the performance goals—no surprises due to the marketplace. The market price appreciation is accounted for through the regular stock option approach and only affects "capital surplus" and the dilution in shareholder's equity.

Example: SECO sets the same performance targets and the same three-year performance period as before. The company also anticipates a $5 increase in the market value of its stock if SECO's earnings are at the projected level during the period. In this instance, SECO awards Kelly a performance cash award for $22,500 and a stock option for 500 shares at $20 per share (the market value on the date of grant).

Tax treatment

The tax treatment for the two pieces of the combination award are exactly as described earlier for each piece separately. The $22,500 performance cash award will be taxed as personal service income in the year paid, and the company will take a corresponding deduction on its tax return at that time. The stock option, when exercised, will result in taxable income to the executive on the difference between the option price and the market value of the stock at the time of exercise. Again, the company is allowed a corresponding deduction.

Assuming SECO's performance is on target in the above example, Kelly is awarded the $22,500 performance cash award early in 1982. He will owe $11,250 in taxes on that award. Out of the remaining cash ($11,250) Kelly will use $10,000 to exercise his option for 500 shares at $20 per share. If SECO stock is worth $25 at the time Kelly exercises, he will owe tax, at personal service income rates, on $2,500 (500 shares times the $5 per share option gain). The $1,250 tax he will owe equals the remaining cash from his performance cash award. The results are summarized below:

	$22,500	performance cash award earned
Less	11,250	taxes due on award
	11,250	
Less	10,000	to exercise 500 share option
	1,250	
Less	1,250	taxes due on $2,500 option gain

Kelly owns 500 SECO shares.

That *exact* result would only occur if the appreciation in the stock's market value at the end of the award period is precisely at the level predicted when the award was made. However, the structure of the plan provides a mechanism to cover most of the executive's tax liability.

Accounting for the combined plan

As with taxes, the accounting follows the procedures stated for each part independently. In the SECO example, the $22,500 performance cash portion would be accrued in 12 equal quarterly installments over the three years. The stock option would not result in a charge to SECO's book income. At the time of exercise, SECO would realize a tax deduction of $2,500 resulting in a $1,150 tax savings which would be accounted for as a contribution to capital surplus along with the $10,000 Kelly paid upon exercise of the option.

The combination performance cash/stock option approach is one way to achieve the benefits of the performance share plan without exposing the company to the risks discussed earlier. It also takes advantage of the favorable accounting treatment for stock options. This results in a slightly more efficient compensation package. Under the combination example, Kelly still realizes an aftertax value of $12,500 (500 shares times $25 market value). SECO's aftertax cost, however, would be only $11,000—$2,500 less than under the performance share or cash plans. This is a result of the lower aftertax cost ($12,150) charged to book income for the $22,500 performance cash award, reduced further by the $1,150 tax savings realized from the option exercise.[2]

IN SUMMARY

Performance plans are a significant departure from the stock option plans that lead to their development. They do, however, offer an alternative approach to rewarding executives for company performance over a period of

---

[2] SECO's tax deductions ($22,500 and $2,500) and their tax values are the same as with performance shares or performance cash.

several years. The plans reviewed above are the most common long-term incentives (other than stock options) in use today. But there are other forms that could be used. Any of the stock plans discussed in earlier chapters have the equity ownership characteristics usually desired in long-term incentives. And most could be combined with performance criteria to create a specific long-term incentive program. (See restricted stock, Chapter 9 and phantom stock, Chapter 6.)

SAMPLE PERFORMANCE SHARE AGREEMENT

1. The Company hereby grants to the Employee, as an incentive to improve the Company's long-term financial results, the right to earn _____ shares of the Company's common stock subject to the performance criteria set forth in paragraph 2.

    The number of shares earned shall be determined, after the completion of a three-year performance cycle, based on the attainment of targeted financial results, expressed in earnings per share as determined by the Company's auditors.

2. For the three-year performance period commencing on January 1, 19____, the Board has determined a target of cumulative earnings per share of $_____. If this level of financial performance is attained, the full number of shares awarded in paragraph 1 shall be deemed to be earned. If cumulative earnings per share are less than $_____, no shares will be earned and all rights to earn such shares will be forfeited. If cumulative earnings per share are at least $_____, 50 percent of the shares specified in paragraph 1 shall be deemed to be earned; if such earnings per share exceed $_____ but are less than $_____, a pro rata portion between 50 percent and 100 percent of such shares will be deemed to be earned.

3. Shares so earned will be paid as soon as practicable following the close of the Company's books at the end of the award period.

4. No shares will be earned or paid unless the Employee has been a full-time Employee of the Company throughout the award period.

12

Executive
expense accounts

Some laymen hold the view that the expense account is the executive's tax-free passport to a life of luxury. This is definitely not the case. Expense accounts have a useful role to play in business life, but they should not be accounted a major element of the executive compensation package.

EXPENSE ACCOUNTS IN RECRUITMENT
AND RETENTION

A liberal expense account policy can help attract prospective executive employees. Most executives will expect to incur some entertainment expenses on their company's behalf, such as lunch with a client, and many must do occasional or frequent traveling. The executive will welcome the assurance that he or she need not bear any of these costs out of salary, that the company will cover all proper charges for meals in comfortable surroundings, for first-class hotels and plane accommodations, and so on.

The company that can offer the prospective executive

employee a generous expense account has an advantage over other possible employers. And it takes something extra to attract an executive who already enjoys a liberal expense account.

The attractive power of the liberal expense account can be seen from this example: Two companies are competing for Brown's services. One offers her a $55,000 salary. The other offers her $50,000 and a $5,000 expense account. Assuming she will actually incur $5,000 in expenses in either job, which arrangement should she choose? Normally, the $50,000 + $5,000 job. Since the net income would be the same in either case, the chief attraction of the expense account arrangement is one of convenience. There would be no tax withholding on the expense account, and tax reporting of disbursements would be less detailed. But there are also small practical tax advantages in the expense account job. There, the executive is more likely to be able to establish to Revenue Service satisfaction that all expense account items were business outlays, and that none were personal items generating taxable income. Thus, Jones of Ecks Corporation and Smith of Wye Corporation may incur exactly the same $5,000 of expenses. Jones has a salary of $50,000 and a $5,000 expense account. Smith has a $55,000 salary and pays her own expenses. It is more likely that the $5,000 covered by Jones's expense account will pass IRS review than the $5,000 deducted by Smith. The IRS might bar Smith's deduction for, say, $800 of her $5,000 outlay, so that Smith is taxable on $800 more than she actually has—an additional tax burden of about $400. Such a tax hardship for the executive whose costs are not covered by a company expense account or reimbursement arrangement could arise, for example, where the job involves travel abroad.

The IRS audit of Smith's deductions might arise as the result of a refund claim by Smith. Tax would have been withheld on Smith's entire $55,000, so her $5,000 deduction for business expenses could mean that she has overpaid her tax through withholding.[1] She would claim a refund of the overpaid tax, which could trigger an audit.

Another tax advantage of an expense account arrangement lies in the fact that expenses covered by an expense account are deducted in computing adjusted gross income. They are not itemized deductions. Thus, an executive can deduct such expenses and still get the benefit of the zero bracket amount.

EXPENSE ACCOUNT PLANNING

Our concern in this chapter will be with planning how the company should set up its expense account for maximum advantage and protection for both company and executive.

Proper expense account planning must reflect awareness of these two rules: (1) company payment of an executive's personal expenses is taxable income to the executive, and (2) company payment or reimbursement of expenses the executive incurs on the company's behalf is normally tax-exempt to him or her. Depending on circumstances, tax exemption is achieved directly through being excused from reporting company-paid sums as income, or indirectly, through reporting such sums but taking an offsetting deduction.

From the executive's standpoint, the goal is to avoid having company payments treated by the Revenue Service as payments of personal expenses, which will result in taxable income. The IRS should be convinced that all outlays were for business reasons on the company's behalf.

The company, for its part, will also want to prove that

---

[1] In some cases, she could claim additional withholding allowances for her itemized deductions. These reduce tax withholding.

its outlays were for business reasons and so are deductible. Technically, its motive need not always be the same as its executive's. A payment of the executive's personal expenses is deductible by the company as a compensation expense (if compensation is reasonable); the company need not prove the outlay was for business entertainment or business travel. But as a practical matter, companies try to establish the business entertainment or travel aspect to spare tax difficulties for their employees. This chapter therefore will explore what expense account policies a company should adopt to assure full tax deduction for all its outlays while at the same time assuring tax exemption on those outlays for its executives.

What travel expenses can be covered

An expense account can properly cover the following travel expenses:

1. Transportation costs from the home area to the away-from-home business location, such as plane, train, or boat fare, or car rental.
2. Meals and lodging while away from home on business.
3. Transportation costs (cab fares or car rental costs), between airport or station and hotel, and between hotel and the business location, or between business locations.
4. Cleaning and laundry costs.
5. Baggage charges.
6. Tips incident to any of these items.

What entertainment expenses should be covered

With entertainment expenditures as with travel expenses, the company wants to be certain that the executive's outlays which it covers or reimburses through the expense account device will be deductible as entertainment expenses. Executives should therefore be carefully instructed as to the ingredients of a deductible entertainment expense, so that they will know exactly what outlays they can make that will be deductible by the company and tax-free to them. The following material shows the categories of entertainment activities a company can authorize the executive to engage in with reasonable confidence that deduction and tax exemption will be available.[2]

"Directly related" entertainment. What is meant here is an outlay where: (*a*) the executive (on the company's behalf) expected to derive income or some other specific business benefit (not just goodwill) in the future, (*b*) business with the person being entertained was actually engaged in during the entertainment, and (*c*) business rather than entertainment was the dominant aspect of the meeting. This would recognize entertainment taking place at sporting events, night clubs, and so forth, if business is actually seriously considered during the entertainment. It would also recognize the costs of meals or drinks at home or in restaurants or bars, with the same business aspect (though cost of meals is deductible in other settings as well, and without the need for actual business discussion; see below). Business need not actually result, as long as it is seriously discussed.

The executive should be discouraged from expense account entertaining at cocktail parties or other gatherings where persons other than business contacts are present, since their presence would prevent or inhibit business discussion. Deduction would not be allowed unless busi-

---

[2] We will not be concerned here with the detailed tax rules on entertainment expense deductions. The material given here is to indicate what entertainment expenses should properly be included in an executive's expense account. A readable account of the entertainment expense rules can be found in the Revenue Service publication *Tax Guide for Small Business.*

ness is actually discussed, and IRS suspicions would be aroused by the presence of nonbusiness guests.

"Associated with" entertainment. Entertainment which precedes or follows a substantial business discussion would qualify. This rule contemplates the situation where, after a business discussion with a customer, prospect, or other business contact, the parties break off for entertainment. Costs of entertainment provided before or after a serious business discussion are deductible even though no business is considered during the entertainment. Ordinarily, outlays for entertaining the spouse of the business contact in the same gathering (and the executive's own spouse, where both husbands and wives are there) are part of the deductible expense. Entertainment may take place anywhere—in the home, at sporting events, night clubs, theaters, restaurants, or elsewhere.

Example: Baker, sales vice president, is conducting negotiations with Whitlock, purchasing manager of a prospective customer from out of town. Following business discussions during the day, Baker, Whitlock, and their wives go out for drinks, dinner, and a hockey game, all at Baker's expense, borne by his company. The costs of these evening activities are deductible entertainment expenses even though no business is discussed. Baker could be properly authorized to incur such expenses under his expense account arrangement.

"Quiet" business meals. This recognizes the entertainment expense status of meals or drinks furnished "under circumstances generally considered to be conducive" to a business discussion. It is not necessary that business discussion actually take place or even be contemplated. It is necessary that the surroundings be appropriate to business discussion (a night club ordinarily would not be), and that the person being entertained has a significant business

relationship to the company bearing the entertainment expense. Thus, the executive could be authorized by the expense account to take a regular customer to drinks or dinner, as a gesture to retain the customer's goodwill, and without any need to discuss business. But reciprocal arrangements, where business associates alternate in picking up the tab for drinks or meals, would not be qualified entertainment.

The meals or drinks could take place in public restaurants and the like or in the executive's own home.

The executive's expenses. In all the situations set forth above, the executive's own expenses, meals, or entertainment costs are deductible by the company and not taxable to him or her, assuming the entertainment has business motivation.

Too luxurious

The Revenue Service bars deduction for expenses of "lavish and extravagant" travel or entertainment. That is, deduction is denied to the extent that travel or entertainment is lavish or extravagant. This would suggest that the reasonable part of any outlay is deductible but that any more than that would be lavish and extravagant. The company could not deduct the entire sum, but only the dollar cost of reasonable accommodations or services. The executive enjoying the lavish and extravagant accommodations could also be required to report as taxable income (without offsetting deduction) the part the company could not deduct. The justification for taxing the executive would be that the lavishness and extravagance was probably incurred for his or her own gratification and lacked a business excuse. It would therefore be a company payment of an employee's personal expenses.

So much for what the law says and what professional practitioners might surmise about it. In fact, however, there is no recorded case or ruling holding any outlay to be nondeductible (or taxable) as lavish and extravagant. Just the reverse.

The Revenue Service says that expenses are lavish and extravagant if they are unreasonable, considering all the circumstances. But they are not lavish and extravagant just because they are for deluxe accommodations in a restaurant, hotel, night club, or resort.

This indicates that unless the amount spent is really ridiculous, it is deductible (assuming an adequate business connection). Haute cuisine at the town's grandest restaurant, a deluxe room at its finest hotel, the limousine between airport and hotel and between places where business is conducted, all would seem acceptable, under the present IRS position.

But this also indicates that the tax rules cannot be relied on to control or set a business standard for company spending. Management must decide on its own what it can reasonably afford to pay, consistent with executive comfort and company prestige. Decision-making here is an ongoing process, as travel and entertainment costs rise.

Club dues and expenses

In most cases, it will not be desirable to have the expense account cover an executive's costs of membership in a social or athletic club.

Membership or initiation fees are not deductible at all, if the membership lasts beyond a year.

Periodic dues or fees also are not deductible at all unless more than 50 percent of the executive's use of the club is for business purposes.[3] Detailed records must be kept of the executive's use of the club. And even if the club is used

---

[3] A provision of 1978 law completely barred deduction for periodic dues or fees at social and athletic clubs which were not country clubs, but this has been described by Congressional officials as an error, which will be corrected.

more than 50 percent for business, the company deducts only that portion of the dues which is allocable to directly related entertainment and quiet business meals.

Amounts spent at the club for entertainment are deductible under the general entertainment expense rules already discussed. For example, greens fees and caddy fees and tips of a round of golf are deductible if business is discussed. Costs of meals or drinks at the club, or of other club activities, could be deductible if they precede or follow substantial business discussion. And meals or drinks at the club could be deductible under the *quiet business meals* rule even though no business discussion takes place. These deductions are allowed whether or not club dues are deductible.

Dues and fees to businessmen's lunch clubs are normally exempt from the above rules on social clubs. They are deductible as ordinary business expenses and are not thought of as entertainment outlays. The dues are therefore often paid directly by the company, and would not be part of the expense account.

Such clubs are conducive to business discussion, so that meals or drinks furnished there would properly be part of an expense account arrangement, under the *quiet business meals* rule.

Business gifts

In the authors' opinion, gifts to business contacts should come directly from and be paid for by the company; they should not be part of the executive's expense account. But some exceptions to this position can be justified: Gifts of candy or flowers to the wife of a business contact, or of liquor to a husband, could appropriately be an expense account item. So could gifts of tickets to some entertainment activity which the executive will not attend.

Deduction for business gifts generally cannot exceed $25 per recipient, which should serve to keep expense account charges within bounds. Deduction for gifts of tickets can be taken either as entertainment expenses or as gifts. As entertainment expenses, they can exceed the $25 ceiling applicable to gifts, if they qualify under the *associated with* rule. But as gifts (subject to the $25 limit) they would not need to meet any of the entertainment tests.

A gift to the spouse (say, the wife) of a business contact is normally counted as a gift to her husband, in figuring the $25-per-recipient ceiling.

RECORD-KEEPING AND SUBSTANTIATION OF EXPENSE ACCOUNT CHARGES

Company expense account policy is to make sure that it can deduct expense outlays and that its executives are not taxable on these amounts. Therefore the company should adopt procedures for full executive accounting to the company for travel, entertainment, and business gift expenditures. The material below sets forth what records and substantiation are needed.

If record-keeping and substantiation requirements are met, the executive is excused from the need to prove independently to a Revenue Agent that he or she is not taxable on a company payment or reimbursement of expenses. Also, these records and supporting documents will give the company the materials it needs to satisfy the IRS that items labeled as travel, entertainment, or business gift expenses were actually that, and deductible as such, and not nondeductible dividends or unreasonable compensation.

The executive is excused from the need to include expense allowances or reimbursements in income or otherwise report them on a tax return if: (*a*) the expenses equal the allowances or reimbursements, and (*b*) the executive is required to and does make an accounting to the company for receipts and outlays. The elements of a proper accounting are the records and substantiation set forth below:

Entertainment expense records should show:

1. The amount of each separate outlay for entertaining, except that such incidental expenditures as taxis and phone calls can be totalled on a daily basis. Tips may be recorded separately or included in the cost of the service rendered.
2. The date of the entertainment.
3. Name, location, and type of entertainment (dinner, theater, and so forth).
4. Reason for entertainment or nature of business benefit derived or expected and, except for business meals, the nature of any business discussion or activity.
5. Data on person entertained which will establish his or her business relationship to the company: occupation, name, title, and so on.

For *associated with* entertaining, which precedes or follows substantial business discussion, instead of the information in item 4 above, the records should show: the date, duration, location, and nature of the business discussion, the business reason for the entertainment or the business benefit derived or expected, and all persons entertained who participated in the business discussion. (The records for such entertaining would also cover items 1-3, and 5.)

Travel expense records should show:

1. The amount of each separate outlay for travel away from home (such as transportation or hotels), but the daily cost of incidental items may be aggregated and set forth in reasonable categories such as: meals; gasoline and oil; cab fares. Tips may be recorded sepa-

rately or included in the cost of the service rendered.

2. Dates of departure and return home for each trip, and the number of days spent on business away from home overnight.
3. Destination or locality of travel, described by name of town or the like.
4. Business reason for the travel or the nature of the business benefit derived or expected.

Records of business gifts should show:

1. Cost of the item given.
2. When the gift was made.
3. Reasons for the gift or nature of business benefits derived or expected.
4. Data on person to whom gift was made which will establish his or her business relationship to the company: occupation, name, title, and so on.

Substantiating expense account records

The elements of travel, entertainment, or gift expense must be substantiated. This is done by an account book, diary, company expense statement, or similar record, whose entries are made at or near the time the outlay was made.

In addition, receipts, paid bills, or other similar documentary evidence is required for lodging away from home (regardless of amount) or for any other outlay of $25 or more, except that documentation is not necessary for a transportation expense where evidence of the cost is not readily available. Documentary evidence, where required, should show amount, date, place, and character of the expenditure. (A cancelled check alone would not be enough.) A hotel bill should show lodging, meals, and telephone charges separately.

Substantiation unnecessary for certain per diem and mileage allowances

Executive and company are excused from the need to provide the substantiation described above (account book, for instance, and documentation) for travel expenses in these situations:

a. The executive receives a per diem allowance of not more than $44 a day. This allowance would cover meals, lodging, laundry and similar items, and related tips; amounts for transportation (air fares, cab fares, and so on) could be covered outside the per diem. An employee who is "related" to his or her employer (that is, a more-than-10-percent stockholder of a corporate employer or certain close relatives of an individual employer) would have to substantiate in any case; the per diem exemption would not apply to such an employee.

b. The executive receives a mileage allowance of not more than 17 cents a mile. Substantiation of such mileage allowances isn't required even if employee and employer are "related." An executive may be given both per diem and mileage allowances or only one of these.

Companies which wish to ease the tax reporting burdens for themselves and their executives should adopt per diem and mileage policies, assuming they can be economically justified. The release from the substantiation requirement does not affect the company's duty to retain the travel expense records on time, place, and business purpose (travel expense items 2-4 above). The amount of the expense would be the per diem and mileage allowances it pays.

Technically, an executive or other employee receiving a per diem or mileage allowance must report for tax purposes the excess of the amount received over actual outlays. This would of course require him or her to keep a record of outlays. In practice, the Revenue Service does not seem to require this reporting for the per diems and mileage allowances described here. Thus, in practice, records of outlays apparently are not necessary.

The company is expected to police the executive's expense account reporting, through "proper internal controls." Some responsible employee other than the executive who incurs the expense must verify and approve the expense account.

According to the Revenue Service, the per diem allowance given should be based on reasonable estimates of actual current costs in the localities where they are incurred. The idea behind this long-standing rule is that $44 may be a proper per diem in one area while $38 may buy the same accommodations and services in another area. In the authors' opinion, the rule should now be considered inoperative because of inflation—that $44 is hardly likely to be an unreasonably high estimate of current costs of meals and lodging anywhere in the United States. (In fact, so long as the reporting rule is limited to $44, it seems of no practical value to any U.S. executive.)

Per diems at a rate higher than $44 a day are allowed in either of these situations:

1. Where the U.S. government pays a higher per diem to *its* employees for travel in the same area.

This usually involves travel abroad. Here, substantiation is excused on per diems that don't exceed what the government pays.

2. On special application. Companies which think the $44 rate, or the U.S. government rate, is too little for travel in particular areas should apply for IRS approval of a higher rate. Requests for approval should give detailed information about the allowance to be paid, with the rea-

sons why the company's situation justifies a higher rate. Address requests to: Commissioner of Internal Revenue, Attention: Income Tax Division, Washington, D.C. 20024.

EXPENSES OUTSIDE THE EXPENSE ACCOUNT

Some firms find it unreasonable to try to cover every executive entertainment outlay under its expense account policy. In some businesses (advertising and public relations are examples), entertainment situations could be so numerous, or so widely varied, as to resist codification in a company program or policing through company accounting procedures.

A frequent solution is for the company to adopt an expense account policy covering certain limited, easily definable expenses. The company then instructs the executive that while many other entertainment outlays are proper and encouraged, they will not be covered by the company. Instead, the executive's salary is set at a level intended to enable him or her to bear needed entertainment outlays outside the expense account.

Reasonable, so far. The company has assured its own deduction: The easily defined expense account outlays will be adequately accounted for and deductible as entertainment expenses. And the executives' salaries will be deductible as compensation expenses. Executives will be tax-exempt on the expense account outlays. But they will have to be able to establish to Revenue Agents their right to deduct entertainment expenses they bear out of their own pocket (that is, out of the salary that was augmented to cover entertainment outlays). In other words, the company has shifted from itself to its executives the entire burden of accounting for entertainment expenses outside the expense account.

The company can ease this burden, without any cost or

inconvenience to itself. A key difficulty when executives try to deduct entertainment expenses is the frequent Revenue Service claim that the deduction properly belongs to the company on whose behalf the outlay was made. For the executive to deduct them, he or she must show that they are expenses of his or her business as a company executive. The company can help here. It can clearly proclaim that its executives are expected to incur substantial entertainment expenses which are intended to be covered by their salaries and for which no company reimbursement will be made. The statement could be in an employment contract or other official company document circulated to executives involved and preserved in company records. A sample statement appears below. Executives whose deductions are questioned can then produce such a statement to help establish that their outlays were required by their business.

MEMORANDUM FROM _____ CORP. PRESIDENT
TO ALL CORPORATE OFFICERS

For guidance of _____ Corp. officers, I wish to state company policy regarding reimbursement of entertainment expenses:

Executives of this company are expected to exercise initiative in promoting company objectives. Salary has been computed taking into consideration that the executive will incur expenses of a kind intended to benefit the company, but which will not be reimbursed by the company.

The company will reimburse costs of transportation, and related meals and lodging, on company business. It will also reimburse costs of lunches with present clients or customers of the firm, where business is conducted during lunch.

The company will not reimburse any other expenditures for entertainment of or gifts to present or prospective clients or customers.

13

Providing health care coverage for executives and their families

Experienced compensation planners have learned that executives face a special handicap when trying to deal on their own with family medical and dental bills. Many executives find that the real cost of health care is higher for them than it is for rank-and-file employees.

Tax deductions reduce the true cost of medical care. If a $55,000-a-year executive could deduct $1,200 of medical expenses, the real cost of medical care to him would be about $612. But in fact, few executives can deduct their dental and medical bills. This difficulty is an unwelcome by-product of their high salaries. Individuals can deduct only the amount of their medical and dental bills which exceed 3 percent of their income. Thus, the higher a person's income, the less chance there is of taking a tax deduction for medical and dental expenses. The high-salaried executive therefore must bear, out of pocket, a larger share of personal and family medical costs than other employees do.

Wise compensation planning on the part of company personnel officers or other management decision makers can overcome this difficulty. The company can set up a plan to pay or reimburse the medical and dental bills executives incur for themselves and their families.

There is no requirement that the executive's sickness or injury be work-connected, though the company can insert this limitation if it wishes (very few do). The company may limit coverage under the plan to executives as a class, or to particular executives, or otherwise, as it chooses. This can keep total costs relatively low. Moreover, it may fix a dollar ceiling on the amount or type of expense which it will reimburse, to keep costs lower still.

HEALTH INSURANCE COVERAGE

Instead of directly reimbursing the executive's medical expenses, the company could pay all costs of health insurance coverage (hospital, medical-surgical and major medical) for the executive and his or her family. The company can tax-deduct insurance premiums, just as it would for direct cash reimbursements. The premiums are not considered taxable income to executives, nor are they taxed when insurance proceeds are used to pay their actual medical bills.

The company can set any limit it pleases on the type of health insurance cost it will reimburse and the amount it will pay.

Some companies may fail to reimburse health insurance premiums because they believe that their executives can deduct such premiums. This company policy should be reconsidered. The special deduction allowed individuals for health insurance costs seldom is enough to do much good at executive levels. One half of health insurance premiums is automatically deductible by individuals up to a maximum deduction of $150. The balance of the premium is treated as an ordinary medical expense, deductible only if the individual's other medical and dental bills are at least 3 percent of income. Thus, an executive may pay $420 for full accident and health coverage but deduct only $150. Actual aftertax cost for this insurance would be about $345.

Combination plans

For many companies, the authors would advise using a combination of insurance coverage and reimbursement of expenses. Typically, the company under study already provides employees—rank and file and executives—with coverage of some expenses under an insured plan. Covered employees may be expected to contribute toward the cost of coverage, at least to the extent of covering their family members.

It is easy and economical for the company to widen health care coverage for its executives while continuing any existing plan it may have. First, the company could pick up the cost of the executives' contributions (if any), paying the premium. In addition, the company can directly pay or reimburse the executive for medical expenses not covered by insurance, such as: expenses falling below some deductible limit in the policy; preexisting conditions; cosmetic surgery; dental bills; medicines; health care equipment such as wheelchairs or contact lenses; added cost for a private room; travel or transportation to doctors' offices or treatment centers, including ambulance service; physician's home or office visits; and routine or periodic medical examinations. The company could also provide special insurance coverage for executives only, such as major medical coverage.

Even if the company does not have or intend to have a plan covering employees generally, it may decide to provide the executive with insurance coverage for normal or major health risks and direct payment or reimbursement of other medical bills. When selecting an insured plan, the compensation planner should keep in mind that executives would prefer one which lets them choose their own physician.

It is wise to spell out to each executive exactly what the company is providing in the way of health care coverage. This can be advisable for legal reasons, as will be seen later, but should be done in any case so they will not feel a need to provide coverage on their own. This is important, since they might pay more than their company does for the same coverage, and might not be able to collect on their policy if already covered by the company's. And the company should emphasize whenever applicable that the executive's family is covered as well, so that these individuals need not buy health insurance on their own.

TAX TREATMENT OF HEALTH CARE COVERAGE

The company. The company can generally deduct all its payments under a health care plan for executives, whether the payments are to an insurance company, directly to hospitals, doctors or other suppliers of health services, or to the executive as reimbursement for his or her own expenses. The only qualifications are that they must be under a health *plan* (more on this later) and the payments when added to other payments and benefits for executives must be reasonable compensation for services.

The executive. While company payments under a health care plan *can* be taxable compensation to the executive, they are exempt from tax in *any* of these situations:

1. The payments are made before 1980.
2. The health benefits are provided under an insured plan, that is, under a policy of health and accident insurance.
3. The plan is nondiscriminatory, that is, it doesn't dis-

criminate in favor of highly compensated individuals. A plan is discriminatory if it excludes rank-and-file employees. Here the tests for discrimination in eligibility are like those for pension or profit-sharing plans discussed in Chapter 14. In addition, in health care plans (unlike pension plans), a plan is discriminatory if benefits are proportionate to compensation.

In any of the above situations, the amount the employer pays to cover medical or dental outlays for the executive and family is exempt from income tax, while the company takes an income tax deduction for the full amount of medical or dental bills it pays or reimburses.

From an economic standpoint, a plan to reimburse the executives for medical expenses should be preferred to simply increasing salaries by the amount of the medical bills. Though a salary increase would not affect the before-tax or aftertax cost to the company, the added salary would be subject to tax at the executive's own high tax rates. The amount of the tax would reduce the amount of funds available to cover medical bills.

Example: Janet earns a salary of $60,000 a year, and has $5,000 of dividends and other taxable income. Family medical and dental bills total $1,800 a year, but Janet can not deduct any of this because it is less than 3 percent of her income (3 percent of $65,000 is $1,950). Thus, Janet must pay the full $1,800 with aftertax dollars.

But assume Janet's company adopted a plan to cover medical and dental expenses of Janet and her family. The $1,800 paid by the company does not increase Janet's income tax. Also, her company can deduct the entire amount, which reduces its income tax by $828 (46 percent of $1,800), making its net cost $972 ($1,800 minus $828). Suppose that instead of covering Janet's medical bills under its medical plan, the company had awarded Janet a $1,800 bonus. The company's net cost ($972) is unchanged, but Janet's tax bill is increased by about $900. Thus, only $900 of the $1,800 is left to pay medical bills, and Janet must provide the balance out of her own pocket.

However, the executive will be taxable with respect to company payments under a plan if *all* of the following conditions exist: The plan is discriminatory, it is an *un*insured plan (the employer is a self-insurer making direct payment or reimbursement of medical bills) and payment is made in 1980 or after.

If the health benefit is available to one or only a small number of executives, the taxable amount is the cost of the benefit. For example, if dental benefits were provided only to executives, and benefits for Tomkins and her family totaled $1,000, she would have $1,000 of additional taxable income.

In other cases, where the benefit is available to a sizable group but is still discriminatory, the taxable amount is determined by a formula. The taxable amount is the cost of the executive's benefit times the total amount of such benefits for all highly compensated individuals and divided by the total of such benefits for all employees.

Medical benefits taxed to the executive would qualify for medical expense deduction subject to the 3 percent floor.

COMPANY PLANNING FOR HEALTH CARE COVERAGE

Companies with discriminatory plans face these alternatives for 1980 and after:

1. Make the plan nondiscriminatory. This means making the benefits that now are limited to executives available to rank-and-file employees. Except in companies with

relatively few rank-and-file employees (such as some personal or professional service organizations), this can prove prohibitively expensive, unless the benefit level is sharply reduced for everyone.

2. Convert a self-insured plan to an insured plan. This can prove a more cost-effective move. Some plans reimburse an executive's premiums for insurance the executive obtains personally. From 1980 on, this would be taxable. Tax could be avoided if the company instead obtained an insured plan and paid the premium itself.

3. Continue the discriminatory plan. The company is allowed full deduction whether or not the plan is discriminatory. The executive is better off financially from benefits provided by the company than if he or she had to pay for those benefits. For example, suppose Tomkins' employer paid $700 of dental costs for her and her family, and suppose she is in the 37 percent bracket. She is taxed $259 on this payment, but she is still $441 better off than if she had to pay the $700 herself.[1]

Company payments or reimbursements aren't subject to wage withholding, even if they are taxable. This means the executive gets the full amount when it is needed most, without reduction for taxes. Taxes are due only later, at tax return time, when the executive will have time to collect the funds to pay the tax.

If the company plan operates on a fiscal year, the executive using the calendar year has income only in the calendar year the plan year ends. For example, assuming a February 1-January 31 plan fiscal year, a payment March 1, 1980 is income in 1981.

Even taxable discriminatory arrangements offer important benefits for executives. But companies should be careful to choose coverage which justifies the aftertax costs.

---

[1] Her tax liability would be less if she can deduct the dental costs under the 3-percent floor.

All the planning recommendations set forth above apply to companies adopting health care plans for the first time, as well as those with existing plans.

SALARY CONTINUATIONS DURING ILLNESS

Most companies continue to pay the salary of any executive who is absent from work because of sickness or injury. Companies which have not yet adopted a plan for providing such continuations (called a sick pay or disability plan) should consider doing so. The company can take an income tax deduction for the full amount it pays the executive directly as sick pay, or for amounts it pays on insurance policies providing sick pay coverage for executives.

Sick pay received is fully taxable, except for a limited exemption for persons under 65 who are retired because of disability.

Some companies may want to combine insured and self-insured arrangements. For example, the company may decide to continue an executive's salary during the first few weeks of absence out of regular payroll, but cover any further salary continuations under a disability policy (which may pay full salary or some lesser sum). Sick pay policy for executives may differ from that for rank-and-file employees.

Here, too, executives should be told exactly what coverage is provided, so they can better appraise the need to provide further disability insurance coverage on their own. If the arrangement pays less than full salary for some period during the absence, some executives may want to take out their own disability policy, to make up the difference. Any amount they collect on their own policy is exempt from income tax, even though they also collect from the company or its insurer. On the other hand, premiums they pay for this coverage are not medical expenses and are not deductible in any amount.

SPECIAL CONSIDERATIONS WHEN COVERING STOCKHOLDER-EMPLOYEES

With the important qualifications set forth above, a company's plan for providing medical expense reimbursement, health insurance or salary continuations may be limited to executives or other key employees as the company chooses. It need not be (though it may be) made available to rank-and-file employees. But there are two special factors to cope with where stockholder-employees will be covered:

1. The tax benefits under these plans are available only if the plan is one for employees. A plan for stockholders only would not qualify; the recipients of benefits would be taxable on company payments and the company should not expect to be allowed a tax deduction for them (though deduction was allowed in one unusual situation). Plans which are limited to stockholders who are also employees can qualify as plans for employees, and have been treated as qualified in some actual situations. But such qualification often involves struggle and even lawsuits with the Revenue Service. The authors instead advise that even a plan intended to be discriminatory should include one or more employees who are not stockholders (or closely related to stockholders) where this is possible. Any non-stockholder-employees included in the plan should have the same rights as stockholder-employees. No persons who are stockholders and not employees should be covered.

2. A company can take tax deductions for health care payments only to the extent that these payments plus the salary and other benefits to the executive don't exceed

reasonable compensation to the executive. In practice, the company's deduction goes unchallenged by the Revenue Service except where the corporate executive is also a stockholder or is closely related to a substantial stockholder. Even here, full deduction usually is allowed.

A complete analysis of reasonable compensation considerations appears in Chapters 3 and 4. In the authors' opinion, the reasonableness test, when it involves health care payments, should apply the rule used for incentive compensation. That is, reasonableness should be judged on the basis of factors existing when the corporation agreed to cover the executive's health care costs, and not on the amount the corporation may happen to have to pay later under its commitment. For example, if the corporation's plan covers expenses which usually run up to $1,500 but which run on one occasion to $20,000 because of medical peculiarities in that case, the additional outlay would not necessarily tend to make unreasonable the total compensation to the executive involved.

This does not mean that the authors believe the company should be allowed to deduct any and all expenses it bears for an executive's catastrophic illness, or that of a family member. It is seldom reasonable for a company to assume unlimited risk. As a matter of business as well as tax protection, the authors recommend that the company put a dollar ceiling on the amount of health care cost it will bear. Where coverage of catastrophic illness is required, this can be provided through insurance.

HOW TO SET UP A HEALTH CARE PLAN

The executive enjoys the tax-favored benefits of medical reimbursement or health insurance payments only if these payments are made under a plan of the employer. A company has a plan only if it has a definite, predetermined commitment to do something specific when a covered employee falls ill. There is no plan if the company can decide on a case-by-case basis whether to extend benefits, and how much to pay, after illness occurs.

The plan need not be enforceable by the employee (need not be part of any employment contract, for example) and need not be in writing. However, the authors recommend that the plan always be set down in writing and always be communicated to employees who will be covered. A plan of a corporation should be a formal act of the board of directors, recorded in the minutes of the directors' meeting and announced to covered employees, or written into the executive's employment contract. The company can have different plans for different employees or groups of employees, and can have one or more plans for some and none for others. A plan of a partnership or sole proprietorship could be expressed in an employment contract, or in another writing communicated to covered employees, but partners or proprietors should not be included in any plan.

The plan may provide for direct payment or reimbursement of expenses, for health insurance, or both—for example, basic health insurance, plus supplemental reimbursement of expenses not covered by insurance. Any of these payments could be limited as to dollar amounts, kind of expense, and period of coverage, as the company may think fit.

Since salary continuations carry no *tax* benefits for current employees, they can be provided apart from the plan, but are often included in the plan anyway.

A sample medical payment plan appears on the following pages.

BOARD OF DIRECTORS
RESOLUTION ESTABLISHING
MEDICAL PAYMENT PLAN

WHEREAS, _____ [name of company] desires to pay or reimburse, directly or indirectly, certain medical and dental expenses of the following employees of the company during their employment with the company.

_____ [names of employees] *

_____

_____

and of the spouse and dependents (as defined in Section 152 of the Internal Revenue Code) of each such employee,

AND WHEREAS, the medical and dental expenses to be so paid or reimbursed shall be those not compensated for by insurance or otherwise, which are treated as medical expenses under Section 213 of the Internal Revenue Code and Treasury Regulations thereunder, except that the amount of such expenses so paid or reimbursed to any employee shall not exceed $_____ [insert any dollar ceiling selected by the company] in any calendar year,

AND WHEREAS the company also desires to continue the salary of each of the above-named employees during a period in which they shall be disabled from performing their duties because of occupational or nonoccupational sickness or injury, for a period of not more than _____ consecutive _____ (and not more than a total of _____ in any _____) [insert maximum period of absence selected by the company] (except that for absences extending beyond _____ days, the compensation for absence after that _____ th day shall be reduced to _____ percent of regular compensation),

NOW THEREFORE, be it resolved that the above plan for paying or reimbursing such medical and dental expenses and for continuations of salary be and hereby is adopted on behalf

*Unless rank-and-file employees are covered, highly compensated individuals will be taxable on benefits paid under this plan (see preceding discussion).

of the Company by its Board of Directors, to become effective as of _____ [use the present date or a future date; do not seek to make it retroactive],

AND BE IT FURTHER RESOLVED that the company at its discretion may directly pay any of the above medical and dental expenses instead of providing reimbursement therefore, and may require as a condition of reimbursement that any employee seeking reimbursement furnish to the company all bills for which reimbursement is sought,

AND BE IT FURTHER RESOLVED that a copy of this resolution be given by _____ [any corporate officer] or designee to each employee named above, which that employee is to read, sign, date and promptly return for retention in the personnel file of that employee,

AND BE IT FURTHER RESOLVED that the officers of the Company shall execute this resolution by all necessary and proper means.

14

Pension and profit-sharing plans designed for executives

A qualified pension or profit-sharing plan is by far the most important benefit a company can provide its executives, apart from the salaries it pays them.

Some practitioners and company officers, unfamiliar with pension or profit-sharing rules, tend to think of such plans as being for employees in general and not for executives. They have heard that qualified plans cannot discriminate in favor of executives, that they must be employee plans, not just *executive* plans.

It is true that a qualified plan cannot discriminate in favor of executives. Unlike the situation with group-term life insurance, most stock options, financial counseling, interest-free loans, and other compensation benefits analyzed in this book, some rank-and-file employees must normally be entitled to pension or profit-sharing benefits also if executives are to receive them.

But it is also true that such plans can be structured to benefit executives, and even specific executives, much more than they benefit other employees. The authors know of a profit-sharing plan which paid three executives over $1 million each. The plan had been designed to suit one of these executives, a major stockholder, though hundreds of rank-and-file employees also had some stake in the plan. He had introduced the plan with the knowledge, or at least the expectation, that through the plan he and his family would retain more of the millions in company earnings put into the plan than if he had withdrawn his share of those earnings in the form of dividends and stock sale profits.

The benefits we will be analyzing here are those of qualified plans, that is, plans set up and operated to conform to the detailed requirements of federal law. The tax rules are the keystone of any plan. Without them, the economic benefits, the distributions of hundreds of thousands of dollars to individual executives, would be out of the question. Pension plans which are not qualified, which do not conform to the tax rules, are therefore of little practical interest to executives.[1]

There are many types of qualified plans. Here we will examine pension and profit-sharing plans (including thrift and savings plans, which are types of profit-sharing plans). Annuity plans (a variant of a pension plan), stock bonus plans (a variant of a profit-sharing plan), and employee stock ownership plans (stock bonus plans or such plans combined with money purchase pension plans), will be disregarded but what is said here will be generally applicable to those plans.

The rest of this chapter will deal with the major opportunities for using pension and profit-sharing plans to build up executive wealth. It will concentrate on how plans can be designed to favor executives, and will also note the legal

---

[1] The authors do not think of deferred compensation arrangements as (nonqualified) pension plans, though some practitioners do. In any case, deferred compensation plans *are* of practical interest to executives and are analyzed in Chapter 6.

and practical limitations on such arrangements. But it should be stressed that the pension and profit-sharing area is extremely complicated—by far the most complex subject discussed in this book. Here we will consider, in some detail, the major benefits and limitations. But no one should attempt to set up a qualified plan, or modify an existing one, without extended consultation with a professional practitioner. Designing a plan which will take full advantage of opportunities available often involves the services of several professionals working as a team: lawyer, accountant, and actuary.

HOW A QUALIFIED PLAN WORKS

A qualified plan, in general, involves these three parties or groups: the employer, the employees who will be covered by the plan, and the trustee who will invest and administer the funds involved. The plan, a formal written document, sets forth the rules governing which employees will be entitled to benefits, when the benefits will become available, and how much they will be. The funds from which the benefits will be paid are amounts contributed by the employer (and sometimes by covered employees as well) and investment earnings on these funds.

The tax benefits of such a plan, which are what makes the plan important as a compensation device, are these:

1. The employer can deduct its contribution to the fund for the employees' benefit in the year the contribution is made. This is a departure from the usual rules in the compensation area, under which company deduction is postponed until the employee collects his or her share.

2. The employee is not taxable on company contributions to a fund for the employee's own benefit at the time the contribution is made, even though the employee has a nonforfeitable right to those contributions. This differs from the general rules for taxing deferred compensation.

3. Investment earnings on the amounts contributed to the fund are not taxable to anyone—employer, employee, or trust—as long as they are held by the trust.

4. Amounts distributed to employees or their beneficiaries at retirement or other times can qualify for tax benefits, including reduced income tax and exemption from estate tax. These benefits will be examined later in this chapter. The company and the trust have no tax liability on the distribution.

Example: Warfield is an executive covered by his company's profit-sharing plan. Company profit-sharing contributions are based on salary. Over the 20 years Warfield has been in the plan, company contributions for him amount to $7,500 a year. Assuming the profit-sharing trust earns a 7½ percent return from investing these contributions, Warfield's profit-sharing account would be worth $324,784.50 after 20 years, and could be much more if amounts forfeited by employees who leave are allocated to the accounts of those who remain. There has been no tax on contributions or earnings over the 20-year period. Warfield could withdraw his entire account in a lump sum, subject to favorable tax rules.

No discrimination

Qualified plans cannot discriminate in favor of executives, who are defined, for qualified plan purposes, as officers, stockholders or highly paid employees.

There can be no discrimination in their favor in coverage. This means a company generally cannot design a plan to cover only executives (or selected executives) and exclude others.

And there can be no discrimination in company contributions or employee benefits. That is, the company cannot set up a plan which covers all employees but gives only nominal amounts to the rank-and-file and massive amounts to the executives.

This ban on discrimination applies to the way the plan operates in practice, as well as to its technical terms. For example, a plan is allowed to exclude employees who have worked for the company less than some minimum period, without being considered discriminatory. But if the company fired all or practically all rank-and-file employees before they could attain that minimum period of employment, so that essentially only executives were covered, the plan would be discriminatory in practice and could not be qualified.

But despite these rules against discrimination, plans can be designed to favor executives. This will be shown in the material that follows.

PENSION OR PROFIT-SHARING PLANS

There are several significant differences between pension and profit-sharing plans, in advantages, restrictions, and practical operating considerations. A company can choose a pension or profit-sharing plan—or no plan—as it pleases. It may have both a pension and a profit-sharing plan, though, as will be shown later, this is not necessarily the way to maximize tax benefits.

The key differences between the two types of plans are these:

1. With a profit-sharing plan, no company contributions are made for covered employees unless there are profits. With a pension plan, company contributions are a fixed cost, like rent, whether or not it has profits. Thus, a company's economic risk is less with a profit-sharing plan. By the same token, benefits to employees may not be very substantial.

2. A pension plan must be a retirement plan. It must

contemplate a distribution of benefits only when the covered employee retires (or dies or becomes disabled). A profit-sharing plan may be a retirement plan, but this is not required. The plan can be set up to distribute benefits during employment, as long as the employee normally must wait at least two years before withdrawing any particular company contribution.

3. If it is intended to provide executives with the maximum possible tax-favored benefit, a pension plan is preferable for older executives while a profit-sharing plan is preferable for younger executives. (The dividing line is about age 45.) This results from the rules governing deduction for company contributions to plans, to be discussed later in this chapter.

4. Some compensation planners believe that a liberal profit-sharing plan may stimulate employees to more productive work for the company, since they will share the benefits. On the other hand, pension plans may tie employees more securely to the company. Profit-sharing benefits usually vest and are distributed, at least in part, more rapidly than pension benefits. Thus, even if a pension plan and a profit-sharing plan are equally generous in terms of company contributions, an employee who leaves before retirement will have more to lose (and therefore will have a greater incentive to stay) under a pension plan.

CHOOSING A PENSION PLAN

Essentially, there are two types of pension plan: the fixed benefit plan and the money purchase plan.

The fixed or *defined benefit* plan is the more common type today. Under this plan, the covered employee will receive a specified benefit on retirement. This is usually an annuity of a specified percentage of the employee's regular salary. The company's contribution is therefore on a basis designed to produce this benefit.[2] This is illustrated in *Pension contributions and benefits* below.

Under the money purchase plan (also called a *defined contribution* pension plan), the company makes a designated contribution for the employee each year. At retirement, the covered employee is to receive whatever retirement benefits the contributed amounts (plus investment earnings in the interim) will buy.

Pension contributions and benefits

The pension benefits that any covered employee will receive are funded by employer contributions and investment earnings on those contributions. The typical defined benefit pension plan contemplates providing specific benefits to covered employees. For example, the plan may promise to pay every covered employee 35 percent of regular salary at retirement at age 65, if the employee has worked for the company 25 years. It would determine (with the help of its professional advisers) the amount necessary to provide the promised amount at retirement, and would make annual contributions toward that amount.

Example: Genero Corporation, a newly formed company, is setting up a pension plan for Baker, its president, and other employees. Baker's current base salary is $64,000 a year, and he is 45 years old. The company's plan promises a pension equaling 37½ percent of base salary, at retirement at age 65.

At current insurance company rates, it would cost $222,439 to buy an annuity paying $24,000 a year for the life expectancy of a man age 65. But of course this

---

[2] Variable benefit plans are, in this sense, fixed benefit plans. They involve a determination to pay a specific benefit but with adjustment for changes in the cost of living, etc.

$222,439 will not be needed until Baker actually reaches age 65, 20 years hence. The company would therefore make annual contributions to Baker's pension fund in amounts which, with investment increments, will build up to $222,439 in 20 years. Assuming the company contributes the same amount each year, and assuming a 6 percent return on investment of these contributions, the company contributes $5,705 a year toward Baker's pension.

When deciding upon the amount of benefit the company will provide, the planner will typically take into account the amount covered employees will receive under Social Security. Thus, if a company considers that retired employees in a particular group should not have to live on less than, say, $16,000 a year, in planning what it would provide it would reflect that the employee might in any case expect to get, say, $6,000 a year under Social Security. (The mere recognition of Social Security benefits in pension planning is not equivalent to *integration* with Social Security, discussed below.)

The reader will recall the rule that contributions or benefits cannot discriminate in favor of executives. This rule does not prevent providing greater benefits for executives than for rank-and-file employees. For example, suppose the pension benefit is to be 35 percent of base salary. This means that the pension for a $70,000-a-year corporate officer will be ten times that of a $7,000-a-year office clerk, yet this is not considered discrimination in favor of the officer. Also, company contributions to fund pensions may be many times larger for the older officers than for the younger employees, without being considered discriminatory. A plan is not discriminatory simply because its benefits bear a uniform relationship to compensation. Plans are commonly designed on this basis.

A defined benefit pension plan can't provide a pension

(annuity) of more than $98,100 a year (or more than 100 percent of average compensation in the last three years of covered employment, if this is less than $98,100 a year). The $98,100 figure can rise with the cost of living, as determined by IRS ($98,100 was the IRS figure for 1979); it is reduced if the retirement benefit begins before age 55 or after less than ten years of employment. The amount which may be contributed is not necessarily deductible. For deductions rules, see page 220.

This pension benefit may be in the form of a joint and survivor annuity, which is more costly than a straight annuity. Put another way, the employer may if the plan so provides fund to a level which will pay $98,100 (or other amount) for the joint lives of executive and spouse and for the life of the survivor (normally the female).

For money purchase (defined contribution) pension plans there is instead a ceiling on the amount that can be *contributed,* see page 232.

Some employers seek to "compensate" executives whose pensions are cut down by the ceiling described above ($98,100 or 100 percent of average compensation). That is, the company will pay the retired executive the difference between the pension he would collect in the absence of this dollar ceiling and the pension he actually gets (the pension ceiling).

While this "compensation" is not forbidden by the pension law—since it is outside the pension plan and enjoys no pension benefits—the employer should prepare for a confrontation with the Revenue Service on its deduction for this amount. It may not be easy to get Revenue Agents to accept that amounts in the nature of pension payments which are in addition to *ceiling* payments under the pension plan qualify as *reasonable* compensation.

Plans can limit benefits for employees who join the firm in their middle years. For example, the basic benefit can contemplate a pension after 30 years' service, with that benefit reduced 1/30th for every year of service less than 30. Thus, assuming a basic benefit based on salary, a 20-year employee will get only two thirds the benefit of a 30-year employee with the same salary.

To design plans based on compensation in favor of company executives, compensation planners should consider definitions of compensation which exclude items that rank-and-file employees receive but executives don't (for example, overtime pay and tips) and which include items executives are more likely to receive (such as bonuses).

How many employees must be included in the pension plan

Pension plan coverage may not discriminate in favor of executives. That is, in deciding which employees will get benefits under the plan, discrimination in favor of executives is barred.[3] But an acceptable, qualified plan can still exclude many employees, and these can in practice be rank-and-file employees, without being considered discriminatory.

There are two tests for deciding whether pension plan coverage is discriminatory: (1) the *percentage test* and (2) the *facts and circumstances test.* The plan is not discriminatory if either test is met.

1. *The percentage test* is an automatic numbers test. If a certain percentage of employees is covered, the plan's coverage automatically qualifies as nondiscriminatory.

In deciding who should be covered, the company may first exclude (*a*) employees under age 25; (*b*) employees who have worked for the company less than one year (less than three years in certain cases); (*c*) for pension plans

---

[3] Discrimination *against* executives is always permitted. A plan can be limited to rank-and-file employees.

only, employees starting employment with this employer within five years of normal retirement age (e.g., over age 60 when normal retirement age is 65); and (d) employees who are members of a union *if* retirement benefits were an issue in collective bargaining.

Usually, employees excluded under the test in (b) are rank-and-file only. But occasionally, such a test would work to exclude a newly-hired executive. The plan would of course be discriminatory if it included the executive but barred other new employees.

A plan is not discriminatory if 70 percent or more of the employees are eligible (disregarding any who are excluded under conditions (a) or (b) above), and 80 percent or more of those eligible actually participate. This means that only 56 percent of those left need actually be covered.

Example: Wheeler Corporation has 125 employees. Of these, 105 (including all 6 executives) work in the main plant; the rest work in other locations. Wheeler adopts a benefit plan calling for matching contributions from employer and employee, which is not open to new employees, employees under age 25, or those working outside the main plant.

The excluded new or "under age" employees—assume 25 of these in all—are disregarded in the percentage computation. The company can also exclude up to 30 percent of other employees. Thus, it could properly exclude the off-plant employees—assume 30 of these. And 20 percent (here, 14) of eligibles that remain could be left out without disqualification, if they choose not to participate (as because they didn't want to join a plan in which they would have to contribute). Thus, a plan covering 56 employees, including all 6 executives, out of a work force of 125 is not discriminatory as to coverage.

2. *The facts and circumstances test* is used for many

plans that fail the percentage test but can still be ruled nondiscriminatory, after considering all the circumstances.

The Revenue Service is the first judge of what is discriminatory, and there is no brief or simple way to describe the checkpoints the IRS consults in testing for discrimination. Professional advisers would use their knowledge of what past IRS and court rulings have allowed, as a guide to what the company should provide. In borderline cases, the matter can be negotiated and adjusted with the IRS as part of the process (discussed below) of obtaining IRS approval of the plan.

As an example of qualification under this test, one company had 109 employees of whom 11 were executives. Its plan covered salaried employees only, and therefore excluded 83 hourly employees. The IRS decided that the plan did not discriminate, even though it covered only 26 employees out of 109, and of these 26 only 15 were rank and file.

Vested and forfeited benefits

Pension plans typically require a minimum period of coverage in the plan before the covered employee becomes absolutely entitled to pension benefits, that is, before any rights become vested. If employment is terminated before the expiration of that period, the employee would forfeit all contributions made on his or her behalf. This period for vesting is independent of any waiting period before the employee is first included in the plan.

Vesting is a key cost element of a pension plan. Vested funds are funds employees are entitled to, at retirement (or sometimes before retirement), even if they quit or are fired before they have worked the time needed to qualify for a pension.

Companies tend to believe that their most valued

employees—and especially their executives—are those who stay longest with the company. This attitude inclines them against liberal vesting arrangements—in which relatively large amounts vest in a relatively short time—and in favor of conservative vesting arrangements.

At a given level of pension *benefit* for those the company wants to benefit, a liberal vesting arrangement is more costly to the company. This is because much of the contributed funds are "wasted," going to those who leave early, whom the company does not want to benefit.

At a given level of pension *cost,* a liberal vesting arrangement reduces the benefit for those the company wants to benefit. This is because a large portion of pension contributions is going to those who leave early.

In other words, a liberal vesting arrangement means either higher company costs overall or a reduced pension benefit for the group to be favored.

Conservative or delayed vesting can therefore be part of a design to favor executives. The law limits this favoritism by requiring the vesting arrangement to meet one of three relatively complex tests. Two of these are especially worth study for the company which means to favor executives. Under one alternative, no vesting is required for the first ten years but 100 percent vesting is required thereafter.

Under another, at least 50 percent must vest where the employee's age plus years of covered service equal 45, and 10 percent must vest annually thereafter (though at least 50 percent must vest after ten years in any case, with 10 percent vesting annually thereafter). This second alternative is the slowest permissible method. (The third alternative, more complicated and more liberal, is omitted here.) But IRS has the right to require more liberal vesting if necessary to prevent discrimination. It has not yet stated the situations in which more liberal vesting is required.

Vesting only vests the benefit accrued under the plan.

A plan might, for example, provide that an employee ac-
crues a pension of 1 percent of compensation for every
year of service up to age 50 and 2 percent of compensation
for every year of service thereafter (called "backloading").
This too can be seen as a way of favoring executives, because they are more likely to stay the course than rank-
and-file employees are. It is possible, within certain limits
in the law, to use backloading to defer the largest contributions for an employee until late in his or her career.
This device reduces the cost of covering those likeliest to
leave early.

Suppose a plan calls for full pension at age 65 after 25
years' service, but company contributions wholly vest after
5 years. Here, if an employee worked less than five years
before leaving, all company contributions would be forfeited. If the employee worked five years or more, company contributions made for the period worked would
vest. The employee would be entitled to pension benefits
based on company contributions during the period
worked, plus investment earnings thereon. This would of
course not equal a full pension, since the employee did not
work the full qualifying period.

Employees whose pension contributions have vested
would not necessarily be entitled to collect the amount
standing to their credit at the time they leave the company. Their vested pension benefits might not become
collectible until they reach the company's retirement age.

If a covered employee leaves before his or her pension
share has fully vested, the contributions and earnings
thereon (or the nonvested part) are forfeited. The forfeited
amount is applied to reduce the amount the company will
contribute in the future for those who remain in the plan.

For example, suppose a company contributes $120,000
annually to the pension plan for its covered employees. If
a covered employee leaves and forfeits $15,000 of past

contributions and investment earnings, this $15,000 is applied as part of the company's next contribution, reducing that to $105,000. Forfeited amounts generally may not be returned to the company and, in the case of a pension plan, may not be allocated among the remaining covered employees.[4]

There are essentially two reasons why pension plans contain forfeiture provisions:

1. To tie employees more closely to the company. Employee mobility is deterred if the employee will lose sizable pension benefits by changing jobs.

2. To keep pension costs relatively low or—looked at another way—to maximize benefits for executives. The cost of covering employees who remain in the plan is borne in part by the covered employees who forfeit their shares. This is a major concern when designing a plan weighted to favor executives. Executives as a class are the group least likely to leave, least likely to forfeit their pension benefits. Thus, where a significant number of rank-and-file employees must also be covered, benefits for executives as a whole are larger (or the cost of the plan is lower) if vesting is long postponed. In short, even though many employees must initially be covered to avoid disqualification of the plan, postponed vesting means that the cost of the plan is only the cost of covering those who remain, and that diminished group will include all or most of the executives.

Contributions by employees

Some plans permit voluntary contributions by covered employees on their own behalf. And in some plans, an

---

[4] This is an important difference between pension and profit-sharing plans, as will be seen in the profit-sharing analysis below.

employee is covered only if he or she agrees to contribute to the plan.[5] These plans are called "contributory" plans.

A contribution by the employee would be invested, like the company's contribution. In a contributory pension plan, the employee's contribution and investment earnings thereon would go to provide retirement benefits in addition to those provided by the company.

The employee gets no tax deduction for contributions to the plan. They are made with aftertax dollars. A contribution which is withheld and deducted from salary is still taxable to the employee.

But there is a major tax advantage in contributory plans, especially to executives and other persons in high tax brackets. The investment earnings on amounts contributed to the plan are not taxable until they are withdrawn, years later. The invested funds grow faster by being free of tax burden during the investment period. They will be taxable when they are withdrawn, but then can be taxed at favored rates (discussed later in this chapter).

Example: Ward is able to invest in either a corporate bond paying 8 percent or in her company's qualified plan whose investment yield is 8 percent. Assuming she invests $5,000 each year for 20 years, and her average tax bracket for that period is 56 percent, she would have $141,350 after taxes at the end of that period if she invested in corporate bonds, and $202,219 after taxes by investing in the qualified plan.[6]

The plan would return the employee's own contributions, plus investment earnings thereon, even if he or she

---

[5] It is, in fact, possible to set up a qualified plan to which only employees contribute.

[6] Assumes special ten-year averaging at *1979* rates. Disregards employer contributions withdrawn at the same time, which would operate to increase the tax, by increasing the income included in the averaging computation.

forfeited company contributions and investment earnings thereon by leaving before these amounts vested.

Contributory plans are another means for favoring executives over rank-and-file employees. High-bracket persons are more likely to have funds to contribute (invest) than rank-and-file employees are. Thus, such plans are especially beneficial to executives. The higher a person's bracket, the more valuable is the tax exemption for investment earnings while they remain in the fund.

Still more favoritism for the executive arises if the plan requires the employee to contribute in order to qualify for a company contribution. Here, the company incurs costs only for employees who have investment funds available.

The Revenue Service has long recognized the potential which contributory plans have for discrimination in favor of executives. It therefore limits the amount which an employee can be required or allowed to contribute under a contributory plan. It says that an employee's voluntary contributions in any year can't exceed 10 percent of the employee's compensation. If an employee *must* contribute in order to qualify for company contribution, this mandatory contribution can't exceed 6 percent of compensation.[7]

The deduction rules

The key deduction rule for pension contributions is the same rule that applies to other company payments in the compensation area. The payment must be an ordinary and necessary business expense and must be reasonable com-

---

[7] The Internal Revenue Service has ruled that voluntary contributions up to 10 percent and required contributions up to 6 percent are acceptable. It is the consensus among pension specialists that these 10 percent and 6 percent figures are maximums, and that plans with larger percentages would not qualify, with the minor qualifications noted at page 239, on thrift and saving plans.

pensation for services actually rendered. Reasonableness here, as elsewhere, is determined employee by employee.

But the determination of reasonableness takes into consideration all the current and past compensation paid the employee (in salary, pension contributions, and so forth), and the value of his or her services in the current year and all previous years. As IRS regulations put it, a contribution is deductible if it, together with other current compensation, "plus all compensation and contributions paid to or for such employee in prior years, represents a reasonable allowance for all services rendered by the employee by the end of the current year."

The first deduction hurdle—ordinary and necessary business expense—is easily surmounted. The Revenue Service is not disposed to question that there is a sound business reason for setting up a pension plan. And the reasonableness hurdle has not been a serious issue in tax litigation. This may be because pension plans usually are submitted to the Revenue Service for approval before they are put into effect (a matter discussed below). This process permits reasonableness questions to be raised and resolved in advance.[8]

Deduction is allowed only if the company's pension contribution is actually paid. The deduction is taken for the year payment occurs. In addition, deduction can be taken for a taxable year even though payment is made the following year, if (*a*) payment is made by the due date for filing the return for the taxable year (including extensions of time for filing) and (*b*) the payment is made on account of that year. This rule permits a company to determine its

---

[8] The approval process does not legally foreclose a later IRS challenge to reasonableness, and such challenges have actually been made. But such challenges have been rare, considering the amounts involved; the approval process may account for this.

income or income tax liability for a year before fixing the amount of its contribution for that year (especially important in profit-sharing plans).

Deduction in the year of payment into the trust (or by the return due date) is actually a concession, a liberalization, granted to qualified plans. Under usual tax rules, deduction would not be allowed until the employee received (became taxable on) the company's payment.

Payment of a company's contribution in property is technically acceptable but is often unwise. The company's transfer of portfolio stock or other property to the pension trust as its contribution to the trust is considered a sale of the property for tax purposes. The transaction amounts to a satisfaction of the obligation to contribute to the trust (a sale). The company is considered for tax purposes as receiving an amount of cash equal to the fair market value of the property transferred. Thus, if the property is worth more than the company's basis for it, the company has a taxable gain—unless the company is transferring its own stock, which is tax-exempt. If the property is worth less than the company's basis for it, the company has a loss which it cannot deduct.

Despite the prospect of a taxable gain on the transfer of property, some companies that are short on cash might want to make such a transfer anyway. They should be able to establish the fair market value of the property involved, and where possible should select property whose value can easily be demonstrated. Property worth less than its basis to the company should not be contributed but should be sold (contributing the proceeds), so the loss can be recognized for tax purposes and deducted.

The amount deducted as a contribution to the pension plan is the property's fair market value (subject to the deduction limits). For example, if Whipple Corporation contributed shares of IBM stock worth $10,000 which it had bought for $6,000, it would have a $10,000 pension contribution deduction and a $4,000 capital gain.

There are further deduction restrictions specially applicable to pension plans. These restrictions are complex and won't be analyzed here. Their purpose is to limit deductions where the company attempts to fund a large part of its pension obligation in a single year. For example, suppose a company sets up a plan to pay a pension at age 65 for employees with 20 years' service. And suppose the plan counts the period an employee worked for the company before the plan was adopted as part of the qualifying 20 years. (Most plans do.) For an employee who worked for 12 years before the plan was adopted, the company could in a single year pay in an amount attributable to those past 12 years as well as the current year. The deduction rules limit its deduction for such payment.

A further limitation: If a company has both a pension and a profit-sharing plan, its deduction for contributions to both in a year generally cannot exceed 25 percent of the other compensation paid covered employees for the year.[9] This deduction ceiling can provide a reason not to add a profit-sharing to a pension plan, since there is no such ceiling on a pension plan alone. Thus, deductions equalling, say, 35 percent of compensation can be allowable if the company has only a pension plan, but only 25 percent is allowable if it has both a pension and a profit-sharing plan.

---

[9] There is an exception to this rule: A larger contribution is deductible where the contribution was necessary to meet certain minimum funding requirements in the law. The minimum funding requirement is to make it possible for plans to accumulate enough assets to pay the prescribed benefit to employees when they retire.

An employer can—and often does—contribute more than the minimum funding requirement. An employer with both a pension and a profit-sharing plan can deduct more than 25 percent of compensation in the case where the amount being contributed to the pension plan is to satisfy the pension plan's minimum funding requirement but not in other cases.

Contributions in excess of deduction limitations may be deducted in later years under deduction carryover rules. Companies tailor the amounts they pay into the fund so as to avoid postponement of deduction.

Distribution of pension plan benefits

Pension plans are retirement plans. An employee's share of the pension fund can be withdrawn before retirement only in case of death, disability, termination of employment or termination of the plan itself.

Pension plans contemplate payment of retirement benefits in the form of an annuity, usually for the life of the employee. However, pension plans may authorize the distribution of the employee's share in a lump sum, which he or she can invest in an annuity or in some other investment (or, of course, no investment). Where the plan gives the employee a choice between an annuity and a lump-sum payment, the choice may be influenced by the tax factors analyzed below.

Annuity. An employee is taxed as follows on amounts he or she collects periodically, in the form of an annuity: If *the employee* did not contribute to the pension fund, everything collected is fully taxable as ordinary income. Thus, if the pension is $600 a month, the employee reports the full amount as income and pays regular income tax on that amount.

If the employee contributed to the pension fund and the amount so contributed is less than will be collected as an annuity in the first three years of the annuity, the employee is exempt from tax on all annuity amounts until he or she recovers the full amount of his or her contribution. Thereafter, the employee is taxable on everything collected. For example, if Barker contributed a total of $10,000 and draws a pension of $600 a month, he is exempt from tax on the first $10,000 of annuity payments (the first 16 months and $400 of the 17th month), and is taxable on all annuity payments thereafter.

If the employee contributed to the pension fund and the amount so contributed is more than will be collected as an annuity in the first three years, the employee is taxable on part and tax-exempt on part of each annuity payment received, for as long as the annuity is paid. The exempt portion or percentage is obtained by dividing the employee's contribution (the cost or "investment in the contract") by the amount he or she expects to collect under the annuity (which would be the amount to be received each year for life expectancy, in the case of a life annuity). Thus, if Thompson who has a 20-year life expectancy when she retires had contributed $30,000 and the life annuity will pay $600 a month, 21 percent ($30,000 ÷ $600 × 12 × 20) of each annuity payment is exempt.

Lump-sum withdrawal. Withdrawal in a lump sum is granted favored tax treatment, if the following two requirements are met:

1. The amount which represents the employee's share (or the balance of that share, if some amounts were withdrawn previously) is distributed within a single taxable year—which in almost all cases is within a single calendar year.
2. The distribution is on account of the employee's separation from employment or disability, or occurs after age 59½.

If the employee contributed to the fund, this contribution is recovered tax-free out of the lump-sum distribution. The balance is taxable as ordinary income subject to a special averaging provision (designed solely for qualified plans) whose effect is to reduce the tax below the amount that would be due at regular rates. *Exception:* For employees who were covered by a pension plan before 1974, the portion of the lump sum attributable to pre-1974 coverage is taxable as long-term gain or as ordinary income subject to special averaging, at the employee's option.

Annuity or lump sum? Whether to take down a lump sum or an annuity will depend on many nontax factors, such as the employee's health and competing investment opportunities. The practical effect of the lump-sum rules is that the tax burden need not be a major deterrent to lump-sum withdrawal. This is ordinarily a once-in-a-lifetime decision, and should be made with the help of a professional adviser.

After employee's death. These are the rules governing pension plan distributions beginning after the employee's death:

For income tax purposes. An employee's heirs are entitled, indirectly, to a $5,000 exemption ($5,000 for all together, not $5,000 for each heir) on what they collect under a qualified plan.[10] This tax exemption is achieved by treating the $5,000 as a contribution by the employee to the fund, whether or not the employee made other contributions. Thus, the first $5,000 (plus any actual contributions the employee made) collected in annuity form is exempt from income tax, and amounts collected thereafter are taxable, assuming $5,000 plus actual contributions do not exceed total annuity payments in the first three years. If they do exceed total annuity payments, the actual contributions plus the "exempt" $5,000 are counted as employee contributions in computing the exempt portion of each annuity payment.

If the employee's heirs make a lump-sum withdrawal, $5,000 is automatically treated as an employee contribution to the plan, reducing to that extent the amount

---

[10] The exemption is $5,000 or the amount of the total annuity or lump-sum withdrawal, whichever is less.

treated as ordinary income subject to averaging (or as capital gain).

For estate tax purposes. There is a further tax benefit for qualified plans. Amounts to be distributed to the heirs of a deceased employee out of his or her pension account are exempt from estate tax to the extent they represent contributions by the employer. For example, suppose the value of Testa's account was $400,000. The company had contributed $160,000, Testa had contributed $40,000, and the balance represented earnings on these contributions. Only $80,000 (20 percent of $400,000) would be included in the estate as subject to estate tax, because Testa's $40,000 contribution represents only 20 percent of the amount contributed. For this estate tax exemption to apply, the fund must be paid out as an annuity or, if paid as a lump sum, the *income tax* benefits for lump-sum distributions must be waived.

Chapter 17 considers ways to minimize the estate tax on executives covered by qualified plans.

Other withdrawals. Withdrawals which are not in the form of an annuity or a lump sum are covered in the analysis of profit-sharing plans.

Plans integrated with Social Security

Integration with Social Security is another way to design a plan to favor executives.

The integration concept starts with the fact that the company already bears part of the cost of a retirement plan for its employees, through its "contributions" or taxes under the Social Security system. It contributes an amount for each covered employee based on his or her compensation, up to the ceiling amount subject to Social Security tax, which is called the Social Security base. Under the Social Security system, a retired person's receipts or pension will depend on the amount of his or her covered salary (the Social Security base when he or she was working, or whatever lesser amount was actually received). Thus, the company could reason, employees are provided, through Social Security, with a pension based on their covered salary. But employees who earn more than the Social Security base are not in the same sense fully covered by Social Security. That is, while Social Security may provide a pension of, say, $7,800 (which represents 44 percent of a $17,700 Social Security base), for an employee who made $17,700 annually, it will provide no more than that for an executive who made $60,000 annually. For the executive, Social Security provides a pension of only 13 percent of salary.[11]

Hence the plan which "integrates" with Social Security. Though integration can be done in various ways, one acceptable way is to design a plan in which the company contributes only for employees whose compensation exceeds the Social Security base amount ($22,900 in 1979). This way, the company incurs pension costs in 1979 only for employees who make more than $22,900, an arrangement which can exclude many or most rank-and-file employees but will cover all executives. The company can draw its plan so that, as the Social Security base amount rises in later years, it ceases to make contributions for employees whose compensation fails to exceed those amounts.

Under integration, combined Social Security and pension benefits for higher paid employees are roughly the same percentage of compensation as Social Security benefits are for the lower paid employees.

---

[11] The authors are not suggesting that this aspect of the Social Security system is unfair. Neither company nor executive has paid any Social Security tax (has made any "contribution") on compensation in excess of the Social Security base.

Integration is available for pension plans, and for profit-sharing plans which are retirement plans. Integration is optional. Many of today's plans are not integrated plans. But integration has been increasing in recent years, because of its opportunities to provide substantial benefits for higher salaried employees at relatively low overall cost to the company.

Insurance benefits

Pension plans are meant to provide retirement benefits. A plan can provide death benefits (life insurance) only if they are incidental to retirement benefits. Life insurance in a pension plan does not enjoy tax benefits. That is, a covered employee is taxed on the cost (determined under Revenue Service tables) of current life insurance protection, and his or her beneficiaries are subject to income tax on the insurance proceeds they receive, up to the policy's cash surrender value just before the employee's death.

CHOOSING A PROFIT-SHARING PLAN

The company may select a profit-sharing plan instead of a pension plan. Or, it may install both plans, at the same time or at different times. Each plan may cover the same or different employees, but the overall result may not discriminate in favor of executives.

Most of the rules governing pension plans also apply to profit-sharing plans. That is, the basic tax rules are the same, and the barrier against discrimination remains.

But there are significant differences between the plans, differences which can in particular situations make profit-sharing plans more attractive than pension plans.

Profit-sharing plans may be retirement plans. But unlike pension plans, they don't have to be retirement plans.

Company contributions for the employee's benefit can be distributed before retirement (or death, disability, termination of employment or termination of the plan). It is only necessary that at least two years elapse between the time the company makes its contribution and the time the employee withdraws it.

Profit-sharing plans which are not retirement plans typically cover a larger percentage of employees than retirement plans do.

Profit-sharing contributions for employees

Profit-sharing plans, of course, contemplate company contributions out of company profits. The plan may define "profits" in any rational way. Profits need not be defined with reference to taxable income. A plan may provide for contributions out of past (accumulated) profits where current profits are lacking. And it may provide that contributions will be made only if profits exceed some particular figure. It may choose any percentage of profits, which in any year may vary with the amount of profit (5 percent of first $100,000 and 6½ percent of next $100,000 for example).

No specific formula for computing the amount of profits to be contributed is necessary. The company may choose a different formula each year, after it sees what its profit picture for the year will be. However, the Revenue Service will not recognize it as a plan unless contibutions are recurring and substantial. A plan which is set up to make a contribution in one year and never again would not qualify.

The authors recommend that the company adopt a specific formula for computing the contributions it is to make to the fund. This is advisable to show that the plan is intended to be permanent, and also can help a bit to overcome IRS suspicions that the plan in question may be discriminatory. Furthermore, it will have more effect as a stimulus encouraging employees to produce profits if they know the company is definitely committed to contribute a certain portion of its profits.

The basic deduction limits already discussed in connection with pension plans apply to profit-sharing plans. That is, the contribution must be paid, it and other compensation must be reasonable, and so on. In addition, there is a specific percentage deduction ceiling for profit-sharing plans. The deduction can't exceed 15 percent of the compensation of covered employees. The deduction rules offer opportunities for carrying over and using in later years both contributions in excess of the 15 percent ceiling and credits arising from contributions below that ceiling. (Pension plans follow different principles, but their deduction rules are in essence more liberal.)

If a company has both a pension and a profit-sharing plan, the deduction for both generally can't exceed 25 percent of the other compensation of covered employees, described above.

The amount a company contributes for covered employees typically is based on their compensation. A plan is not considered as discriminatory in favor of executives if company contributions bear a uniform relationship to the compensation of covered employees. Thus, a profit-sharing contribution for a $90,000 a year executive can be ten times the contribution for a $9,000-a-year clerk without being discriminatory.

Company contributions could also be based on other factors, such as age or length of service.

A number of compensation planners have tried, without success, to design qualified profit-sharing plans based on both compensation and years of service. This would tend to favor executives by taking advantage of the fact that they are paid more and also that they, as a class, are likely to have worked longer for the company. Basing company contributions on either of these factors can be acceptable. Using *both* can result in a discriminatory, nonqualified plan.

A defined contribution plan (a term which includes profit-sharing plans and money purchase pension plans) can't contribute in any year for any participant more than $32,700 (or more than 25 percent of the employee's compensation, if this is less than $32,700), subject to these qualifications:

a. The $32,700 figure can rise with the cost of living, as determined by IRS. $32,700 was the figure for 1979.
b. The limit on contribution is technically a limit on additions to the participant's account, and so includes: actual employer contributions; that part of amounts forfeited by other employees who leave the plan, which is allocated to the participant in question; and an additional though minor amount where the participant makes a voluntary contribution.

The amount which may be contributed is not necessarily deductible. For deduction rules, see below.

Vesting and forfeiture

The vesting provisions of a profit-sharing plan must meet the requirements imposed on pension plans which are described beginning at page 215. In practice, the vesting provisions of profit-sharing plans which are retirement plans will resemble vesting provisions of pension plans.

Where the profit-sharing plan is not a retirement plan, company contributions for covered employees are likely to begin to vest sooner than with pension plans. Thus, a plan might vest a percentage of a year's contribution after, say, three years, with an increasing percentage in later years. For example, 60 percent of a contribution might vest the third year of coverage, 80 percent the fourth year, and 100 percent the fifth year.

Contributions and earnings thereon that are forfeited by employees who leave before all contributions on their behalf are fully vested generally cannot be returned to the company. The plan may provide that forfeitures go to reduce future contributions of the employer. This is mandatory for pension plans; it is one of two options in a profit-sharing plan. The alternative is to allocate the forfeitures among employees who remain. This is the preferred option where it is intended to have the profit-sharing plan favor executives, and is one factor which could incline a company to choose a profit-sharing over a pension plan.

There are three ways commonly used to allocate the forfeited amounts:

1. In the way company contributions to the plan are allocated. Thus, if contributions are allocated to each employee on the basis of length of service, forfeitures of contributions and earnings can be so allocated.

2. In proportion to the compensation of each covered employee. This is the same as (1) if the company's contributions are in proportion to the employee's compensation. Thus, if an employee forfeits $20,000 upon leaving, the account of a $90,000 executive gets $10 of this for every $1 that goes to the account of a $9,000 secretary.

3. In proportion to the size of the account of each covered employee. This in practice has proved most favorable to executives, and is now the least likely to be accepted by the IRS as nondiscriminatory. The concept is this:

With a plan in which company contributions are proportionate to compensation, an executive's account in the plan will be leveraged upwards by these two factors: (*a*) contributions for the executive are larger in the first place, and (*b*) he or she is likely to have been in the plan longer, so that a larger number of contributions were made on his or her behalf. Thus, the account of a $90,000 a year executive may be *30* times larger than that of a $9,000 a year secretary, and not just ten times larger, because the executive will have been covered longer. If an employee leaves and forfeits say, $12,000, the executive's account gets $30 of that forfeiture for every dollar allocated to the secretary's account.

The authors know of an IRS-approved plan containing such a favorable allocation formula (from the executive's standpoint), and a sample clause reflecting such a formula appears at the end of this chapter. But the Revenue Service has in recent years become more concerned that such a formula might amount to prohibited discrimination in favor of executives. It has therefore sharply narrowed the situations in which it will approve such plans. Apparently, only plans having a sizable number of participants (several hundred or more) should seriously hope for IRS approval of an allocation formula based on the size of the accounts of employees who remain.

The dollar ceiling on profit-sharing plan contributions described above also applies to allocations of forfeited amounts. This serves to restrict amounts that can be allocated even if the IRS should have approved other aspects of the allocations formula.

As with pension plans, company contributions (and employee contributions, if any) are invested by the trust. Unlike the rule with pension plans, a covered employee may be given the right to suggest the securities in which the funds are to be invested. This right has proved of more interest to executives than to other covered employees.

Distributions or withdrawals from profit-sharing plans

If a profit-sharing plan is designed as a retirement plan, distributions from the plan are treated in the same way as distributions from a pension plan. Thus, if the distributions are received periodically, in the form of an annuity, the rules covered in the pension analysis would apply: each annuity receipt is taxable in full unless the employee also contributed to the fund, in which case all receipts for a limited period, or a portion of the receipts for the duration of the annuity, are tax-exempt. If, instead, the employee share is withdrawn in a lump sum, the rules previously analyzed for lump-sum withdrawals would apply: tax-exempt return of the employee's own contribution, with the balance taxable as ordinary income subject to a special averaging provision, and with possible capital gain benefits. (See pages 224-27.)

But profit-sharing plans need not be, and frequently are not, retirement plans. The employee will be allowed to withdraw all or some part of vested amounts periodically or otherwise, independently of retirement.

Amounts the employee has the option to withdraw could be considered made available to him or her for tax purposes. He or she would be considered to have constructively received those amounts. For example, suppose Brown has a profit-sharing account of $20,000, representing company contributions and earnings thereon, after five years in the plan. Assume that $12,000 of this account has vested and the plan permits employees to withdraw vested amounts after five years. Under constructive receipt principles, Brown could be taxable on $12,000 even though he makes no withdrawal, since $12,000 is made available to him.

To prevent subjecting Brown to a tax on funds not

withdrawn, plans typically impose a penalty for withdrawing. For example, the plan might permit withdrawal of vested amounts except that the employee must forfeit 6 percent of the amount withdrawn (which drops back in the fund for allocation as other forfeitures are allocated). Such a penalty or forfeiture prevents constructive receipt, since an amount is not considered made available if there is a substantial penalty or detriment for withdrawing it. Other, less common, ways to prevent constructive receipt would be to foreclose the employee from company contributions for a substantial period after withdrawal (which is a penalty in another form) or to require a committee approval of withdrawal, based on need, to pay for medical care or education, for example (here no amount is made available until committee approval is given).

Amounts actually withdrawn are fully taxable as ordinary income, without any annuity, special averaging or capital gains tax benefits.[12] The employee is taxed on the amount received, and is not taxed on forfeited amounts not collected.

For withdrawals of employee contributions and earnings thereon, see *Thrift, savings, and other contributory plans*, below.

Some plans permit an employee to borrow part of his or her profit-sharing account. Borrowed amounts are not taxable income. Interest paid on borrowed funds is usually at a low rate, and is tax-deductible.

Withdrawing company stock. In some profit-sharing plans, employees may have the opportunity to take some or all of their lump-sum distributions in the form of company stock. Here, there is a further opportunity for postponing tax on the employee.

---

[12] The special "ten-year" income averaging for lump-sum distributions from pension and profit-sharing plans is unavailable here, but the general five-year averaging can be used.

Normally, an employee is taxed on the fair market value of property received, in the year received. But where he or she receives stock in the company, tax is imposed partly in the year received and partly in the year he or she sells it. In the year the stock is received, the tax is on the amount the profit-sharing trust paid for the stock. Then, in the year he or she sells it, tax is imposed on the selling price less the cost to the trust.

Example: When Grey retires, he receives a lump-sum profit-sharing distribution of 2,000 shares of stock in his employer. The profit-sharing trust's cost for these shares averaged $20 a share. When Grey received them, they were worth $50 a share.

Grey is taxed on $40,000 ($20 a share) in the year he receives them. If he sells all shares three years later at $52 a share, he is taxed on another $64,000, that is, $104,000 minus $40,000.

Distribution at death.   Amounts distributed to an employee's heirs at the employee's death would be taxed under the rules beginning on page 226 governing after-death distributions from pension plans.

If a profit-sharing plan is not a retirement plan, there may not be any fixed time at which withdrawals must be made. Thus a plan may be designed to permit withdrawal of vested amounts after a certain time, but not require any withdrawals while the employee remains employed. This feature has also been used to favor executives by generating a saving in estate tax, a tax which often applies to estates of executives but seldom to those of rank-and-file employees.

The company may not have any mandatory retirement age for its executives. Thus, the executive may continue employed (at a diminished pace, if desired) beyond normal retirement age, and still be employed at death. Profit-sharing distributions received by his or her heirs can be exempt from estate tax, to the extent allocable to company contributions. There would be no such estate tax exemption had he or she received the distribution during life and held the funds at death. The authors know of an instance in which such a profit-sharing arrangement saved several million dollars in estate tax for a single individual. For more on tax planning arrangements to save executives' estate taxes, see Chapter 17.

THRIFT, SAVINGS, AND OTHER CONTRIBUTORY PLANS

The terms *thrift plan* and *savings plan* do not have a uniform meaning to all companies. As used here, both are contributory profit-sharing plans, that is, profit-sharing plans to which both company and employee contribute. The company's contribution comes from current or past profits, and the employee's from his or her own cash contributions or payroll deductions. (If the company's contributions were independent of profits, the arrangement would be, and would have to qualify as, a money purchase pension plan.)

The term *savings plan* has been applied to a plan in which employee contributions are voluntary, that is, where the company will make contributions for each covered employee and the employees may make further contributions on their own behalf. The term *thrift plan* has been applied to a plan in which employee contributions are mandatory; that is, where an employer will make contributions on the employees' behalf only if employees also contribute a certain minimum amount for themselves.[13] (It should be understood that such contributions are manda-

---

[13] Many practitioners use the term "thrift and savings plan" or "thrift plan" alone, without distinction between mandatory and voluntary plans.

tory only in the sense that employees must contribute, on their own behalf, in order to obtain plan benefits. Contributions on their part are not a condition of their employment.) In such a plan, an employer might match employee contributions at the rate of 50 cents on the dollar, dollar for dollar, $1.50 on the dollar, and so on.

Employees get no tax deductions for their contributions to contributory plans. The tax attraction is the fact that investment earnings on such contributions are exempt from tax until withdrawn. So they grow faster and result in a larger aftertax fund when they are withdrawn, as is illustrated on page 219.

Voluntary plans cannot permit employee contributions in excess of 10 percent of their compensation. However, if the plan permits contributions up to 10 percent and a participant contributes less than 10 percent this year, he or she can be allowed to make up the underpayment in a later year along with a full 10 percent contribution for that later year as well. In this situation, contribution for a single year can exceed 10 percent if contributions for all years don't exceed 10 percent.

Mandatory plans cannot require the employee to contribute more than 6 percent of his or her compensation.

The employer can establish both a voluntary and a mandatory arrangement, which in combination can permit contributions of more than 10 percent. For example, there can be a 3 percent required contribution plus a voluntary contribution up to 10 percent.

Contributory plans, like other plans, will limit the times at which amounts can be withdrawn, for the convenience of plan administration. But contributory plans must also consider provision for withdrawal of the employee's contribution even though company contributions may not be withdrawable.

The plan cannot require forfeiture of the employee's

own funds.[14] It would, however, be reasonable to restrict the time at which employees may withdraw their own contributions, and restrict the amount they may withdraw and still remain in the plan.

The tax rules governing withdrawals of employee contributions as part of an annuity or lump sum have already been covered (pages 224-27). In other withdrawal situations, the return of the employee's own contribution is exempt from tax. Any excess over the amount contributed is fully taxed ordinary income.

The rules set forth above apply to contributory profit-sharing plans generally, and not just to thrift and savings plans.

OTHER PENSION AND PROFIT-SHARING CONSIDERATIONS

IRS approval of the plan

A *qualified* pension or profit-sharing plan is one which meets the requirements of the law. An *approved* plan is something more. It is a plan which the IRS has ruled is a qualified plan. To tax practitioners and pension and profit-sharing specialists, the distinction is vital: A pension or profit-sharing plan involves a huge investment. The company makes substantial contributions each year, or at any rate, frequently. These contributions are invested by the trust for a long period—often decades—and can grow to enormous sums. Amounts distributed to employees frequently run to six figures.

The entire edifice is built on a foundation of tax benefits: immediate tax deduction for company contributions with current tax exemption for the employee; tax-exemp-

---

[14] Since these funds are invested, and investments sometimes drop in value, the employee may actually get back less than he or she put in, but this would not be a forfeiture.

EIGHT WAYS PLANS CAN
FAVOR EXECUTIVES

The following list highlights the ways in which pension or profit-sharing plans can be designed to favor executives:

1. In selecting the type of plan, pension or profit-sharing. A liberal pension plan is preferable to a liberal profit-sharing plan for persons over 45 or so. Thus, a pension plan can be selected, which will favor executives if they are significantly older than the average employees are.

2. In using the opportunity to favor executives by basing company contributions or benefits on employee salary.

3. In using the opportunity to exclude rank-and-file employees based on their compensation below a certain amount, or cover them at a low rate, through integration with Social Security.

4. In using the opportunity for covered employees to make voluntary contributions on their own behalf, since earnings on contributions are tax-exempt until withdrawn. This chiefly benefits executives, who may otherwise be taxed at high rates on their investment earnings, and who are more likely than other employees to have funds available for investment.

5. In using the opportunity to exclude employees (chiefly rank and file) who do not make contributions on their own behalf, in a mandatory contributory plan.

6. In using the *limited* opportunity to exclude employees (chiefly rank and file) on the basis of age, length of service, union membership, and so forth.

7. In using the opportunity in a profit-sharing plan to allocate the forfeitures of those who leave to benefit those who remain, including executives, on the basis of their salary or (in limited cases) the size of their profit-sharing accounts.

8. In using the opportunity (especially in a profit-sharing plan) to obtain an estate tax exemption (which especially benefits executives) through remaining employed until death.

tion for investment earnings while held by the trust; and various tax benefits to the employee or the employee's estate on withdrawal. The edifice topples if the plan is not qualified. The company's immediate deduction, or the employee's current tax-exemption, is lost; investment earnings become taxable as earned; and the tax benefits on withdrawal are forfeited.

With so much at stake, the company naturally seeks assurance that its plan will be treated as qualified. The Revenue Service is willing to provide such assurance. That is, it is willing after examining the plan and satisfying itself that the plan is qualified to issue a commitment (a determination letter, sometimes also called a ruling) that its Revenue Agents will treat the plan as qualified. It will do this for existing plans and, more important, for contemplated plans before they go into effect. The commitment is effectively binding on the Revenue Service if the information given to the Revenue Service fairly and fully states the facts of the matter, and the plan is not deviated from thereafter.

Obtaining IRS approval is not a legal necessity. The plan must of course conform to the statutory conditions for qualification. Sometimes, however, taxpayers (and their tax advisers) disagree with the IRS on what these conditions actually require. A number of plans have been ruled qualified in court, over IRS objection. But seeking IRS approval is considered by practitioners to be a practical necessity in almost all cases. It is the authors' own experience that the IRS is reasonable in granting approval.

Subchapter S corporations

The devices described above for favoring corporate executives are available for executives of Subchapter S corporations with these major qualifications:

1. A stockholder-employee is subject to tax on that portion of the corporation's deductible contribution on his or her behalf that exceeds $7,500 (or 15 percent of his or her compensation, if less). The amount on which stockholder-employees are taxed becomes their investment in the plan so that neither they nor their beneficiaries will be subject to income tax on *that* amount when plan benefits are distributed.

2. Amounts forfeited by employees who leave may not be allocated to stockholder-employees. The compensation planner should therefore design the plan so that forfeitures reduce employer contributions.

3. In computing the contribution or benefit where stockholder-employees are covered, the compensation taken into account for any employee can't exceed $100,000. The effect of this provision is to limit the favoritism of stockholder-executives, either by reducing their benefits or by increasing the company's costs through a corresponding increase in benefit for other employees.

Example: Assume a Subchapter S corporation with 11 employees covered by its profit-sharing plan. One is Bailey, its president and controlling stockholder, who was paid $200,000; the others are nonstockholders who were paid an average of $10,000 each.

The maximum profit-sharing contribution that can be paid on Bailey's behalf without a tax on Bailey is $7,500, which is 3¾ percent of $200,000. Therefore, Bailey would want a plan that contributes 3¾ percent, which would be $7,500 for him and $3,750 in all for all other employees combined, at a cost of $11,250. But the rule above says that only $100,000 of compensation may be taken into account. This means that if the plan sticks to the 3¾ percent rate, the contribution for Bailey is only $3,750, which is 3¾ percent of $100,000 (still $3,750 for all other employees). If the tax-free contribution for Bailey is to be $7,500, the plan must call for contribution at the rate of 7½ percent (7½ percent of $100,000, the maximum taken into account, is $7,500), and the contribution for the other employees rises to $7,500, at a total cost of $15,000.

A stockholder-employee is defined as an employee owning more than 5 percent of the Subchapter S corporation's stock, counting stock owned by spouse, children, grandchildren, and parents.

Partnerships, proprietorships, and the self-employed retirement plan

All the rules and opportunities discussed earlier in this chapter apply to pension or profit-sharing plans established by partnerships or proprietorships, if the partners or proprietors are excluded.

The rules are substantially different if proprietors or partners are to be covered. Practically all devices for favoring executives in corporate plans are denied to plans covering proprietors or partners whose partnership interest is more than 10 percent.

Master or prototype plans

Some companies may choose to participate in a master or prototype plan. These are qualified and approved pension or profit-sharing plans sponsored by banks, insurance companies, mutual funds, trade associations and other entities. Joining such a plan is cheaper than setting up the company's own plan. On the other hand, the company's own plan can be tailored to its, and its executives', own situations, and can offer much more in aftertax benefits than master plans do. Furthermore, front-end charges of an insurance company's master plan have been known to equal costs of a tailor-made plan.

SAMPLE PENSION OR PROFIT-SHARING
PLAN CLAUSES

Eligibility

Each employee of the Company shall be eligible to commence participation in the Plan as of the earliest entry date on which he (i) has attained age twenty-five (25), and (ii) completed at least one year of service with the Company, ending on or prior to such entry date; PROVIDED, HOWEVER, that if such employee has separated from the service of the Company, and not returned prior to such entry date, he shall not commence participation prior to his date of re-employment. The entry dates shall be the last day of the sixth and twelfth months of each fiscal year.

In the determination of whether an employee has completed a year of service for participation purposes, the initial year for each employee shall be the year beginning on said employee's employment commencement date, as defined in Paragraph _____ hereof. In the event that said employee fails to complete one thousand (1,000) hours of service in that initial period, said determination shall be based upon succeeding years beginning with the first anniversary of his employment commencement date.

Allocation of company profit-sharing contributions and forfeitures in proportion to employee compensation

The Employer's contribution for each Plan Year, together with any forfeitures for such year, shall be allocated among the Participants who were such or who became such on the first day of an Accrual Computation Period and who shall have completed a Year of Service during such period, in the same proportion that his total compensation for such period bears to the total compensation paid to all Participants for such year.

In no event shall any amount be allocated to an Employee which would result in such Employee receiving an Annual Addition to his account exceeding the lesser of $25,000.00 or twenty-five percent (25%) of his annual compensation. Any portion of the Employer's contribution not allocated to the

SAMPLE PENSION OR PROFIT-SHARING
PLAN CLAUSES *(continued)*

Employee by reason of the foregoing restriction shall be allocated among the remaining Participants in accordance with the allocation formula set forth in the preceding paragraph.

Contributory plans—employee contribution voluntary

For the purpose of increasing his retirement benefits, a Participant in any Plan Year may make contributions, in addition to those being made by the Employer, to his Participant's Contribution Account. The making of such contributions shall be voluntary on the part of the Participant and he shall have no obligation to continue them or to maintain them at any level. A Participant's Voluntary Contribution in any one year may be an amount which, together with all Voluntary Contributions made by the Participant to this Trust and any other qualified Employee Benefit Plan of this Employer in all prior years, if any, will cause his total contributions for all years to equal, but not exceed ten percent (10%) of the aggregate basic compensation received by that Participant for all years that he has been a Participant under the Plan. In no event, however, will a Participant be permitted to make a contribution for any year to the extent that the portion of the contribution in excess of the lesser of (a) six percent (6%) of his annual compensation or (b) one half of such contribution, when added to the Employer's contribution and forfeitures credited to his account causes the annual additions to his account under this plan to exceed the lesser of twenty-five percent (25%) of his compensation or $25,000.00. Such contributions shall be unmatched by, and independent of, contributions made by the Employer. Notwithstanding any other provision of this Trust, amounts contributed under this Section, increased or decreased by net gains or losses, together with interest thereon, shall be fully vested in the Participant and shall be distributed to him or his beneficiaries. The Participant may at any time direct the Trustee to pay to him some or all of his contribution made in accordance with this Section, but no interest shall be allowed with respect to the contributions so withdrawn, and amounts so withdrawn shall not be subsequently repaid to the Trust. If a portion of a Participant's Voluntary Contributions shall have been invested in a policy, the transfer of the policy to him shall be deemed the return of that portion of his contribution which was invested in the policy. Any increments already earned on amounts withdrawn shall be paid to the Participant upon severance or retirement.

Contributory plan—employee contribution mandatory

Each participant shall contribute to the trust fund an amount equal to _____ percent of the total compensation paid him by the company for that year.

Allocation of forfeitures in proportion to account balances

Any amounts forfeited in accordance with Section _____ hereof shall be allocated to the accounts of remaining participants in the proportion that each participant's balance in his account on the date of allocation bears to the total balances in the accounts of all participants on that date.

In no event shall an amount be allocated to a participant which would result in such participant receiving an annual addition to his account exceeding the lesser of $25,000.00 or twenty-five percent (25%) of his annual compensation. Any portion of a forfeited amount not allocated to the participant by reason of the foregoing restriction shall be allocated among the remaining participants in accordance with the allocation formula set forth in the preceding paragraph.

Continued employment after "retirement age"

Normal Retirement: Upon attaining normal retirement age, a participant shall be one hundred percent (100%) vested in the balance of his account. If the Company and the participating employee agree, he may remain in employment after attaining his normal retirement age. In such case, his retirement shall be deferred until said employment terminates; and during this deferral period he shall continue to participate in the Plan in all respects.

SAMPLE PENSION OR PROFIT-SHARING
PLAN CLAUSES *(concluded)*

Death: Upon the death of a participant during employment, one hundred percent (100%) of the balance of his account at death shall be fully vested in him and paid to his designated beneficiary or to his executor or administrator, as provided in Paragraph _____ hereof.

15

The most valuable fringe benefits

No single definition for the term fringe benefits seems to satisfy everyone. What some companies and personnel specialists call fringes, others classify as necessities—pensions and vacations, for example.

The fringe benefits analyzed in this chapter should not be considered to include everything that might be made available to executives in the way of fringe benefits. Rather, the chapter covers those fringes (not discussed elsewhere in this book) which offer the most significant benefits to the executive, at relatively low cost to the company because of its right to deduct its fringe benefit outlays.

FINANCIAL COUNSELING FOR EXECUTIVES

Financial counseling is one name given to an attractive fringe benefit offered by many of the nation's largest corporations. It is a package of financial advisory and planning services, performed by a team of professionals employed by firms engaged in the business of providing such services, for a fee, to company management. Some firms specialize in financial counseling exclusively; for others, financial counseling is a highly developed branch of their many activities.

An employer will engage a financial counseling firm to provide counseling services to selected executives at a fee per executive, to be paid by the employer or, occasionally, partly by employer and partly by executive.

The services provided vary somewhat from one counseling firm to another. Then, too, the employer hiring the consulting firm may ask for special services, or reject some services not considered appropriate to its own executives. But the services financial counselors typically provide executives deal with:

The executive's estate plan. The counselors determine the expected size of the executive's estate, assist in planning how it should be disposed of at death (including will-drafting advice), suggest suitable insurance arrangements and the proper balance between term insurance and other forms, advise on estate dispositions and will clauses that tend to minimize federal estate taxes, state inheritance taxes, and probate expenses, and provide guidance in assuring the estate's liquidity at the executive's death to carry the beneficiaries during the probate period and to cover outstanding debts.

The executive's tax returns. Attorneys or accountants on the counseling firm's staff may prepare the executive's federal, state and city income tax returns, and gift tax returns where applicable. The general review of the executive's financial affairs, which is the starting point of the financial consultant's analysis and recommendations, typically includes an examination of the executive's past income tax returns.

Consultants have sometimes turned up past reporting errors that favored the government; corrections of these errors generated tax refunds. More often, however, the past reporting defects needing correction would require additional tax payments. Prompt correction of these mistakes, as recommended by the consultant, has in some cases forestalled embarrassment or more serious difficulty with the Revenue Service.

The executive's compensation package. Many executives skilled in the most arcane aspects of corporate finance are embarrassingly unsophisticated about their own rights and profit opportunities under company plans. The counselor will outline the benefits, risks, and tax consequences of such common (but, to some executives, mysterious) company plans as stock options, deferred compensation, shadow stock, split-dollar life insurance, group term life insurance, thrift or savings plans, and profit-sharing withdrawals. Thus, one financial consultant reportedly saved an executive $67,000 in income taxes by recommending that a qualified stock option be exercised in installments over a period of years instead of all at once.

The executive's investment portfolio. Advisers from the consulting firm will suggest suitable new investments or switches. One major element of their advice may be an investment in a tax shelter, such as a low-rent housing project.

The financial counseling firm's work is extremely detailed and complicated, calling for the services of attorneys, accountants, investment and insurance advisers, and on occasion professional estate planners and fiduciaries. It is, appropriately, expensive: Costs of $3,500 to $4,000 per executive are common for the complete counseling program, and the executive's situation may thereafter be periodically reviewed (annually or semiannually) at an additional $1,000 or so for each review.

The selection of a counseling firm requires care. First,

there should be complete assurance that each executive's confidences will be protected. There is the further need to be sure that the consulting firm is not promoting any interests of its own when it recommends any particular stock, tax shelter, insurance arrangement or other investment, or that any such interests are fully disclosed. Also, the executive must feel that the advice given is in his or her own interests and independent of the company's preferences. Indeed, the employer which engages an outside consulting firm must accept the possibility that its executives may become less closely tied to the company economically and not more so. For one thing, advisers typically counsel executives to diversify their portfolios by getting rid of some of their company stock. Also, the consultant may criticize the company's present balance of cash compensation versus other benefits, and may urge changes which the company may or may not wish to hear.

A factor contributing to the growth of financial counseling was the claim some counseling firms made that the services were tax-exempt to executives. These firms were aware that many companies had provided in-house legal and accounting services and investment advice for their executives for decades, without tax problems—that is, with no tax to the executive. Tax "exemption" there generally resulted because the services were performed by corporate employees whose salaries were included in the general "salaries and wages" line of the tax return. Little or no Revenue Service challenge arose because there was nothing to indicate that company accountants, lawyers or investment analysts were attending to executives' private affairs at company expense. But financial counseling services are much more open to Revenue Service scrutiny, since the services are separately billed by an outside firm.

This feature had a predictable result: a Revenue Service

decision that the executive must report and pay taxes on the counseling services. Specifically, the Revenue Service considers that the amount the employer pays to the consulting firm is taxable as additional compensation to the executive on whose behalf the payment is made, and furthermore is subject to withholding tax.

However, a substantial measure of tax benefit and, in effect, tax exemption, is still available for financial counseling services, since the Revenue Service will allow the executive what can amount to sizable deductions offsetting the income from services. Specifically:

1. Amounts paid for services directed to tax matters are deductible. Individuals are allowed to deduct costs of services in tax return preparation, tax disputes, tax advice, and tax planning. The amount allocable to tax matters could be a substantial portion of the bill, since the consultant, besides preparing tax returns, would give necessary tax advice connected with investments (especially tax shelters) and estate planning. It would therefore be appropriate for the consulting firm to expressly allocate the appropriate portion of its bill for each executive to tax advice. Of course, the larger the portion properly allocable to tax advice, the smaller the amount which is actually taxable to the executive.

2. Amounts allocable to investment advice would also in effect be exempt from tax to the executive, since an offsetting deduction for the cost of such advice would normally be allowed. The company should ask the consulting firm for a specific allocation to investment advisory services in each bill. Investment advice generally declined in importance as a service during the 1970s because of the stagnant stock market.

3. Costs allocable to explaining company stock option and other benefits to the executive would seem to be tax-

exempt to him.[1] The consulting firm should allocate a part of its bill to such services. The executive would be taxed on the balance of the cost of the counseling, since offsetting deductions for costs attributable to other services would not be allowed.

Example: Suppose the bill for consulting services to Walters, Apex Corporation's financial vice president, is $3,500, of which $2,000 is for tax and investment services and therefore in effect exempt from tax. The company treats the $3,500 as additional compensation to Walters, and withholds an additional $1,260 from Walters' cash pay to cover the withholding liability on $3,500 in Walters' bracket. At the end of the year, it shows $3,500 as part of Walters' wages in the Form W-2 withholding statement given to Walters, and also includes the $1,260 in the amount withheld. On Apex's corporate income tax return, it would treat the $3,500 as salary to Walters (under "compensation of officers"), which is deductible to the extent that it, along with Walters' other compensation, is reasonable.

Walters would report the $3,500 along with his other salary income and claim a credit for the full amount withheld. He would also take a deduction (under "miscellaneous deductions") for the $2,000 allocable to tax and investment services, so that he is taxable only on the $1,500 balance. (The required withholding on the entire $3,500 may cause withholding to exceed the executive's tax liability. To prevent this, the executive could file a revised Form W-4 with the employer to increase his or her withholding allowances and thereby reduce withholding on future salary payments. Otherwise, a refund of the

---

[1] This is the authors' opinion. The Revenue Service has not publicly discussed this.

excessive tax could be claimed when the tax return is filed.)

The aftertax cost of the $3,500 of consulting services for Walters is therefore $1,890 for Apex. The services are worth $3,500 to Walters, but he pays only $750 in tax for them (assuming he is in the 50-percent bracket).

Any company offering such services to its executives should warn them of the Revenue Service rule treating the cost as taxable compensation (with some offsetting deduction).

This tax liability may deter some executives from accepting the offered services. Services refused would not be taxable income. But in most cases they should not refuse. Financial counseling gives the executive a systematic review of personal financial affairs, which probably have been neglected for years, and helps examine current and future career plans and estate plans. More important, it can produce actual, visible, immediate profits and tax savings for the executive far outweighing any tax cost.

The company is free, from a tax standpoint, to give or withhold such services to executives or other employees as it chooses. Companies typically limit it to top executives, and sometimes to selected top executives. (Some companies furnishing executives with such services expected objections from stockholders. But there seems to be little vocal objection.)

No plan or other formality is required when setting up financial counseling for executives. But it is wise to include a waiver to be signed by executives who accept financial counseling. This waiver would represent the executive's agreement not to hold the employer liable for the consequences of following any advice furnished by the counseling firm.

INTEREST-FREE AND LOW-INTEREST LOANS TO EXECUTIVES

Today, when mortgage interest rates reach 9½ percent and rates on personal loans reach 12 percent, an interest-free or low-interest loan from the employer can be a fringe benefit of considerable value to executives.

For the executive who could use $50,000 or so to help buy a home or exercise some stock options, an interest-free loan from the company may be worth some $4,000-$6,000 in interest cost saved (though its aftertax worth is somewhat less, since interest payments usually are deductible).

Interest-free and low-interest loans are also used as inducements on the hiring line. One well-known executive accepted a top position when the offer to sell him stock in the company substantially below its market value was sweetened by a low-interest loan for the stock's purchase price.

Tax professionals generally agree that the employee who borrows from an employer is not taxable on the amount of interest the company does not charge (or, of course, on the principal amount). For example, if a company makes a $100,000 loan interest-free to an employee at a time when the rate on similar loans is 12 percent, it is clear to most tax practitioners that the $12,000 (12 percent of $100,000)-a-year value of that loan is not taxable income to the employee. If the employer were to charge, say, 4 percent, the $8,000 value of that bargain rate (12 percent of $100,000 less 4 percent of $100,000) would not be taxable. Of course, the employee could not tax-deduct any interest not actually paid.

These tax specialists also agree that the company should not be considered as receiving interest income with respect to interest not charged to employees (and could not treat that amount as a deduction).

The IRS position on interest-free loans to executives is cloudy. It has made no public announcement on the question, and it lost the only court cases which squarely raised the issue of loans *to executives.* It has also lost two somewhat analogous issues—a corporation's interest-free loan to a stockholder who was not an employee, and an interest-free loan by joint venturers to a co-venturer as compensation for putting the venture together.

The consensus in the tax profession appears to be that there is enough official support for tax-free treatment to make interest-free and low-interest loans acceptable elements of a compensation package, but that the IRS has not given up on its apparent opposition.

The situation is a bit different on a loan to an executive who controls the company. Since IRS *has* publicly announced that despite a court defeat it still considers interest-free loans to controlling stockholders to be taxable, it will probably try to tax loans to executives who are controlling stockholders. Also, IRS is authorized to treat interest-free loans from a corporation to its controlling stockholder-executives as resulting in taxable interest income to the corporate lender with an offsetting deduction to the borrower. The authors have seen no example of this, probably because it would seldom result in a net increase in tax revenues.

An alternative to risking IRS attack on an interest-free or low-interest loan to an executive would be to make the loan at full commercial rates but increase the executive's salary correspondingly. For example, suppose the commercial interest cost on an $50,000 personal loan would be $6,000. The company could grant the loan, charging full ($6,000) interest, but increase the executive's salary by

$6,000. The executive's increased salary is offset by an interest deduction, leaving the executive in the same tax position as with an interest-free loan. The company's interest income is offset by a compensation deduction (though the corporation should take care to establish that the compensation is reasonable, applying the standards in Chapter 3).

For executives with heavy borrowings to buy or carry their investments, the forgiven interest in a low-interest loan may seem more attractive than a corresponding increase in salary. Under the tax law, a person's deduction for interest on borrowings connected with his or her investments can't in any year exceed the sum of $10,000 plus the net income from all investments; the excess is carried over for deduction in another year.

Example: Gold intends to borrow $220,000 at 10 percent to buy land which will be security for the loan. Assuming she has no other investment interest and no investment income, $12,000 of her interest cost would be nondeductible.

If she got a $22,000 increase in salary, her $10,000 interest deduction would offset $10,000 of that salary, but the $12,000 balance would be taxable.

But suppose instead she got a $220,000 interest-free loan. She has no nondeductible (or deductible) interest. There is no *taxable* increase in her compensation.

Here is the weakest point of the low-interest loan, should IRS mean to attack such loans. One theory for treating low-interest loans as nontaxable is that *if* they were considered taxable income, an offsetting interest deduction would have to be allowed. But an offsetting deduction would not necessarily be required where *actual* interest would be nondeductible. This position has not yet been officially voiced by IRS.

It should be understood that the employee's tax exemption on the amount borrowed (the principal amount) is assured only if the transaction represents a true loan and is not disguised salary or bonus. While a $20,000 interest-free loan is tax exempt, $20,000 which is actually salary is taxable income to the employee, and is deductible by the company to the extent it is reasonable for the services rendered.

If a loan is intended, it should be made in a businesslike way, with all, or at least most, of the formality appropriate to loans in business settings. It should be in writing and should have a fixed repayment date or installment payment schedule. It is reasonable to make it a secured loan, if the money is lent to provide funds to purchase a house (it could then be a mortgage loan), or company stock (the stock itself might be security for the loan; for more on the problems here, see Chapter 8). If any interest will be charged, specify the amount and payment dates.

Including the above provisions does not guarantee that the payment will be treated as a loan. The Revenue Service is always free to seek to prove that it was really compensation. But observing all due formalities helps to incline the Revenue Service—and if necessary the courts—to treat it as a loan.

Many companies limit their interest-free or low-interest loans to certain specific employee purposes: to buy a home, company stock directly or through exercise of a stock option, a car or life insurance, to pay the tax on such taxable benefits as bargain stock purchases, or to pay family medical bills or school tuition. Even companies with no regular loan policies may make loans to executives who move to new job locations. Such loans are to help the executive buy a new home or, when made as a low-interest second mortgage loan on the old home, to help the executive carry it until it can be sold for a suitable price.

One elaborate transaction known within the tax profession involved a large company's purchase of a luxury home which it sold to its chief executive with no down payment, no amortization of principal, low interest (4 percent), and principal due many years hence (apparently after the executive's planned retirement, when the house probably would have been sold). There is no public record that the executive was taxed on the low-interest element of this transaction or any other part.

Company considerations on interest-free loans

Though the company faces little danger of adverse tax treatment on an interest-free loan, there may be other unwelcome aspects worth considering before such a loan is made:

1. Some companies have had trouble obtaining repayment of funds they have lent. Their executives looked on the money as theirs, without strings. While this seems to be a problem that could be avoided by adequate communications before the loan is made, the strain and embarrassment at repayment time has soured some firms on making loans.

Some companies which make such loans provide for repayment by means of payroll deductions, while others expect separate repayment in installments. A requirement that the outstanding loan balance be paid in full on termination of employment is a common feature.

2. Corporate loans to executives who are officers may be subject to legal restrictions under state law. The rules vary widely. California law allows loans only with stockholder approval, while Delaware expressly allows the loans without such qualification, and New York allows them by strong implication.

Even where loans to officers are allowed, restraints may

be imposed on loans to executives who are directors. It is important to check local law before lending to executives who are officers or directors.

Some companies which have decided against lending to their employees try to get outside lenders to make loan funds available. The likeliest source for such loans is, of course, the company's own bank. Leverage applied by the company can cause the bank to make loans to company executives on terms not available to the public at large. There is no case on record in which this has been treated as resulting in compensation to the executive; the executive would deduct any interest paid. The executive can be expected to pay off a bank loan more readily than an employer loan, though some companies have still felt obliged to make good on bank loans on which their executives have defaulted (company payments here being considered taxable compensation to the executive, if still employed there).

EXECUTIVE DINING ROOMS

Lunches served in the executives' dining room are a tax-favored fringe benefit for the executive who receives the lunches, and are fully deductible by the company. Employees, including executives, are not subject to tax on the value of meals furnished them free of charge on company premises if the meals are provided to meet the business convenience of the company. This business convenience test is satisfied with respect to the executives' dining room if the executives gathered there for lunch discuss business concerns during meals.

In most firms, business discussion in the executives' dining room can be taken for granted, and need not be structured by the company. (In any case, business discussion need not take place every day.) But it is wise for some personnel or other management officer to make occasional checks that business matters actually are raised at lunch, and to make an occasional record of matters discussed, in the event of a possible Revenue Service question.

The company's cost of the lunches would be deducted as a business expense. Though some companies provide lavish and elegant meals in luxurious surroundings, there seems to be no recorded instance of a Revenue Service challenge to the amount of the company's deduction for such magnificence.

Thus, a company could provide an executive with a lunch worth $7 some 200-250 times a year. Though he receives $1,400-$1,750 in value, the executive is completly exempt from tax, while the company deducts the cost of the meal and so bears only about 54 percent of the true cost.

Another reason some companies provide an executives' dining room: to control executive's lunchtime alcoholic intake. Many, perhaps most, executives' dining rooms are liquor free. Limiting liquor consumption seems a sound business reason for providing an executives' dining room, entirely apart from any business discussions during meals. There is, however, no official decision on this point, and some firms (Wall Street brokerage and investment bankers come to mind) are known for the breadth and grandeur of their wine cellers, displayed and drawn upon at lunchtime.

Some companies use the executives' lunchtime as an opportunity to introduce new ideas. Guests from government, universities, or other industries are invited, who may serve as catalysts for new thinking. For other firms, the executives' dining room serves to keep executives on the company premises and available in emergencies.

Sometimes, the executive is charged for the meal, usually a nominal amount, or in any case much less than its true value. The bargain element in the meals is not taxable, again assuming business discussions take place during meals.

The Revenue Service technically requires that the meals be furnished on the company premises. This has in practice been stretched (by a court, over Revenue Service objection) to include a rented hotel suite, and could on the same theory be extended to a private room in a restaurant or club. But it seems advisable to follow the IRS requirement if possible: to use company premises if they are available, and if not, to avoid a public room in a restaurant.

No plan or formalities of any kind are required to establish an executives' dining room. But be prepared to show that business discussions typically take place during meals. Some companies have had unpleasant experiences with their company dining rooms. The negative feelings of employees who were not invited were sometimes sufficiently strong to outweigh the advantages to the company and the executives who were included. A few firms discontinued their dining rooms for this reason.

COVERING EXECUTIVES' MOVING COSTS

Wise employee relations policy will completely relieve executives of any out-of-pocket expenses of moving to the area of a new job. Such moves, however welcome they may be when they represent a promotion or a more attractive or exciting location, still bring physical discomfort and family disruption. They should not also involve added expense to be paid with aftertax dollars.

Typical company-paid costs of moving executives from one job location to another are explored below. The analysis applies to the move of a single executive or a small group, and also to moves of the entire top management on a shift of corporate headquarters. A company can cover most moving costs with full deductibility for its outlays and full tax exemption for the executive. If a company limits its outlays to these tax-favored items, the actual cost of moving is limited, in effect, to about 54 percent of what it spends. For the company that wants to provide moving expense benefits or protection beyond the tax-favored items, suggestions are offered for restructuring the arrangement to qualify for tax benefits. There is no barrier to discriminating in favor of executives in the moving expense benefits provided.

To illustrate the rules, we will take the case of Crawford, the company's regional sales manager located in Dallas, who is named national sales manager and transferred to company headquarters in New York City.[2] Crawford has a wife and three children, and owns a home in Dallas which cost him $82,000 two years ago. All the company moving expense payments or reimbursements described below are deductible by the company and tax-exempt to Crawford (and to his family) except where otherwise expressly stated. Tax exemption for the executive is accomplished by treating company payments or reimbursements of expenses as compensation income to him but allowing him an offsetting deduction.

Basic moving expenses

1. Travel fares for Crawford and all his family (but not servants) and including costs of meals and lodging en route. If the travel is done by auto, costs of gasoline, oil, tolls, etc. are included in the exempt amount. In any case, travel must be by the most direct route available and in the shortest time commonly required. Expenses of holiday stopovers, side trips, or detours are not covered.

2. Costs of transporting household goods and personal

---

[2] Somewhat more liberal rules apply to moves abroad.

effects. This covers costs of packing and crating and also insurance and storage for up to 30 days after the goods are moved from the old homestead and before they are moved into the new.

3. House hunting costs. This covers costs of round-trip travel from the area of the old job to that of the new, to search for a new residence to buy or rent. The trip can be by the executive alone, or with spouse or others of the family, or by family members unaccompanied by the executive. Thus, Crawford and his wife could travel round-trip from Dallas to New York to look for a new home in the New York area, and either or both of them could make return trips as necessary for further searches or to negotiate or close deals. Furthermore, the costs are covered even though no new residence is taken because of the trip, but is only found after the move to the new location.

4. Temporary living costs. These are outlays for meals and lodging up to 30 days in the area of the new job location, following the move there but before moving into permanent quarters. For example, suppose Crawford arrived before the redecorating work on his house was finished. He and his family lived in a suburban New York motel and ate in restaurants there for 11 days until the house was ready, at a cost of $95 a day. Company reimbursement of this $1,045 cost could be tax-exempt.

5. Home sale expenses. Company payment or reimbursement of certain kinds of costs connected with disposing of a former home or acquiring a new one qualify as tax-exempt to the executive. These are certain costs of buying or selling a home, or acquiring or breaking a lease. Specifically, items that can be covered tax-free include: brokerage commissions, attorney fees, title search, title insurance, appraisal fees, escrow fees, mortgage "points" paid for services (appraisal, processing, and so forth, but not "points" paid as interest), transfer taxes, payments to a landlord for release from a lease, and fees or commissions for obtaining a lease, a sublease, or an assignment of a lease.

Taxable amounts. The executive is tax-exempt on company payments or reimbursements of the above items if the amounts are reasonable. This reasonableness requirement does not preclude first-class travel or meals. There seems to be no recorded case where company payment of travel fares, meals and lodging was treated as partly taxable to the executive because it was extravagant and unreasonable.

But for some moving expense items there are additional limits. The exemption for house hunting expenses, temporary lodging, and selling or leasing costs combined is limited to $3,000. Furthermore, the exemption for house hunting and temporary living costs combined cannot exceed $1,500. Thus, if $2,600 were spent as selling costs and $600 on house hunting (no temporary lodging costs), $3,000 would be exempt and $200 would be taxable. If $1,200 went to selling costs and another $1,800 to house hunting and temporary lodging combined, $2,700 ($1,200 plus $1,500) would be exempt and $300 taxable.

No exemption is allowed unless the new place of work is at least 35 miles farther from the old home than the old place of work was. This in essence denies exemption for moves connected with job transfers between nearby towns or between the city and the suburbs. For example, if an executive commuted 12 miles to work at the old job, the new job would have to be more than 47 miles from the executive's old home before the move to a new home would qualify for exemption. The length of the commute between the new home and the new job is irrelevant.

Also, in most cases exemption is barred unless the executive works full time, in the general area moved to, for at least 39 weeks of the 12-month period following his or her arrival.

Moving for personal reasons can be tax exempt. Executives sometimes pressure their companies to move them to a particular location which they happen to prefer for reasons of climate, recreation, and the like. This helps account for the corporate offices springing up on the California coast. Company payment or reimbursement of expenses of such moves made for the executive's own health, comfort, convenience or other personal reasons is still tax-exempt, since the executive can deduct these costs, assuming the regular exemption tests are met (chiefly, that the executive is employed full time 39 weeks of the year following arrival).

In this situation, the company would treat its payment of moving expenses as additional compensation to the executive, rather than as an ordinary business expense. The company therefore could deduct this payment only if the amount paid, together with other compensation, is reasonable.

Other moving costs

6. Home sale "losses." Many company payments connected with the executive's sale of his or her old home or purchase of a new one, while deductible by the company, are taxable to the executive as additional compensation. These taxable payments usually result from company efforts to protect the executive from loss on "forced" sale of a home, the loss attributable to the fact that the executive must sell under a time pressure, without being able to wait for a fair price. The company may therefore pay the difference between the fair market value of the property and what the executive actually collects on sale. (This was an IBM practice for a time.) The amount an executive receives from the company under this arrangement is taxable compensation income whether the amount collected on sale is more or less than the house cost.

For example, suppose Crawford sells his Dallas house

for $79,000 and his company pays him $3,000 to cover his loss on the sale. The $3,000 is taxable even though his total collections on sale ($79,000 plus $3,000) do not exceed his $82,000 cost of the house. The $3,000 loss he sustained on sale is not deductible, so it cannot offset the $3,000 of income.

Or suppose the company determined that the fair market of the Dallas home was $85,000, but Crawford got only $83,000 on sale, so his company made up the difference with a $2,000 check to cover this moving "loss." The $2,000 is taxable as additional compensation income. It cannot be treated as additional capital gain on sale, and cannot be exempted from tax (tax deferred), as capital gain would be, if he bought a new home for $85,000 or more.

Where it appears that the executive will not get full value on sale of the old house, the company could rescue the executive by buying the house at a fair market value determined by independent appraisal (or an average of independent appraisals). This avoids any loss resulting from the "forced" aspect of the sale, though it would not protect the executive from loss attributable to any decline in value of the property below its cost. The executive's profit on sale to the company is capital gain, which can be tax-deferred if the executive buys a replacement residence; the loss on the sale is not deductible. Making the selling price equal the independent appraisal (or average of appraisals) tends to discourage the Revenue Service from claiming that the selling price was inflated to include some disguised compensation.

The company would face fewer time pressures than the executive in arranging the sale of the house, and therefore could hold out for a suitable price (and might rent it out meanwhile). It probably should treat profit or loss on the house as ordinary income or loss for tax purposes (though this is not entirely clear).

IBM abandoned its previous practice of making taxable payments to reimburse executives for loss on sale of their homes and adopted the tax-favored course: buying the executive's home. But not all companies are willing to tie up funds in purchases of homes of moved executives. Some firms therefore have adopted these alternative approaches:

a. The company appraises the property and in effect guarantees that appraised value to the executive. The executive then seeks to sell it. If it is sold for more than the appraised value, the company keeps the excess; if for less than the appraised value, the company makes up the difference, but the executive must accept any offer the company considers reasonable.

This plan, when used by a large insurance company, resulted in taxable income to the executive to the extent of the company's payment of the difference between the appraised value and the lower sales price. This was not considered the tax equivalent of a sale to the company, even though the company could have made a profit on the arrangement. The executive was still the owner of the house until it was sold, so the company's payment was taxable compensation.

b. The company arranges to have a real estate firm buy the home. A number of large firms have entered this field, and some small local firms may also be interested. Under the arrangement, a price for the executive's house is set by appraisal (maybe by the real estate firm, maybe by independent appraisal), and the executive can take this price or seek to sell it elsewhere. Assuming the house is sold to the real estate firm, the employer corporation thereafter may pay an amount to the firm as a commission, or may cover all or part of the firm's loss on sale of the executive's house if the firm should fail to sell it at a profit. There is as yet no published Revenue Service ruling on this arrangement, and its tax treatment is far from clear. One view would treat amounts paid the real estate firm by the company as made for the benefit of the executives selling their homes, taxable to them as additional salary and deductible by the employer only as compensation, subject to reasonableness tests.

Under the alternative view, the company's payments are considered made for services performed for the company in lieu of costs the company would incur if it bought the homes directly. This would make the payments deductible business expenses of the company and nontaxable to executives. In the authors' experience, the latter view has been adopted by companies on numerous occasions without challenge from revenue agents.

7. Pay and bonus for moving. Crawford was paid for the days off from work which he spent house hunting and moving. He also received an extra four weeks' pay as a "bonus" to cover special moving expenses, such as telephone and appliance installation costs. Such payments are taxable income to Crawford and his special moving expense outlays ordinarily are not deductible. The company should set the amount of the "bonus" high enough to cover both the special moving expenses and the executive's tax on the bonus. All these amounts are treated as compensation, and are deductible by the company subject to the reasonableness tests.

8. Mortgage differential. The mortgage interest rate on the house Crawford sold was less than the rate on the house Crawford bought in the new location. His employer reimbursed him for the extra interest expenses (mortgage differential) that would be incurred in the three years following purchase of the house, in a lump sum. This lump sum is taxable compensation to Crawford in the year received. He can deduct interest on the mortgage as paid. For the company, a good argument could be made that the mortgage differential is an ordinary business expense of moving employees, and not compensation subject to the reasonableness test.

9. Low-interest loans.   Interest-free and low-interest loans to executives in home sale and home purchase situations were considered earlier in this chapter.

Company deduction.   An IRS publication says that the employer treats reimbursements for moving expenses as compensation for services, subject to the deduction tests of reasonableness, etc., discussed in Chapter 3. The authors consider this rule questionable except where the move is made for the executive's convenience. Moving an executive or other employee from one location to another is usually seen by the company as a normal cost of operating a business; it has no thought of compensating employees for services when it pays the costs of moving them. An employee's moving expenses depend on family size, distance travelled, and quantity and type of household goods, all factors which have nothing to do with the value of the executive's services. Newly hired employees may have performed no services when their moving expenses are reimbursed.

However, this IRS position apparently is not enforced. The authors know of no instance in which moving expense reimbursements have been treated as nondeductible excessive compensation.

MAKING THE EXECUTIVE'S CHARITABLE DONATIONS

Helping to meet the executive's charitable obligations is a fringe benefit popular with a number of large companies.

Some firms agree to contribute to charities selected by their executives, up to specified dollar maximums. For others, the company may grant executives and other employees a kind of charitable allowance based on their performance on the job. Thus, one worker may be allowed to designate a charitable donee of $500 while another worker (an executive, for example) might be able to designate a charity to receive $5,000. Still another common charitable program has the company match charitable contributions of executives (or other employees) dollar for dollar up to a specified maximum.

Company contributions may be made in the name of executives or other employees, but they are by company check, payable to the charity. Amounts donated are not taxable to executives or other employees selecting the charitable donees, and they get no tax deduction for amounts contributed. All deductions are taken by the corporate employer, and are subject to its own deduction limit (generally 5 percent of its taxable income).

DEATH BENEFITS

Company payments to the spouse or heirs of a deceased executive qualify for tax benefits.

The spouse or other beneficiary is exempt from tax on up to $5,000 of death benefits, if the deceased employee would have had no right to receive the payments personally had he or she lived longer, or the right to receive them was subject to forfeiture.

The $5,000 exemption is a single exemption for all beneficiaries, not $5,000 for each. If company payments exceed $5,000, the $5,000 exemption is allocated among recipients in proportion to the death benefit they receive. Thus, if a widow receives $9,000 and a son $6,000, she is exempt on $3,000 and he on $2,000.

Besides this limited income tax exemption, voluntary or forfeitable amounts paid to the spouse or other beneficiary are exempt from estate tax regardless of amount.

Since income and estate tax exemptions are available only for amounts which the company pays voluntarily, or which are forfeitable by the executive, executives sometimes seek contractual arrangements which make payments forfeitable. It is of course logically unwise for an executive with, say, a deferred compensation agreement to transmute a guaranteed payment under that agreement into a payment which could be forfeited by some future action or inaction. But it is in fact sometimes done, for the tax advantage, by executives who believe there is little danger that the amount will in fact be forfeited. Executive death benefits will often greatly exceed the $5,000 which is exempt from income tax. Thus, the income tax planning technique by executives who foresee little risk of actual forfeiture would be to make $5,000 forfeitable and the balance guaranteed. (But remember that a guaranteed amount won't be exempt from *estate* tax.)

Amounts are made forfeitable by attaching conditions to them so that the executive loses the right to receive them in the event of resignation or termination for cause. This might be done with a deferred bonus or other deferred compensation payable in installments; the executive would forfeit any unpaid balance upon termination. Amounts which could become nonforfeitable in the future (through performance of services, lapse of time, or some other event) are treated as forfeitable until nonforfeitability occurs.[3]

Nonforfeitable death benefits qualify for the $5,000 income tax exemption if they are paid under qualified pension or similar plans.

---

[3] The rules on forfeitability (substantial risk of forfeiture) in Chapter 9 do not apply here.

Amounts which the spouse or beneficiary receives which exceed $5,000 can still be exempt from tax if they represent gifts by the company. The Revenue Service usually treats the excess as taxable income, either as compensation for the deceased executive's past services, or as dividends where the beneficiary is a stockholder (for example, where the spouse has inherited the stock of a stockholder-executive). But courts often find the payments to be nontaxable gifts where they are made based on the beneficiary's need.

Death benefits paid as compensation for services are deductible by the company. They can be compensation even though they are not required under a contract or other formal plan. The company's deduction is subject to the reasonable compensation ceilings, but deduction has been allowed for sizable sums. For example, deduction was allowed for $40,000 paid over a two-year period to the widow of a $40,000-a-year president.

Companies occasionally treat payments in excess of $5,000 as gifts. Their motive here is to improve the chance that the widow or other recipient can treat receipts as a tax-free gift. Gift treatment by the company does not guarantee gift treatment for the widow. Also, deduction for the first $5,025 of such a gift payment, though not absolutely foreclosed by the Revenue Service, is doubtful. And in any case, deduction is barred for the excess over $5,025 of amounts treated as gifts.

To summarize, payments of not more than $5,000 under a voluntary or forfeitable arrangement as compensation enjoy full tax benefits: income tax exemption to the beneficiary, estate tax exemption for the estate, and deduction for the company. Departure from this arrangement risks loss of some benefits to someone.

Companies sometimes take out an insurance policy on an executive's life, naming the company itself as beneficiary. This is done so that the company will have the funds at the executive's death to cover any death benefit obligation. The company will not be allowed to deduct any of its premiums, but will not be taxable on the proceeds. When it uses the proceeds to pay death benefits, its payments and the beneficiaries' receipts will get the tax treatment described above.

OTHER FRINGE BENEFITS VALUED BY EXECUTIVES

Company payment of business or professional dues.   A company's payment of dues for the executive's membership in a business association (such as the American Management Association, the American Bankers Association, or the Sales Executives Club) or a professional association (a bar association or CPA society) is deductible by the company and tax-exempt to the executive. Thus, an executive who would maintain an association membership in any case can be relieved of the need to pay the cost of membership with aftertax dollars. Company payment for subscriptions to business or professional journals would get the same treatment.

Dues paid for membership in downtown luncheon clubs (such as New York's Banker's Club) are likewise deductible by the company and tax-exempt to the executive. Such clubs are considered to have a business purpose for the company, since business discussion and contacts of potential importance to the company take place there. (Deduction of the cost of meals is another matter, as is deduction of dues to a country club, yacht club or other social club. These matters are considered in Chapter 12.)

Company payment of officer liability insurance.   An executive isn't subject to tax on, and the company may take a deduction for, company payment of the cost of insurance indemnifying its executives for expenses arising from their wrongful acts (or allegedly wrongful acts) committed in their official capacities, including breach or neglect of duty, wrongful act or omission, error, misstatement or misleading statement, or "any matter claimed against them."

Lavish office furnishings. The Revenue Service does not seek to tax an executive on the value of office creature comforts furnished, however splendid they might be. Also, company deductions for such grandeur generally are not questioned, except that it cannot take depreciation deductions on antiques and works of art which do not decline in value with the passage of time.

SEC FRINGE BENEFIT DISCLOSURE REQUIREMENTS

Companies registered with the Securities and Exchange Commission are required to disclose the remuneration of their officers and directors. Disclosure is made in registration, proxy and information statements and annual reports. Remuneration includes noncash remuneration—that is, fringe benefits.

"Remuneration" for SEC purposes is similar but not identical to "income" for tax purposes. Noncash remuneration which must be disclosed even though it is not or may not be taxable income to executive recipients includes:

a. *Low-interest or interest-free loans from the company.* Tax treatment here may still be doubtful but so far it has not been held taxable, as discussed earlier in this chapter.

b. *Loans by a third party* to an officer where his or her company in some way compensates the lender—e.g., a bank loan where the company maintains or increases compensating balances. This has apparently not arisen as a tax issue.

16

How to use
life insurance

In any survey of executive dissatisfaction with the federal tax structure, one of the most frequently heard complaints is that today's high taxes prevent executives from building up a substantial estate to leave to their families. No single compensation arrangement can completely relieve this concern, but one kind of company-furnished benefit—life insurance—is uniquely suited to executives' needs. Life insurance proceeds are, of course, an element of the estate that the insured individual leaves the family, yet life insurance is more highly favored for tax purposes than other forms of investment for the executive, for several reasons.

First, insurance proceeds collected by the executive's beneficiaries at death are completely exempt from income tax. For example, if $30,000 was paid in premiums on a policy that paid $100,000 at death, there is a $70,000 profit on the insurance investment, all of which is exempt from income tax.

Second, insurance proceeds can also be exempt from federal estate tax and state inheritance tax. Unlike the income tax exemption for insurance proceeds, however, the estate and inheritance tax exemptions are not automatic; tax saving action is necessary, as shown later in this chapter.

Third, the current premium cost of life insurance coverage can be provided to the executive in two tax-favored ways:

1. Group term life insurance.
2. Split-dollar life insurance.

These tax benefits for insurance premium costs do not apply to premiums a company pays on other straight or term life insurance for the executive. Any employee, including an executive employee, must include in taxable income any premiums the company pays on insurance covering his or her life if either (a) the employee names the beneficiaries of the life insurance or (b) the beneficiaries are named by the company but are those the employee would be likely to choose, such as spouse or children, or a trust for their benefit, or the employee's estate or executor. The premiums are additional salary income to the executive, and are deductible as additional salary by the company (subject to reasonable compensation ceilings). This can still be an economic benefit for the executive (as shown in convertible term insurance below) but it is not a tax benefit.

GROUP TERM LIFE INSURANCE

This is a way to provide substantial life insurance coverage for employees, without tax cost to them and with full deduction for the company. It is possible to limit coverage to executives, keeping down the overall cost to the company, or to cover executives for larger amounts than other employees.

For complete tax exemption, insurance must be term insurance, and the executive's coverage may not exceed $50,000. The actual cash value to the executive of getting term insurance coverage free through his or her employer, instead of having to buy it with aftertax dollars, will depend on how much the insurance the executive would buy would cost at his or her age; $50,000 of term insurance could reasonably cost between $350 and $1,250 in various age brackets.

Additional benefits are available for coverage in excess of $50,000. Here, the executive continues to be exempt from tax on the cost of the first $50,000 but is taxable on the cost of each $1,000 of coverage in excess of $50,000. However, the taxable amount is substantially less than the actual cost of such coverage, because the taxable amount is dictated by a table provided in Revenue Service regulations.[1] The amounts in the table are less than the company actually pays. Yet the company can still deduct its actual cost, and not the lesser amount its executive is taxed on. Deduction seems to be subject to reasonable compensation ceilings.

Example: Caldwell, in his 50s, is a $38,000-a-year vice president at Dunmow Corporation. He has $100,000 of coverage under Dunmow's group term plan. The insurance costs Dunmow $15 per $1,000 of coverage, or $1,500.

Caldwell is exempt from tax on $50,000 of insurance coverage, but is taxable on the cost of any excess (assuming he pays nothing for his coverage), so he is taxable on the cost of $50,000. But cost is figured under Revenue Service tables which tax Caldwell at the rate of $8.16 per $1,000, or $408. Thus, Caldwell gets value of $1,500 and

[1] See the end of this chapter for this table and how it is used to compute an executive's tax.

pays tax on $408. In Caldwell's probable tax bracket (after itemized deductions, and so forth), his actual cost of this $100,000 of coverage, the tax cost, is about $151.

Dunmow would still deduct its $1,500 cost (subject to reasonable compensation limits). Its deductible cost is not limited to the $8.16 per $1,000 used to figure Caldwell's tax.

If the executive pays part of the cost of coverage in excess of $50,000, the amount paid reduces dollar for dollar the taxable amount.

Example: Assume that in the above example Caldwell got $100,000 of coverage but had to pay for $20,000 of it, while his company paid for the $80,000 balance. Since Caldwell pays $300 ($15 per $1,000, for $20,000), he is taxed on only $108 ($408 minus $300).

Having Caldwell pay for part of his own coverage is, of course, less attractive to him than if the company covers the entire $100,000, since the executive must pay out $340 ($300 plus $40, the tax cost of $108 of taxable income), instead of $151. Still, it has advantages where the company is willing to pay only part of the cost of coverage over $50,000, or where the company will pay the entire cost of a specific amount but the executive wants more. This route, therefore, is preferable to providing the extra $20,000 of term insurance on his own, and outside the plan. Thus, if he got $80,000 under the plan and $20,000 elsewhere, at a cost of about $440 (figured at $22 per $1,000 since he could not get the benefit of group rates), his cost would be $532, that is, the $92 tax on $249 (the taxable income from the $30,000 of group insurance in excess of the exempt $50,000), plus $440 paid for the extra $20,000 of insurance.

Other group term insurance benefits

The executive's spouse and dependents can be given tax-free life insurance coverage up to $2,000 each. If coverage for any such person exceeds $2,000, the executive is taxable on the cost of the entire coverage of that person.

Retired executives—that is, executives who no longer work for the company and who have reached retirement age—are tax-exempt on all their coverage, even if it exceeds $50,000.

While permanent insurance is not tax-exempt, a policy provision allowing the executive to convert the policy from term to permanent when he or she leaves the company will not make the coverage (up to $50,000) taxable. Some companies do not welcome this convertible feature, thinking it provides something of an incentive to change jobs.

Group term insurance for executives only. There is no express provision in the tax law which prevents companies from granting group term life insurance to executives only, and excluding all other employees. But Revenue Service regulations somewhat inhibit company efforts to make such insurance "executives only."

First, there must be a group. To the Revenue Service, this means that the company cannot individually select those to be covered. Rather, those covered must be a class or classes of employees (or, of course, all employees). This, however, does not prohibit the company from limiting coverage to, say, all officers, or all department heads, or all employees making over $25,000, or all employees over age 50 with more than 15 years' service, or some other reasonable classification which may cover only those intended to be benefited. Also, it is not necessary that they be covered by a single master policy; a group of individual policies for each covered individual is also acceptable.

Second, the group covered must not be limited to *stockholder*-employees.

Third, in most cases the group must consist of ten or more persons. This rule admits of a few exceptions. The Revenue Service accepts groups of less than ten, where there are fewer than ten full-time employees and all full-timers are covered. (There is, by the way, sometimes a practical difficulty with small groups. Some insurance companies are reluctant to write sizable group policies for groups of fewer than ten members.)

To summarize the effect of these rules, a company can, as an economy measure or for other company policy reasons, exclude rank-and-file employees from group term coverage if (*a*) it covers a group of employees, selected on the basis of position (officers, department heads, managers, etc.), salary, age, length of service, and so on, (*b*) the group is not limited to stockholders, *and* (*c*) there are at least ten in the group.

For example, suppose a company has 110 full-time employees, including 6 officers (of which 4 are stockholders) and 5 department heads. Limiting group term coverage to the six officers is not allowed under the above rules (since the group is less than ten), but limiting coverage to all officers and department heads would be allowed.

However, a company could provide group term coverage for all employees, or one or more classes of employees, and still favor executives by giving them greater coverage. Thus, the company could adopt a plan which provides group term coverage which is a percentage of salary (assuming that percentage applies uniformly to all covered employees). For example, the company could provide $2 of coverage for every $1 of salary (a uniform 200 percent), so that the $8,000-a-year employee gets $16,000 and the $50,000-a-year executive gets $100,000.

Or, instead, coverage could be provided based on salary

brackets if the brackets are set by the insurance company rather than the employer. These brackets allow considerable flexibility. For example, employees in a $10,000-$20,000 bracket could be given $20,000 of coverage while those in the $20,000-$30,000 could be given $50,000.

The company could not individually select the amount of coverage for particular employees, but must use the uniform percentage system, the bracket system, or some other formula. A sample plan of group term insurance appears at the end of this chapter.

SPLIT-DOLLAR INSURANCE

This is another form of tax-favored insurance for the executive. It is a way whereby the company and the executive split the costs and the benefits of the insurance. It is permanent, not term, insurance and is used especially for younger executives or managers who are unable to afford a large insurance commitment on their own. Under a split-dollar arrangement, the company and the executive each are obliged to pay part of the premium cost of insurance on the executive's life, but after the early years of the policy the executive normally no longer has to pay anything.

The company pays that part of the annual premium which equals the increase in the policy's cash surrender value for the year. For this payment, the company becomes entitled to receive at the executive's death that part of the insurance proceeds which equals the policy's cash value (which in the policy's later years may exceed the company's actual investment in the policy).

The executive pays the balance of the premium due, that is, the total premium less the portion paid by the company (and disregarding for the moment dividends on the policy, which are considered below). This means, in practice, that the executive pays a substantial part of the premium cost in the first three or four years, and little or nothing thereafter. (See below for company loans to help pay these premiums.) At death, the executive's beneficiaries will collect the entire proceeds of the policy except for the cash surrender value which is paid to the employer.

The amount to be collected by the executive's beneficiaries declines each year as the cash surrender value mounts. This is why split-dollar insurance is so often designed specifically for the younger executive. The split-dollar arrangement gives maximum protection while the children are young, which drops as they get older and the amount needed for their support until they can become self-supporting declines. (The same sort of thinking lies behind recommendations of some insurance advisers and salespersons that executives should carry large amounts of term insurance while their children are young, which can be terminated as the children get older. Decreasing term insurance is sold on this basis.)

The policy may technically be owned by either the company or the executive. The authors generally advise that the executive own the policy, but with adequate protection for the company's investment. (Thus, the policy may be assigned to the company, as shown in the sample split-dollar arrangement at the end of this chapter.

Like other life insurance proceeds, the proceeds of split-dollar life insurance come to the beneficiaries (including the company as beneficiary of the cash surrender value) free of income tax. Moreover, the insurance proceeds can be made exempt from estate tax in the executive's estate, see below. But there is a tax liability, and there are several tax and business planning opportunities, connected with payment of the insurance premiums.

The executive is subject to tax on part of the premium cost of split-dollar coverage. The Revenue Service considers that, to a degree, a split-dollar insurance arrangement uses the employer's payments for the executive's benefit. This makes the payments compensation, in part. Specifically, the executive is taxable on an amount equal to the cost of one-year term insurance for the amount of coverage in that year, reduced by the amount of premiums he or she actually pays.

Example: A $100,000 policy is taken out for Davis, on on which her share of the first premium is about $600. Her share of the $100,000 is reduced by the cash surrender value of the policy (which goes to her employer), so her coverage is about $93,000. She is taxable on the cost of $93,000 of term insurance for one year, at her present age, but this taxable amount is reduced by the $600 premium she pays. In practice, she would therefore have little or no taxable income this year.

But two years later, she pays only about $200 of premium cost, and her share of the policy is now about $80,000 (since the cash surrender value is now about $20,000). She is taxable on the cost of $80,000 of term insurance at the age she is two years hence, reduced by the $200 she paid as premium. Now she is taxable on about $400. So for this year her split-dollar insurance costs her $356 as a single person in the 39 percent bracket, that is, $200 plus the $156 tax on $400.

The cost of term insurance, used to determine the amount taxable to the executive, is prescribed by a Revenue Service table. (The table, which is not the same as that used for group term life insurance, appears at the end of this chapter.) In general, the table reflects a cost of term insurance which is less than the actual cost of such insurance. This means that though executives are taxed on their split-dollar insurance benefits, they are taxed on less than the true value of what they get, and thereby make a tax saving on the premium cost as well as on the proceeds.

The Revenue Service recognizes the possibility that the cost figures in its table may sometimes be higher than some insurance companies actually charge. Therefore it permits the tax to be computed by using the rates actually charged by the insurance company involved, where these are lower than those in the Revenue Service table.

Policy dividends.   The rules described above assume that any dividends on the policy are paid to the employer, or go to reduce its premiums. Such dividends are not taxable to the employer. If policy dividends are paid to the executive, they normally are taxable income to him or her. (They would be exempt from tax to the extent that the premium the executive paid that year exceeded the value of his or her term insurance coverage for that year.) Dividends payable to the executive are sometimes used to buy additional insurance. Some executives do this because they want to offset, in part, the drop in insurance coverage that occurs automatically as the cash surrender value, payable to the employer, increases. Dividends so used normally are also taxable income to the executive.

Employer's tax treatment; financed life insurance.   The employer is not allowed any tax deduction for its split-dollar insurance premium. It will collect the cash surrender value completely free of income tax, but it gets no current deduction for the premiums paid to create that cash surrender value.

Though the company will get back the amount it put into the policy when the executive dies (and sometimes a bit more), some companies are reluctant to tie up their funds that long. They therefore may want to take care of some of their premium cost by borrowing against the cash surrender value.

This practice of borrowing against the cash surrender value to pay a premium—called "financed life insurance"—minimizes the company's cash commitment in split-dollar arrangements. It does not affect the tax treatment of the premiums or the proceeds. But there are limitations on a company's tax deduction for interest it pays on funds borrowed to buy or carry financed life insurance. In general, the company cannot deduct interest on financed life insurance, whether the loan comes from the insurance company or another source, unless at least four years' premiums out of the first seven years' premiums are paid without borrowing. Also, in the years in which the premiums are paid with borrowed funds, the amount borrowed against the cash surrender value cannot exceed one year's premium. Thus, the company could pay premiums from its own cash funds the first two years, and then in the third year borrow the amount of that year's premium, deduct any interest on that borrowing for that year, borrow again in the fourth year the amount of that year's premium (and deduct interest), pay the premium in the fifth year without borrowing (but deduct the interest on the two previous loans still outstanding), and so on.

After the seventh year, the company can borrow the balance of the cash surrender value, if it wishes. It then is not limited to borrowing only a single year's premium.

There are several other exceptions (besides the four-out-of-seven-year exception) to the rule barring the company's interest deduction, but they are of little practical value. Interest on financed insurance may be deducted if the insurance is connected with the company's business, but the Revenue Service doesn't consider split-dollar insurance business-connected. Interest on financed insurance is also deductible (even if no other exception is met) if it is less than $100 a year. But this $100 ceiling is quickly passed if there is a sizable premium, or more than one year's premium, or several executives are covered.

Company insurance loans to the executive.   The executive covered by split-dollar insurance must make a sizable premium payment in the first year, and further premiums in the following year or two. A company loan of the amount needed for these premiums may therefore be in order. This loan may be made interest-free, without tax consequences to either lender or borrower. (See the analysis of the interest-free loan as a fringe benefit in Chapter 15.) If the company will charge interest, the executive can deduct this for tax purposes. It is not subject to the financed insurance limitations above.

Split-dollar for executives only.   The company may limit split-dollar coverage to executives, or to selected executives, or to any other employees as it chooses. No plan is required and no formalities of any kind are prescribed. Terms of a sample split-dollar arrangement, involving a policy owned by the executive, appear at the end of this chapter.

How one split-dollar plan worked.   The accompanying table shows the economic and tax results of an actual split-dollar arrangement examined by the Revenue Service. The arrangement involved an executive, aged 45 when the policy was taken out, who was covered by a ten-payment life policy with a face amount of $100,000, on which policy dividends are credited to the employer. Column 9 shows the amount taxable to the executive for the policy year indicated. Note that in this case taxes are due (after the tenth year) even though no premiums were paid in those years. Thus, the executive is enjoying insurance coverage attributable to company payments in previous years.

CONVERTIBLE TERM INSURANCE

The young executive with a growing family may feel the need for a sizable amount of insurance and yet be unable to afford much in the way of straight life coverage. For this

(1)	(2)	(3)	(4)	(5)	(6)	(7)	(8)	(9)
Policy year	Cash value per $100,000	Gross premiums	Amount provided by employer, Y	Amount paid by employee, B	Proceeds payable to employee B's beneficiary	Cost of insurance per $1,000	Value of insurance to employee, B (6) × (7)*	Value provided by employer, Y (8) − (5)
1	$ 7,291.00	$7,899.50	$7,291.00	$608.50	$92,709.00	$ 6.30	$584.07	$ -0-
2	14,775.00	7,899.50	7,484.00	415.50	85,225.00	6.78	577.83	162.33
3	22,465.00	7,899.50	7,690.00	209.50	77,535.00	7.32	567.56	358.06
4	30,375.00	7,899.50	7,899.50	-0-	69,625.00	7.89	549.34	549.34
5	35,791.00	5,268.50	5,268.50	-0-	64,209.00	8.53	547.70	547.70
6	41,356.00	5,268.50	5,268.50	-0-	58,644.00	9.22	540.70	540.70
7	47,080.00	5,268.50	5,268.50	-0-	52,920.00	9.97	527.61	527.61
8	52,977.00	5,268.50	5,268.50	-0-	47,023.00	10.79	507.38	507.38
9	59,062.00	5,268.50	5,268.50	-0-	40,938.00	11.69	478.57	478.57
10	65,356.00	5,268.50	5,268.50	-0-	34,644.00	12.67	438.94	438.94
11	66,385.00	-0-	-0-	-0-	33,615.00	13.74	461.87	461.87
15	70,462.00	-0-	-0-	-0-	29,538.00	20.73	612.32	612.32
20	75,373.00	-0-	-0-	-0-	24,627.00	31.51	776.00	776.00

*The figures in column (8) represent the figures in column (6) multiplied by the corresponding figures in column (7) and divided by $1,000.

situation, some companies have decided to join their young executives in arranging for convertible term insurance.

A substantial amount of convertible term insurance, say $60,000, is taken out for the executive, and the cost is paid by the company. In later years, when the executive's salary has risen so that he or she can afford $60,000 of straight life coverage, the executive converts the policy to straight life and thereafter pays the premium cost personally.

This arrangement offers economic benefits to the executive, but no special tax benefits. The insurance here is not group-term insurance. The executive therefore is subject to tax on the actual cost of the term insurance paid by the company; the company can deduct its payments as additional compensation. The economic benefit lies in the fact that instead of paying the cost of the term insurance with aftertax dollars, the executive pays only the tax on an amount of income equal to that cost.

Example: Youngblood, age 32, is furnished $60,000 of convertible term insurance by his employer. Five-year convertible term insurance at age 32 costs $5.19 per thousand, or $311. Assuming Youngblood is in the 37 percent bracket (taxable income between $29,900 and $35,200 on a joint return), his cost, the tax cost, of this company-paid insurance is $115, instead of the $311 cost if he had provided it out of his own pocket.

SAVING ESTATE TAX ON LIFE INSURANCE

Proceeds of insurance on a deceased executive's life generally are included in his or her estate for estate tax purposes and therefore may be subjected to estate tax. But estate tax can be avoided by taking these two steps:

1. The executive's estate or executor should *not* be named as beneficiary. Name instead the spouse, child or

other individual the executive seeks to benefit, or a trust for such beneficiary,

2. The executive should give away all rights in the policy (in most cases, these are given to the beneficiary) or have the beneficiary take out the policy initially.

Some executives will understandably consider this second step a drastic one. The authors agree. Insurance can be valuable property, which should not be surrendered lightly, even to the beneficiary. But it is essential for insured executives to give up all rights to policies if they mean to keep insurance proceeds out of their estates for estate tax purposes. Giving up all rights means parting with the right to surrender the policy for cash, the right to borrow against it, the right to change the beneficiary, and other rights.

In the case of a transfer of a straight life policy (including an endowment policy or accelerated payment life policy) which has been in existance for a substantial period of time, the transfer of the policy to avoid estate tax can occasionally subject the executive to federal gift tax. Employers today rarely provide such policies, so gift tax planning for this situation need not be considered here (but the tax saving techniques explored in Chapter 17, on planning the executive's estate, are applicable).

To avoid estate tax on group term life insurance, both the policy and state law must permit the insured executive to make an irrevocable assignment of all rights under the policy (including the right, if any, to convert the policy to permanent insurance) and the executive must actually make such an assignment. The tax profession is not unanimous that estate tax can ever be avoided on group term life insurance (on the theory that each year's premium payment by the employer is a gift by the executive, so that the entire proceeds are included in his or her estate at death). The authors do not share the view that the estate tax cannot be avoided here, and in any case, transferring all rights to group term insurance does no tax harm. Gift tax is seldom a factor since the value of term insurance is relatively small.

Saving state inheritance tax on insurance

While the rules vary from one state to another, state inheritance tax on life insurance is normally at least as easy to avoid as federal estate tax. In many states, inheritance tax is avoided simply by naming as beneficiary the insured person's spouse or child. In others, there is no inheritance tax on insurance if there is no federal estate tax on it.

INSURANCE FOR THE COMPANY

The personnel planner must distinguish the insurance arrangements discussed above, which benefit the executive, from those designed to benefit or protect the company. Thus, so-called key man insurance covers the company against loss of a valued executive by providing a cash fund to the company at his or her death; the executive is not directly affected by this transaction. Or, the company may arrange insurance to fund its obligation to executives or their beneficiaries under deferred compensation contracts or death benefit arrangements. Here, too, while the insurance proceeds may eventually be spent on the executive's behalf, he or she is not directly affected by the insurance aspect. The executive's tax treatment, and that of his or her beneficiaries, is governed by the nature of the underlying transaction (e.g., death benefit rules), and not by life insurance rules.

SAMPLE GROUP TERM LIFE INSURANCE ARRANGEMENT

No formal plan of group term life insurance is required. A group term arrangement limited to executives could be adopted by a board of directors resolution, as follows:

Upon motion duly made, seconded and carried it was RESOLVED that the corporation provide and pay the costs of term insurance, for a group of employees consisting of _____ [all officers and heads of department]* [all employees whose annual salary, including commission and bonus, shall exceed $_____] [all employees over age _____ who shall have been continuously employed by the corporation for not less than _____ years] in an amount for each employee within the group which shall equal [$_____] [_____% of the annual salary of the employee].

SAMPLE SPLIT-DOLLAR INSURANCE ARRANGEMENT

The letter below reflects a split-dollar arrangement in which the policy is owned by the executive:

Mr. [Executive]   [Date]

[Home Address]

Dear Mr. _____,

This letter, when signed by you and returned to us, will constitute our mutual agreement with respect to a policy of life insurance in the amount of $100,000 which it is understood will be issued to you by _____ Life Insurance Company:

1. You will apply for the policy and become the sole owner thereof, with the entire right, except as hereinafter set forth, to designate the beneficiary or beneficiaries of the policy and the manner in which proceeds of the policy will be distributed.

2. The premiums on the policy will be paid as follows: For

---

*The group selected under any of these formulas, or any other suitable formula, should include at least ten persons, at least one of whom is not a stockholder.

convenience, a check covering the entire annual premium will be drawn by us and forwarded to the insurance company. However, you will pay us the amount of the premium for the first year, reduced by the cash value of the policy on its first anniversary. For all succeeding policy years, we will pay an amount which, when added to all previous payments made by us, will equal the cash value of the policy at the end of that policy year, and you will pay, not later than the due date of the premium for that year, the amount which equals the balance due of the net premium (gross premium less policy dividends) for that year.

3. The entire amount of our payments under this policy shall constitute an indebtedness, without interest, from you to us. As security for the repayment of this indebtedness, you will deliver to us physical possession of the policy and will execute and deliver to us a collateral assignment of the policy in accordance with the manner of assignment approved by the insurance company.

You or we may cancel this agreement upon _____ days written notice to the other.† Within that _____-day period, you may satisfy the indebtedness, in which case we will cancel the indebtedness and collateral assignment and return to you physical possession of the policy. If you should not satisfy the indebtedness within that period, we shall have the right to surrender the policy for its cash value, recover therefrom the amount of your indebtedness to us, and turn over to you any amount in excess thereof which we shall have received.

4. At your death while this agreement is in force, the indebtedness shall be satisfied out of the proceeds of the policy, and the balance of the proceeds shall be distributed to or for the benefit of your beneficiaries as you shall have designated.

Very truly yours,

_____

[Employer]

Accepted:

by _____

_____   President
[Executive]

†Provision covering termination of employment.

IRS TABLE OF TAXABLE GROUP TERM
INSURANCE COSTS

The table below shows the figures used to compute the cost of group term insurance taxable to executives. The table is used where the executive has insurance coverage in excess of $50,000. (A one-month period is shown in the table so it can be used where the executive is covered for varying amounts during the year.) The rate is the same whether the executive is male or female.

The taxable amount for a full year (assuming the same coverage throughout the year) is the cost per $1,000 in the executive's age bracket, times 12 (months), times the amount in thousands of coverage in excess of $50,000.

Thus, if Brown is age 37 and is covered for $70,000, the taxable cost for a year is $33.60, that is, $.14 (the rate for 35 to 39) X 12 X 20 (70 [thousand] less 50 [thousand]).

	Cost per $1,000 of protection for one-month period
Under 30	8 cents
30 to 34	10 cents
35 to 39	14 cents
40 to 44	23 cents
45 to 49	40 cents
50 to 54	68 cents
55 to 59	$1.10
60 to 64	$1.63

IRS TABLE FOR COMPUTING SPLIT-DOLLAR INSURANCE COSTS

The figures used to compute the cost of one-year term insurance for purposes of taxing the executive covered by split-dollar life insurance are shown below.

The taxable amount is the premium cost figure shown opposite the executive's age times the amount in thousands of his or her interest in the policy in that year, minus the amount the executive paid during the year toward the premium.

Thus, if Harris is age 34, the policy's face amount is $100,000, the cash surrender value (payable to his employer) is $15,000, policy dividends go to the employer, and Harris paid a premium of $150, Harris is taxable on $106.70, that is, $3.02 (the rate per $1,000 at age 34) times 85 (100 [thousand] less 15 [thousand]) or $256.70, minus $150, the premium Harris paid.

Uniform one-year term premiums for $1,000 life insurance protection

Age	Premium	Age	Premium	Age	Premium
15.	$1.27	36.	$ 3.41	56.	$14.91
16.	1.38	37.	3.63	57.	16.18
17.	1.48	38.	3.87	58.	17.56
18.	1.52	39.	4.14	59.	19.08
19.	1.56	40.	4.42	60.	20.73
20.	1.61	41.	4.73	61.	22.53
21.	1.67	42.	5.07	62.	24.50
22.	1.73	43.	5.44	63.	26.63
23.	1.79	44.	5.85	64.	28.98
24.	1.86	45.	6.30	65.	31.51
25.	1.93	46.	6.78	66.	34.28
26.	2.02	47.	7.32	67.	37.31
27.	2.11	48.	7.89	68.	40.59
28.	2.20	49.	8.53	69.	44.17
29.	2.31	50.	9.22	70.	48.06
30.	2.43	51.	9.97	71.	52.29
31.	2.57	52.	10.79	72.	56.89
32.	2.70	53.	11.69	73.	61.89
33.	2.86	54.	12.67	74.	67.33
34.	3.02	55.	13.74	75.	73.23
35.	3.21				

17

Planning the executive's estate

Put simply, an estate plan is a program, adopted during a person's lifetime, for the distribution of his or her property at death. The estate plan must make adequate provision for the family, and may need to include arrangements for maintenance of the family while awaiting probate of the will and satisfaction of bequests. It will involve the selection of a reliable executor to carry out the deceased person's intentions. It will try to insure liquidity of the estate, so that current liabilities of the deceased and his or her estate can be satisfied without forced selling. It will attempt to minimize the taxes imposed on the estate, so that the heirs can enjoy a larger share of the property left behind. And so on.

Estate planning is a vastly complex operation on which many scholarly treatises have been written. The complexity arises partly because the rules of property ownership, probate, estate administration, and state inheritance taxation vary from one state to another. It also comes about partly because of the many differing ways individuals decide to divide up their property at death.

Some estate planning complexities are peculiar to executives, or are especially common or severe among executives:

For many executives, the planning process is difficult because it's hard to determine the value of what they own now or what the value of that property is likely to be at their death. Many executives are heavily committed in the stock of their companies, which usually are closely held. Since there is no public market for such stock, valuation is difficult and the value arrived at often fluctuates.

Another, related difficulty: When the executive dies and the need arises to sell some of his or her assets (either to pay obligations or because estate administration otherwise requires it), it may not be easy to sell or redeem stock in a closely held corporation. Lack of liquidity is an especially serious problem with executives' estates for just this reason.

A valuable asset in the estate of many executives may be unexercised stock options. If the option can't be transferred, the executor will want to exercise it (assuming the option plan permits exercise by the estate), but the estate may lack the funds to pay for the stock (which may well be the reason the *executive* didn't exercise the option).

Executives are often moved from one plant or office to another, around the country or around the world. The migrant executive may own property in several places. Therefore, more than one state or country may claim the executive as a resident and seek to subject his or her estate to its probate and estate administration laws and taxes.

For problems of valuation of an executive's stock ownership in a closely held corporation, the estate planner may work out contracts whereby the corporation or fellow stockholders agree to buy some or all of the executive's stock at death. The price can be based on book value, or some formula, which can make it somewhat easier to predict the value of that stock at death and will assure that the stock can be converted to cash at that time.

For stock options in the estate, the executor can be specially authorized to borrow funds to exercise the options.

To ease illiquidity and to provide funds to exercise options, the estate plans can include substantial amounts of life insurance.

For the migrant executive, the estate planner can advise on how the executive can clearly establish residence (domicile) in the place the executive intends to live. This is especially important for the executive thinking of retirement or semiretirement in another state.

Each of these planning aspects—of valuation, liquidity, funding option purchase, fixing domicile—is important and should be discussed and worked out carefully. But the estate planning aspect we mean to stress here is the one which all executives can be assumed to hold in common: the wish to minimize the government's tax collections from their bequests.

It is well known by now that the federal government, through the instrument of the estate tax, is the largest single beneficiary in many estates. Few individuals who possess substantial wealth can completely avoid the imposition of this tax on their estate.[1] But there are many ways to reduce this tax. We will explore those most useful for executives.

We will be considering practical, proven arrangements

---

[1] Briefly, the federal estate tax is a tax on the net value of a person's assets. Net value would be assets less liabilities, as further reduced by the amount left to the spouse (subject to certain important qualifications), the amount left to charity, and certain other deductions.

For 1979, thanks to an estate tax credit, no estate tax is imposed if the net value of the estate is $147,333 or less (and assuming no gifts subject to gift tax were made after September 8, 1976). After 1980, no estate tax is imposed where the estate's net value is $176,625 or less (again assuming no post-September 8, 1976 taxable gifts), because of the credit. The estate tax is imposed on the amount of the estate, considered as a separate entity, rather than the amount left to any particular individual.

for tax saving, concentrating on executives with estates of $1 million or less. Nonetheless, this word of caution should be given: Tax saving is only one element in an estate plan. There will be other financial concerns. Moreover, family considerations, not economic considerations, should control.

A successful estate plan is often the work of a team of skilled professionals: attorney, accountant, insurance and investment advisors and, occasionally, a corporate fiduciary. Companies that wish to help their executives in the design of a satisfactory plan often engage a firm of financial counselors who are especially skilled in estate planning for executives. (See Chapter 15 on this.)

PLANNING FOR EXECUTIVE BENEFITS

An essential element in any estate plan is a determination of the assets that the individual can be expected to own at death, and an assessment of their probable value. The individual and the estate planner will therefore begin by making a list of what the individual owns. Estate taxes are often unnecessarily high, and distribution to beneficiaries unnecessarily skimpy, because the estate plan failed to take into account some valuable property items not brought to the planner's attention.

This is a common error in the planning of executives' estates. The plan is designed without reflecting all of their benefits as executives. The estate plan should therefore give full recognition to the following important items of executive compensation and executive wealth.

Life insurance proceeds.   These include the proceeds of company-sponsored life insurance, such as group term or split-dollar insurance, along with any insurance the executive provides independently. Tax planning considerations to eliminate estate and inheritance taxes are noted below.

Pension, profit-sharing benefits.   These include the

amount standing to the executive's credit in company pension, profit-sharing, thrift or other qualified plans. Tax planning considerations to minimize estate taxes are discussed below.

Death benefits. Some companies provide tax-favored death benefits (apart from insurance, pensions, and so forth). Such benefits may be a flat sum, or the continuation of the executive's salary to spouse or heirs for a period after the executive's death. (See Chapter 15.)

Deferred compensation. If executives with deferred compensation arrangements die before collecting all deferred amounts, the arrangement generally requires that the unpaid balance be paid to their estates or heirs. (See Chapter 6.)

Company stock. Executives should take account of all company stock they own, whether it was received as direct payment for services (whether or not it is "restricted" stock), or bought under a bargain purchase arrangement, an installment purchase, or a stock option. (See Chapters 7-10.)

Stock options. Unexercised stock options may have value and should be brought into the estate plan if they can be exercised by the executive's estate or heirs. (See Chapter 10.)

Social Security death and survivorship benefits. These are available to the families of executives as well as others.

Company loans. These may fall due at or shortly after the executive's death. The estate plan should arrange funds to cover any repayment liability. (See Chapter 15.)

Life insurance

Life insurance, provided by the company, is one of the most common of all executive benefits. Thousands of executives are covered by company-sponsored, tax-favored, group term life insurance or split-dollar life insurance, or both. Some executives also are given convertible term policies or other policies which provide welcome insurance protection though they offer no income tax benefits.

Every estate plan must take account of all the executive's life insurance coverage, whether provided by the company, by the executive alone or, as in the case of split-dollar insurance and some group term insurance, partly by each. The executive must be advised that family insurance benefits may be sharply cut down by federal estate taxes and state death taxes unless protective action is taken during the executive's lifetime.

Briefly, federal estate tax on life insurance is avoided if the owner assigns (gives away) all rights in the policy, normally to his or her spouse, some other beneficiary (but *not the estate*) or a trustee. This action is considered in Chapter 16.

In many states, the state inheritance tax on life insurance is avoided simply by naming as beneficiary the insured person's spouse or child or, sometimes, trusts for them. In states with stricter rules, state inheritance tax is still avoided if there is no federal estate tax on the insurance (because it was assigned away).

Executives can consult their own insurance agents for the mechanics of assigning their life insurance policies.[2] But in connection with company-sponsored life insurance—and especially group term life insurance—many companies voluntarily point out to their executives the tax saving aspects of policy assignments and, with help from their insurance companies, make insurance assignments easy to accomplish.

---

[2] The executive should of course have first discussed the wisdom of such an assignment with an attorney or other estate planning adviser.

Pension, profit-sharing accounts

If the executive participated in a qualified pension or profit-sharing plan, the estate or heirs will be entitled to receive the balance in the executive's account at death. The entire amount is included in the estate for estate tax purposes if the estate is named the beneficiary of this property interest. But only the amount in the account which is attributable to the executive's own contributions to the plan (if any) is subject to estate tax if some beneficiary other than the estate is named and the account can be paid in the form of an annuity or through distribution of an annuity contract.

Example: Suppose the company made total contributions of $300,000 as Brown's share of a profit-sharing fund to which Brown contributed nothing. And suppose Brown's share in the fund is worth $600,000 at his death. If Brown had named his estate as beneficiary, this $600,000 would be included in his estate. If he had named, say, his son Gerald as his beneficiary, and the plan provides for paying the $600,000 as an annuity, it would be exempt from estate tax. Depending on the size of Brown's estate, this simple move could save tens of thousands of dollars in estate tax. Assuming Brown died in 1979, the $600,000 represents his entire taxable estate, Brown never made any taxable gifts, and Gerald was his only heir, this move saved $154,800 of estate tax:

If the company and the executive both contribute to the pension or profit-sharing fund, the amount attributable to the executive's own contribution is included in the estate in any case. Here, if Brown had contributed $150,000, then $200,000 ($150,000/$450,000 [$150,000 from Brown + $300,000 from the company] X $600,000) is included in his estate for estate tax purposes even if he designates a beneficiary other than his estate. In this case, assuming $600,000 is the entire taxable estate, and Brown dies in 1979, naming Gerald as his beneficiary saves $83,800 of estate tax.

This estate tax benefit is available only for amounts not withdrawn by executives from their pension or profit-sharing funds during their lifetime. Amounts in an executive's possession are subject to estate tax. Thus, some executives favor profit-sharing plans and employment policies which together will enable them to work on beyond what is ordinarily thought to be retirement age. They seek to die in harness, with their profit-sharing account intact in the profit-sharing trust, so that their beneficiaries will enjoy the estate tax saving. A sample profit-sharing plan provision which reflects this arrangement appears in Chapter 14.

Lump-sum cash distributions as well as annuity distributions *can* be exempt from estate tax. But to achieve this estate tax exemption the recipient (heir or beneficiary) must waive the income tax benefits for lump-sum distribution (described in Chapter 14).

It can happen that the beneficiary of an executive's pension plan is not required to bear the burden of the estate tax. For example, Kramer might leave his pension interest and certain other assets to his widow and the residue of his estate to his son with the provision that estate taxes are to be paid out of the son's share (the residue). (This is a tax-saving clause, see further discussion below.) In that case, Kramer's widow might take the pension proceeds in a lump sum and claim the income tax benefits, since the resulting estate tax will not be borne by her share.

Where at least part of the estate tax will be borne by the beneficiary of the pension, which is the usual case, the beneficiary will need to compare the estate tax cost (or saving) with the income tax saving (or cost) of the decision between lump sum and annuity. The income tax on a lump-sum payout to the beneficiary under the ten-year averaging computation described in Chapter 14 can be less than the income tax on annuity payout. In relatively modest estates, a lump-sum payout could be exempt from estate tax thanks to the combination of the estate tax marital deduction and the estate tax credit (both discussed later in this chapter), and could also qualify for income tax benefits through averaging. The planner of the company's pension or profit-sharing plan should provide for an option to take an annuity or a lump sum, and the estate planner should consider granting such an option to the beneficiary.

PLANNING BEQUESTS THAT SAVE ESTATE TAXES

Here we will consider ways in which executives can leave wealth to their families at the lowest cost in estate tax.

Bequests to spouse (marital deduction). Amounts a person leaves to a spouse are exempt from estate tax up to about half the value of the estate by means of the estate tax marital deduction.[3] (For convenience, we will assume the person making the bequest is a man, since husbands normally predecease their wives, but the rules apply equally to wives who predecease their husbands.) The marital deduction equals the amount the spouse gets at the dece-

---

[3] Not always exactly half. The maximum estate tax marital deduction is the greater of half the estate or $250,000, with this qualification: The estate marital deduction is reduced by the excess of the gift tax marital deduction (for lifetime gifts to the donor's spouse) allowed the deceased individual over 50 percent of the gifts made to the spouse. Thus the estate tax marital deduction of half the estate (or $250,000 if greater) is reduced by from 0 (where gifts to the spouse were $200,000 or more, or where no taxable gifts were made) up to but never more than $50,000.

dent's death, or about half the value of the decedent's estate, whichever is less.[4]

The marital deduction is a major element in any program for saving estate taxes. But the executive must be aware that it is allowed only for property which his spouse, upon his death, will take as absolute or effective owner. The property should be left to her outright, without qualifications or, failing that, should meet *both* these conditions:

a. She has full rights to current income from the property.
b. She has the right to dispose of the property itself during her lifetime or at her death.

Bequests which satisfy both these tests would include a legal life estate to the spouse with the remainder to her estate, or income to her in trust for life with the trust corpus payable to her estate, absolutely or at her option. If she is given only a life estate, the marital deduction would not be allowed.

The marital deduction is based on the size of the entire estate (technically, the *adjusted gross estate*), and not just the assets covered by the will. Such items as insurance proceeds and jointly-owned property may be part of the adjusted gross estate, increasing the allowable marital deduction, even though not mentioned in the will.

Property left to a spouse outright, or under conditions satisfying the above tests, will be subject to estate tax in her estate if she owns it at her death. Yet in general only half the husband's estate can qualify for marital deduc-

---

[4] The marital deduction is not allowed for community property—the system in Arizona, California, Idaho, Louisiana, Nevada, New Mexico, Texas, and Washington—but community property laws produce a similar estate tax result. Also, the marital deduction *is* allowed for *separately* owned property in community property states.

tion. Anything left to her in excess of that amount is taxable in her husband's estate and in hers as well, if held by her at death. Where the husband wants to give her a larger-than-50-percent share of his estate, while still avoiding the second estate tax (on the wife's estate), he could (1) leave her half his estate, either outright or by a bequest satisfying both tests and, (2) leave her a life estate or life income interest in other property.

This way, during her lifetime she will enjoy more than half the income from the husband's property, and will be able to dispose of the half left to her. But her estate will not be subject to estate tax on property in which she had only a life interest.

For medium-sized—about $500,000—and smaller estates of married executives, this is the typical estate plan. The executive concludes that his spouse will need all or almost all the income his estate will produce to live on. This plan minimizes estate tax in his estate but grants his spouse all the income from all his property.

Example: Cunningham dies in 1981 leaving a wife, two adult children, and an estate of $540,000. If he left all of it outright to his wife, the estate tax would be $30,600 and she would collect $509,400 (disregarding state taxes and probate costs). Assuming she owned that much at her death in 1983, and she did not remarry, estate tax at *her* death would be $112,278 on her $509,400 estate, which would leave $397,122 after taxes for their children (or her other heirs). Total estate tax would be $142,878.

But suppose instead Cunningham left half his estate ($270,000) outright to his wife and the balance (less estate tax) to his wife in trust for life with the remainder to their children. Here, the estate tax at his death is still $30,600. Assuming that his wife at her death owns the $270,000 given her outright and leaves this to the children, and assuming further that the amount passing to the children from the trust is $239,400 before tax ($509,400 in all passing at her death *before* tax, the same as in the situation above), the estate tax on *her* estate is $30,600, imposed on the $270,000 *she* leaves to her children. Total estate tax in *this* case is $71,200, for a $71,678 estate tax saving.

The children get $71,678 more this way than if the entire estate had been left to Cunningham's wife, yet she can have the same amount of income during her lifetime (less trust expenses for the $239,400 in trust).

Bequests to children (orphan's deduction). A limited amount of bequest to an individual's children is exempt from estate tax. The exemption applies only where the deceased individual leaves no surviving spouse (which means the estate has no marital deduction), the deceased person's child has no other known living parent, the child is under age 21, and the child acquires rights in the bequest comparable to those needed to support a marital deduction (with minor exceptions). The amount of the deduction can't exceed $5,000 times the number of years the child is under age 21 at this parent's death.

This deduction in fact plays little part in estate planning:

a. Planning is seldom necessary to obtain it. A person whose estate would otherwise be subject to estate tax would normally leave an amount qualifying for deduction to his or her minor children in any case.

b. Where both parents are dead (or one is dead and the other's whereabouts are unknown), the children usually are adults.

Bequests to grandchildren, etc.: Generation skipping. Suppose Bowers, an executive, has a son Ralph, and a grandson Tom. Bowers dies, leaving his property to Ralph, which is reduced by the estate tax on Bowers' estate. Some years later Ralph dies leaving his property (including what he inherited from his father) to Tom, which is reduced by a second estate tax on Ralph's estate.

Generation skipping is the device which tax practitioners and other estate planners have worked out to avoid this second estate tax. Instead of leaving his property outright to Ralph, Bowers leaves Ralph a life estate or life income interest, with the remainder or principal payable to Tom at Ralph's death. This form of bequest does not reduce Bowers' estate tax. But it eliminates any estate tax on Ralph, with respect to interests acquired from Bowers. Ralph has only a life interest, one which terminates at his death, which is not subject to estate tax.

Generation skipping could be accomplished by Bowers' leaving the property first to his spouse for life (marital deduction is not allowed for such a bequest), then to his son or daughter for life, and then to his grandchild. The only estate tax here (apart from any estate tax when the grandchild dies) is on the executive's own estate.

Generation skipping is of little or no interest to executives with medium-sized or small estates because any future estate tax saved (to the first or "skipped" generation) isn't worth the bother of tying up so relatively small an inheritance. Executives with larger estates can still be interested in this device. While highly complex rules exist to tax generation-skipping transfers, they don't affect transfers to the executive's grandchildren (skipping their parents) of up to $250,000 for each of the executive's *children.*

Example: Foley leaves $1 million to each of her three children in equal shares for life, remainder to their children (her grandchildren) in equal shares. Her children's estates would be exempt from the generation-skipping tax to the extent of $250,000 each ($750,000 in all).

Assigning the estate tax burden

It is appropriate for the executive to specify by will exactly which bequests should bear the burden of federal estate taxes and state death taxes, and which should be exempt from such taxes. This is essentially a matter of state law; ordinarily, state law accepts and applies such directives.

Thus, if Philips leaves half his estate to his son and half to his nephew, with the federal estate tax to be borne solely out of the nephew's share, this directive will normally be honored, assuming the nephew's share is adequate to cover the estate tax. The son would get half the estate, and the nephew would get the balance, less estate tax on the entire estate.

Such a directive, properly applied, can also operate to reduce estate tax. The marital deduction (or the charitable deduction) is larger if the surviving spouse's share (or the charity's share) is exempted from having to bear part of the estate tax. The increased deduction reduces the taxable amount.

LIFETIME GIFTS IN ESTATE PLANNING

Estate planning is not limited to designing clauses in wills or other documents which will become effective only upon the executive's death. Many executives should consider adopting a program of making sizable gifts within the family during their lifetime.

Gifts during life can be subject to the federal gift tax, which can in practice be viewed as a part of the estate tax and is designed to limit avoidance of estate tax through lifetime gifts.

Nonetheless, substantial lifetime gift giving is possible in ways which avoid both gift and estate tax, or in ways in which, while they may incur gift tax, can still produce an overall tax saving. This is true even though the gifts are made to the giver's spouse, children, or other family members who would share in the estate under the will, or if there was no will. A program of lifetime gifts should also be explored as a means of avoiding state death taxes and reducing probate costs.

Example: Taylor, age 60 and a divorced father of two, has an estate of $500,000 which he expects will grow to $700,000 at his death. If through lifetime gifts which avoid gift tax he could reduce his estate to $550,000, this would yield an estate tax saving of $55,500.

In addition, it is probable that state death taxes and probate costs will be smaller on a $550,000 estate than on a $700,000 estate.

There is no gift tax unless the donor's gifts to any one person during the year total more than $3,000. This rule, called the *annual exclusion,* makes it possible for an executive to avoid gift tax on gifts made to save estate tax by keeping annual gifts to $3,000 or less (per recipient).

Techniques to save gift taxes

1. Instead of making a $5,000 gift this year, which would trigger a gift tax if the lifetime exemption has been exhausted, one can avoid gift tax by giving $3,000 this year and $2,000 next year. If giving property worth $5,000 instead of cash, give a 3/5ths interest this year and the balance next year.

2. Another way to save gift tax is to spread the gifts

among the members of the family the executive intends to benefit. For example, instead of making a gift of $12,000 to his son, which could incur a gift tax, Mack could give $3,000 each to his son, his son's wife, and their two children, thereby avoiding gift tax.

3. The husband-wife split gift is a third gift tax saver.[5] A gift by husband and wife together is treated as made half by each, if they wish, even though only one of them owns the property being donated. For example, if Charles owns property worth $6,000 which he gives to his son, Phil, it is treated as a gift of $3,000 by each spouse if Charles's wife Maude joins in the gift. Assuming they make no other gifts to Phil that year, the split gift device, coupled with the annual exclusion, completely avoids gift tax on the gift.

4. A marital deduction is allowed on a gift to a spouse.[6] The first $100,000 in value of gifts to a spouse is exempt from gift tax. The next $100,000 of gifts is fully taxable. For gifts in excess of $200,000, *half* the value of the gift is taxable. The $100,000 and $200,000 amounts above are lifetime, not annual, figures. However, the first $3,000 in gifts to a spouse in each year is exempt from gift tax (under the annual exclusion), so that only gifts in excess of that amount in any year are counted against the $100,000 or $200,000 figures. For example, if Howard's gifts before 1979 never exceeded $3,000 a year but he gave his wife $70,000 in 1979 and $50,000 in 1980, the total amount subject to gift tax would be $14,000 ($120,000 less the sum of $3,000, $3,000, and $100,000); tax is imposed only in 1980.

When computing estate tax on Howard's estate, following his death in 1984, $114,000 ($120,000 less the sum of

---

[5] Technically unavailable for gifts of community property, but the tax result is the same for joint gifts of such property.

[6] Except for a gift of community property, but the tax result of such a gift is about the same.

$3,000 and $3,000) would be added to the amount in his estate and a credit would be allowed for gift tax paid.

OTHER TAX-SAVING TECHNIQUES

The following tax-saving moves are used by estate planners even though they may incur gift taxes.

1. Transferring property expected to appreciate in value. The executive may own stock, real estate or other assets reasonably expected to go up substantially in value before his or her death. This is especially likely for stock in or assets of the executive's own business, and the executive's home and vacation residence.

Property which an individual gives away during life, whether or not it is subjected to gift tax, is exempt from estate tax if he or she lives at least three years after the date the gift was made, regardless of the value of that property when he or she dies.[7] Thus, there is an overall tax saving from giving away property which appreciates in value *after* the gift, even though the gift is hit by a gift tax. For example, suppose a gift of property which is worth $100,000 when the gift is made and $300,000 when the giver dies. The gift tax of, say, $34,000 (on $100,000) may reflect an estate tax saving of, say, $108,000 for an overall saving of $74,000.

Such a tax-saving move entails the obvious risk that if the donated property *declines* in value after the gift, the overall tax burden may be higher than if the property were retained and subjected to estate tax.

2. Transferring high-income property. Related to suggestion 1 is the transfer of property which produces high income which the executive doesn't need for living expenses but will invest. The accumulated (invested) income will increase the estate for estate tax purposes. Giving the

---

[7] Technically, it is not part of the gross estate for estate tax purposes. It can, however, figure in the computation of the estate tax.

income-producing property away can result in an estate tax saving that outweighs the gift tax. Also, if the gift is to a family member in a lower income tax bracket, as it often is (e.g., to the giver's child), income tax can be saved as well.

3. Saving estate tax on gift tax.   Amounts paid out as gift tax are excluded from the giver's estate, except where he or she died within 3 years of making the gift. This provides a further tax motive for making lifetime gifts, as can be illustrated in this example.

Example: Assume that Green has a $1 million estate January 1, 1981. He has made no taxable gifts when he dies in March 1984, leaving an estate of $1 million. His estate tax is $298,800.

Now assume instead Green made a $500,000 gift in January 1981. He pays a $108,800 gift tax on this. On his death in March 1984, his estate is $391,200 ($500,000 less $108,800). To compute the estate tax due, add back the $500,000 taxable gift to that (total $891,200), compute estate tax on that ($303,368), subtract the gift tax paid ($108,800) and the applicable credit ($47,000). The result—$147,568—is the estate tax due, which with the $108,800 gift tax is still $42,442 less than if no gift were made.

The above example requires the unrealistic assumption that between 1981 and 1984 Green lived as easily on the income from $391,200 as from $1 million. Put another way, it assumes that the size of Green's estate didn't change from January 1981 to March 1984. For these reasons—

a.   A saving here is most significant when the gift is of property expected to appreciate or produce sizable income as in suggestions 1 or 2 above.

b.   This tax saving move is most effective when very

large amounts are involved. An estate tax saving of several million dollars reportedly occurred on a multi-million dollar gift made by a member of the du Pont family.

This saving is unavailable if the giver dies within three years after making the gift. This is because both the gift *and the gift tax* then become part of the estate for tax purposes.

WHAT AND HOW TO GIVE

Giving the family home. The family home has proved an especially attractive candidate for lifetime giving because of the great increase in residential values experienced since the Depression. This would be a gift of property expected to appreciate in the future (see suggestion 1 above), which could make use of the annual $3,000 exclusion and, in the case of a gift to the giver's spouse, the gift tax marital deduction. Payments on the mortgage after the gift could also escape gift tax through use of the annual exclusion (and, if necessary, the marital deduction). If a husband gives the home to his wife free of restrictions on her ownership, and dies before she does and more than three years after the gift was made, the house will be exempt from estate tax even if he continued to live in the house with her after making the gift.

Joint ownership. Suppose Wiley buys property in his and his wife's names as joint tenants or tenants by the entirety, or transfers property which was his alone to himself and his wife as joint tenants or tenants by the entirety. This form of co-ownership[8] has the attraction that at the death of one of them, the entire property will pass to the other without the cost or delay of probate.

---

[8] It is not community property.

In the case of the family residence or other real property, only half the value of the property is included in the estate of the first joint owner to die (say, the executive) if the executive had made an election after 1976 to subject the creation of the joint ownership to gift tax. This would mean that a gift tax return must be filed, and a gift tax paid if due. The principal *tax-saving* motivation for such an election would be that described in suggestion 1 above—the transfer of property (in this case, a half interest) expected to appreciate in value. Later capital additions by the executive are automatically subjected to gift tax, without need for an election each time.

In the case of property other than real property, simply taking property in or transferring property into joint ownership after 1976 *can* have the same tax result without need for the election made with respect to real property. But this doesn't apply to the most common form of "joint" ownership—joint bank accounts where each joint owner can withdraw the full account. Here, an outright gift of the bank account would be preferable for tax purposes.

The contemplated benefit of joint ownership arises where the person who creates the joint ownership—in our case, the executive—is the first to die. If the executive's spouse dies first, creation of the joint interests just means unnecessary expenses and taxes.

Gifts to children.   An estate-planning program of lifetime gifts is likely to emphasize gifts to the executive's children. Gifts of securities or cash to children typically are made under the simplified procedures of the Uniform Gifts to Minors Act. This law is generally applicable throughout the United States. Once such a gift is made under this law, the income from the donated property ordinarily is taxable to the child and not to the donor. But the person obligated to support the child (usually, the child's father who also usually is the donor) is taxable on the income if it is used for the child's support.

If the donor (again, usually the father) names himself as the custodian of the gift to the child, and dies while the child is still a minor, the value of the amount held as custodian is likely to be subjected to estate tax in the custodian's estate.

When deciding what kind of property to give to a child or other donee, consider favoring gifts of income-producing property such as securities, rather than valuable but non-income property such as land held for investment. Income earned on the property after the gift is not taxable to the donor. If the income is received by the donor's child, taxes due on this income will be less (because of the child's low bracket) than if it were received by the executive donor. Also, the income paid to the donee would not be part of the donor's estate, and therefore would not be subjected to estate tax in his estate.

18

Government standards for executive compensation

This chapter explores how the government's voluntary anti-inflation program monitored by the Council on Wage and Price Stability affects executive compensations, and discusses the tools the government can use to encourage compliance. No firms are exempt from the program, though only about 400 of the largest will be monitored by the council.

As the basic rule, pay for executives and other management employees may not increase by more than 7 percent in a year (technically, a "program year," defined below).

The allowable amount of increase is not determined employee by employee. Instead, for executives, a "management unit" is used. Broadly, management employees are those with supervisory duties not covered by a collective bargaining agreement.

To comply with the pay standards, the pay rate for the last quarter of the program year must not be more than 7 percent above the pay rate for the base quarter.

For calendar year companies, the base quarter is the quarter ending September 30, 1978; for others, it is the last complete fiscal quarter ending before October 1, 1978. The program year is the 12-month period following the base quarter.

Thus, for calendar year companies (or companies with a fiscal year ending September 30) the pay rate for the quarter ending September 30, 1979, should not be more than 7 percent over the pay rate for the quarter ending September 30, 1978.

The pay rate for management is the pay divided by the estimated number of hours worked.

Example: Suppose Apex Co. has five management employees who were paid a total $75,000 during the quarter ending September 30, 1978. And suppose they worked an estimated 2,500 hours. The rate of pay for management is $30. Assuming the same employees and hours (and disregarding promotions), they could be paid a total $80,250 in the quarter ending September 30, 1979 (a $32.10 rate) without violating the guidelines. If they worked 2,700 hours in that quarter, they could be paid $86,670.

The 7 percent ceiling does not limit raises to any particular employee. As long as pay within the management unit does not rise more than 7 percent, the company can pay any executive within the unit what it pleases. Thus, with ten executives and other management employees whose annual rate during the base quarter was $50,000 each, the company could give nine of them a 2 percent raise (to $51,000) and the tenth a 48 percent raise (to $74,000).

Note that the system of measuring pay increases takes into account the rate of pay in the last quarter of the program year, rather than the rate of pay *over* the program year. For example, if executive Wheeler (assumed for simplicity to be a management unit) of a calendar year company should have an annual $80,000 salary during July 1-

September 30, 1978, an annual salary of $85,600 during July 1-September 30, 1979, would not violate the pay standards (assuming no change in hours worked). It would not matter, for purposes of the pay standards, whether he got his raise, say, October 1, 1978, or July 1, 1979. But Wheeler would get $4,200 more for the year if the raise had occurred October 1, 1978. Thus, the policy for companies that want to pay the maximum allowable amount is to make raises early in the program year.

Pay subject to the pay standards includes virtually every item of compensation the executive receives: salary (including cost-of-living adjustments); bonuses and other annual incentives; long-term incentives generally; and job perquisites which give rise to taxable income (such as company-furnished cars for commuting and company-paid financial counseling). Pay also includes employer contributions for employee benefits which are not currently taxable, such as pension, profit-sharing, thrift, and similar plans; and health and accident benefits or insurance, and life insurance. Not counted as pay are moving expense reimbursements; cost-of-living differentials on transfer to a higher-cost area pursuant to an established practice; or employer contributions to social security. See also the discussion below on *When pay standards may be exceeded.*

Annual incentives (bonuses) and contract increases

Compensation under annual incentives is treated as pay and included with other pay in determining the rate of increase.

In making a determination of the pay rate increase where annual incentives are involved, the compensation planner does not necessarily use the quarter the incentive payment is *received.* The general rules are these:

If the payment is under a previously announced and

consistently administered plan, incentive awards are treated as pay over the period *earned.* Thus, a bonus paid in January for work done the previous year is treated as pay received evenly over that previous year—so that one fourth of the amount is received each quarter of that previous year.

If there is no such plan and no objective performance standard, the award is treated as pay when it is *received.*

Exception: If payment of such an award is deferred, it is treated as pay when accrued by the employer. In this case, an award in, say, January 1979, is treated as pay for 1979 (not for the previous year), so that one fourth of that award is treated as pay in each quarter in 1979.

Some companies may have plans paying an amount determined under formulas based on profits which were already in force when the voluntary standards were announced in October 1978. Still, with the exception below, companies should keep the annual bonuses within the 7-percent pay ceiling. To do this, companies should estimate what profits will be in the coming year, and make the corresponding calculation of the bonus to be paid on those profits. This projected bonus (spread over the period earned under the rules above), along with all other pay, should not in the last quarter of the program year be more than 107 percent of the amount in the base quarter.

Exception. Where bonuses under the predetermined formula prove to be higher than projected because *profits* are higher than projected, but the company's profit projection was not unreasonably low, the 7 percent ceiling can be exceeded.

Example: Moore Corporation paid its management group $800,000 (salary and bonus) in the base quarter. It projected a level of profits which would produce a bonus of $40,000 applicable to the last quarter of the program year, and increased salaries by $16,000, so the total projected increase was $56,000 (7 percent of $800,000). But profits in fact produced a bonus allocable to the last quarter of the program year of $52,000. Moore can pay *both* the bonus and the $16,000 salary increase without violating the pay standards if its original profits projection was not unreasonably low.

Deferred compensation

Deferred compensation is treated as pay for the period in which it is earned (the period that services to earn it are performed), not when it is paid. Thus, the pay standards would be violated if pay for the management group in the base quarter is $600,000 and pay in the last quarter of the program year is $636,000 (a 6 percent increase, assuming no change in hours worked) but with a further deferred $75,000 to be paid three years hence.

When pay standards may be exceeded

Promotions.   Pay attributable to legitimate promotions is excluded in determining pay rate increases.

Annual pay plans for employee groups.   Certain pay increases required under formal annual pay plans covering "recognized employee groups" (e.g., corporate officers) can be excluded in determining pay rate increases. Exclusion applies where the plan was in operation on October 1, 1978, or (with some qualifications) had been communicated to employees before October 22, 1978. Where the required increase totals more than 7 percent, the excess over 7 percent is excluded.

Health benefits.   Increases in company costs of providing existing health benefits are treated as pay up to a 7 percent annual cost increase. The excess over 7 percent is not treated as pay. Costs of changed (e.g., new) benefits, however, are treated as pay.

Pensions. Cost increases for defined benefit (pension) plans are not treated as pay unless they result from changes in salary or benefits.

Future value incentive plans. This is a term used to cover stock options, performance share plans, performance unit plans, stock appreciation rights; plans providing restricted stock or other restricted property; and phantom stock plans. It refers to plans under which units (which may also be called options, shares, awards, or investment amounts) are granted whose value to the executive recipient will not be known until some future time. The rules are these:

1. Any units granted before October 25, 1978, are excluded from the pay standards.

Example: Hailey was granted 1,000 stock appreciation rights in 1976 which were worth $50 each when exercised in 1979. This $50,000 is disregarded in determining pay under the pay standards.

2. If a pre-existing plan is continued (or is modified, or a successor plan is adopted) during the program year, the *number of units* granted may not exceed 107 percent per recipient of the number granted in the 12 months preceding the program year or the annual average of units granted in the last five years. Note that this is a limitation on the *number* of units, not the dollar value. However, if the units have value at the time they are granted, the value at that time is counted as pay. Value is the fair market value when granted minus the purchase price per share.

Example: During the year before the program year, Begg Corporation granted the management group options to buy 5,000 shares of Begg stock. This was more than the average in the four preceding years. During the program year it may grant the management group options for up to 5,350 shares without violating the standards. A grant of options for more than 5,350 shares would violate the standards even though the options had no value at the time of the grant. If the options had value (the stock's value at the time of the grant) exceeding the purchase price by, say, $5 a share, this value counts as pay.

If a company introduces a new plan during the year, for which it has no historical precedent, the value of any units granted during the year counts as pay. In this case, the value to be used is not simply the difference between the fair market value *at the time of the grant* and the purchase price. Rather, the value is to be determined in accordance with generally accepted accounting principles.

Hardship relief.   If the pay standards would create "situations of undue hardship or gross inequity," the council may grant an exemption from the standard or make appropriate adjustments in the standard.

How the government induces compliance

Several means of encouraging or inducing compliance through government pressure or influence have been announced. These include:

a. A policy of government procurement—the purchase of goods and services—only from firms that observe the wage and price standards, to the extent possible.
b. Lifting import restrictions in industries where wage or price increases exceed the standard.
c. Restricting cost passthroughs or rate increases in industries subject to regulatory agencies.
d. Restricting wages and prices where administrative regulations set minimums.

    e. Publicizing "specific inflationary situations," naming individual firms. In some situations, the "offending" company must itself do the publicizing. Thus, companies subject to SEC regulations must disclose their noncompliance (since noncompliance limits their opportunities for government contracts).

The government's legal authority to take some of these actions has been questioned. In any case, it uses these powers sparingly.

Index